American SPEAK OUT

Pre-Intermediate Student Book

with DVD/ROM and Audio CD MP3

Pearson

Antonia Clare • JJ Wilson

CONTENTS

DVD-ROM: DVD CLIPS AND SCRIPTS INTERVIEWS AND SCRIPTS

LISTENING/DVD	SPEAKING	WRITING
	ask and answer questions about vacations and weekends	
listen to stories about offers of marriage	ask and answer personal questions	write about an important year in your life; improve your use of linking words
understand routine exchanges	make conversation	
Miranda: watch an extract from a sitcom about a woman called Miranda	talk about important people in your life	write about your best friend
listen to interviews about jobs	talk about what motivates you at work	write an email about work experience
	talk about dangerous jobs	
listen to a man talking about his job	talk about your perfect job	
The Money Programme: Dream Commuters: watch an extract from a documentary about commuting	describe your work/life balance	write a web comment about work/life balance
listen to a radio program about going out in New York	talk about your future plans	write an email invitation
	discuss how you spend your free time	
understand some problem phone calls	make and receive phone calls	
Going Local: Rio: watch an extract from a travel program about visiting Rio de Janeiro	plan a perfect day out	write an invitation for a day out
listen to someone describing how he used his hidden talent	talk about hidden talents	check your work and correct mistakes
	talk about rules in schools	
	give advice and make suggestions for language learners	
Supersized Earth: The Way We Move: watch an extract from a documentary about developments that have changed the world	talk about inventions	write a forum post about inventions
	tell a travel anecdote	
understand travel advice	discuss travel	write an email describing a trip or weekend away
understand and follow directions in a city	ask for and give directions	
Full Circle: watch an extract from a travel program	present ideas for an award	write an application for an award
	talk about your lifestyle	
listen to a radio interview with a food expert	discuss food preferences	write about food
listen to conversations between a doctor and her patients	explain health problems	
Horizon: Monitor Me: watch an extract from a documentary about health	talk about healthy habits	write a blog post about health advice

CLASS AUDIO AND SCRIPTS

CONTENTS

	LISTENING/DVD	SPEAKING	WRITING
	listen to a radio program about a woman who changed her life	talk about a life change	use paragraphs to write about a decision that changed your life
		talk about why people tell lies	
	understand short, predictable conversations	learn to check and confirm information	
	My Family and Other Animals: watch an extract from the beginning of a movie about a family that moves to Greece	talk about new experiences	write a blog/diary
		talk about a project that people should invest in	
	listen to a discussion about salaries	talk about why you should earn more	write an opinion piece
	listen to conversations in stores	describe items; go shopping	
	soleRebels: watch an extract from the news about an Ethiopian business	present a money-making idea	write a competition entry for a business investment
	listen to a radio program about green ideas	talk about green issues	write about your views on the environment
		give your views on life in the city or the country	
	listen to people discussing quiz questions	talk about different animals	
	Joanna Lumney in the Land of the Northern Lights: watch an extract from a documentary about the northern lights	talk about amazing places	write a travel blog
	listen to conversations about different cities	discuss qualities of different places	use formal expressions to write an email
		discuss alternative punishments to fit the crimes	
	listen to people complaining	talk about problems in a school	
	Mary's Meals: watch an extract from a documentary about an Internet sensation	talk about an important issue	write about an issue
	listen to people talking about how they keep in touch	talk about things you've done/ would like to do	improve your use of pronouns
		talk about future consequences	
	listen to a discussion about the Internet	give your opinion	
	Panorama: Is TV bad for kids?: watch an extract from a documentary about giving up television	talk about technology you couldn't live without	write a web comment about technology
		talk about your favorite movie	
	listen to people talking about fame	talk about being famous	write about a famous person
	listen to people making requests	make requests and offers	
	Lewis Hamilton: Billion Dollar Man: watch an extract from a documentary about Lewis Hamilton	talk about your ambitions	write about your childhood ambitions

LEAD-IN

CLASSROOM LANGUAGE

1 A Complete the questions with the words in the box.

say	to	does	you	are	do

1 What ______ this mean?
2 How ______ you spell it?
3 What page ______ we on?
4 What's the answer ______ number 6?
5 Can ______ repeat that, please?
6 How do you ______ this word?

B Match questions 1–6 above with answers a)–f).

a) OK. Which part? The whole sentence?
b) It's a type of food.
c) Page 63.
d) You don't say the "k." Listen: "knee."
e) The answer is b.
f) B-a-n-a-n-a.

SPELLING

SL.1

2 A Listen and write down the words you hear.

B Listen again to check.

C Write down ten words in English.

D Work in pairs and take turns. Student A: say your word and then spell it out. Student B: write it down.

PARTS OF SPEECH

3 Match the parts of speech in the box with the words in bold.

~~verb~~	adjective	auxiliary	adverb	noun
article	preposition of place			

1 I **studied** here last year. *verb*
2 We have **a** new teacher.
3 This is a great **school**.
4 The class is **in** Room 14.
5 **Do** you like speaking English?
6 The teachers are **helpful**.
7 I work **quickly**.

TENSES AND STRUCTURES

4 Find one example of each of these things in the text below.

1 present simple
2 present continuous
3 present perfect
4 past simple
5 *going to* for future plans

My name is Yoko. I was born in Japan, but at the moment I'm living in the United States. I've been here for six months. I'm going to visit my uncle in Canada next year.

QUESTION WORDS

5 Complete the questions with the words in the box.

who	where	what	when	why	how

1 ______ is your name?
2 ______ is your best friend?
3 ______ do you come from?
4 ______ is your birthday?
5 ______ do you come to school: by car or by public transportation?
6 ______ are you studying English? Do you need it for your job?

AUXILIARY VERBS

6 Underline the correct alternative.

1 What *do/does/are* you do?
2 Where *do/does/is* she live?
3 What *do/does/did* they do yesterday evening?
4 I *am not/don't/doesn't* know the answers to these questions.
5 The library *don't/not/doesn't* open on Sundays.
6 We *don't/didn't/weren't* go on vacation last year.
7 *Is/Are/Do* you studying at the moment?
8 John *doesn't/isn't/aren't* using the computer, so you can use it.

VOCABULARY

7 Complete the word webs with the words in the box.

car	salesclerk	bookstore	lawyer	bakery
uncle	tomato	grandmother	bike	doctor
supermarket	sugar	train	cousin	pasta

family

food

jobs

stores

transportation

public transportation / on vacation
salesclerk or salesperson / bookstore

public transport / on holiday
shop assistant /bookshop

1 life

SPEAKING
- 1.1 Ask and answer questions about vacations and weekends
- 1.2 Ask and answer personal questions
- 1.3 Make conversation
- 1.4 Talk about important people in your life

LISTENING
- 1.2 Listen to stories about offers of marriage
- 1.3 Understand routine exchanges
- 1.4 Watch an extract from a sitcom about a woman called Miranda

READING
- 1.1 Understand an article about the secrets to happiness

WRITING
- 1.2 Write about an important year in your life; Improve your use of linking words
- 1.4 Write about your best friend

What do you look for in a friend?

INTERVIEWS

1.1 FEELING GOOD?

G question forms
P stressed words
V free time

VOCABULARY
FREE TIME

1 A Think about three things that make you happy (e.g., *my family, walking on the beach, eating good food*). Work in pairs and compare your ideas.

B Complete phrases 1–5 with the verbs in the box.

~~go~~ eat have play spend

1 *go* shopping/on vacation/for a walk
2 ____ time with family/money/time alone
3 ____ out/with friends/good food
4 ____ free time/a barbecue/a party
5 ____ a sport/a musical instrument/games

C Work in pairs. Do any of the activities in Exercise 1B make you happy? Add some more activities to the list.

READING

2 A Read the magazine article. Which of these things do you do already? Which could you do more of?

B Work in pairs. Which of the seven ideas do you think are the most/least important for you? Do you have any other ideas to include?

the Seven Secrets to Happiness

Everyone has a different idea of what happiness is, but most of us want to be happier. So, what can we learn from looking at the habits of happy people? Here are seven things to make you happy.

1 Sleep More Most people don't get enough sleep. If you want to feel good about life, then try to sleep for at least seven hours a night.

2 Exercise You don't need to run for 20 mi. or go to the gym every night, but a small amount of exercise will help you feel happy. Go for a short (10–15 minute) walk somewhere beautiful. It wakes up your brain.

3 Give to Others Research shows that giving money or time to help others makes you feel happier. Buying someone an unexpected present or spending some time doing volunteer work will give you a feeling of joy.

4 Be Interested Love what you do and try to learn something new. People who are curious and learn new things experience feelings of satisfaction and happiness.

5 Spend Time with Family and Friends This is probably the most important thing you can do. People who have a strong network of social relationships are not just happier; they live longer, too!

6 Focus on the Moment Try to find opportunities each day to enjoy the small things in life. Spend a little time on your own and just enjoy the moment.

7 Smile! Smile more (even when you're feeling sad). Smiling can actually make you feel better. People who post big smiley photos of themselves on Facebook actually feel happier because they see the photo every day and it reminds them of happy times.

volunteer work — voluntary work

GRAMMAR
QUESTION FORMS

3 A Read the questions. Think about your answers.

1 How many hours do you usually sleep?
2 Are you good at sports?
3 How much time do you spend exercising? Where do you go?
4 What do you do that really interests you?
5 When did you last learn something new? Where were you?
6 What small things in life do you enjoy?

B Work in groups. Ask and answer the questions.

4 A Complete the questions in the tables.

Questions with Auxiliaries			
question word	**auxiliary**	**subject**	**infinitive**
Where	1 ______	you	go?
2 ______	did	you	last learn something new?

Questions with *be*			
question word	***be***	**subject**	**adjective/noun/ verb + *-ing*, etc.**
	3 ______	you	good at sports?
4 ______	were	you?	

B Circle the correct word in bold to complete the rules.

RULES
1 In questions with auxiliaries, put *do/does/did* **before/after** the subject.
2 In questions with be, put *am/are/is/was/were* **before/after** the subject.

▶ page 128 LANGUAGEBANK

5 A Put the words in the correct order and add an auxiliary or *be* to make questions.

1 many / your / how / in / people / family?
2 see / often / you / parents / how / your?
3 family / with / you / spending / your / time / enjoy?
4 last / your / when / celebration / family?
5 who / best / friend / is / your?
6 you / often / eat / friends / how / out / with?
7 friend / your / live / where / best?

S1.1 **B Listen and check.**

C STRESSED WORDS Look at audio script S1.1 on page 168. Underline the stressed words. Listen again and repeat.

How many people are in your family?

D Work in pairs. Ask and answer the questions.

SPEAKING

6 A Work in pairs. You are going to interview other students. Look at the prompts and make questions about each topic. Choose a third topic to talk about.

B Work in groups. Ask and answer the questions.

Vacations

How long? Who?

What? Where?

Weekend

What? Where?

Work / Study? Get up?

????

Why? Where? What?

C Tell the class. Who do you think:

1 has the best vacations?
2 has very busy weekends?
3 enjoys staying at home?
4 exercises the most?
5 sleeps the most?
6 really knows how to enjoy themselves?

sports sport

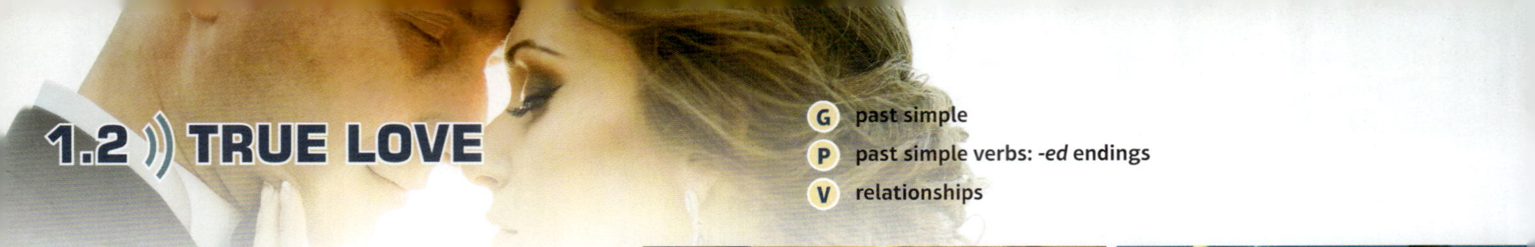

1.2 TRUE LOVE

G past simple
P past simple verbs: *-ed* endings
V relationships

SPEAKING

1 Work in pairs. Discuss the questions.

1 Do you believe in love at first sight? Why/Why not?
2 Where are good places to meet new people?

VOCABULARY

RELATIONSHIPS

2 A Read sentences 1–8. These describe the stages of a relationship. Match the phrases in bold with definitions a)–h).

1 He **proposed (to her)**.
2 They **got along** well.
3 They **got married**.
4 They **got engaged**.
5 They **met**.
6 She **accepted**.
7 He didn't **have a girlfriend**.
8 They **fell in love**.

a) agreed to marry
b) asked her to marry him
c) began to love each other
d) have a romantic relationship with a girl
e) said yes
f) had a good relationship
g) first knew each other
h) became husband and wife

B In what order do these things usually happen? Put the phrases 1–8 in Exercise 2A in order.

1 He didn't have a girlfriend.

C Write three true sentences about yourself or a friend. Use the phrases in bold in Exercise 2A.

I met my best friend, Piri, at a conference. We got along well immediately.

American Speak Out TIP
Words like *get* and *have* are used in lots of different phrases in English. Keep lists of these phrases and add new phrases when you learn them. Write down all the phrases you know with *get*. Compare your list with your partner's.

LISTENING

S1.2 **3 A Look at the pictures. They show how three people proposed to their partners. What do you think happened? Listen and check.**

B Listen again and answer the questions.

1 In Story 1, where did the boyfriend propose?
2 Why did she say, "It was almost a disaster"?
3 In Story 2, which country were they in?
4 What happened on the boat?
5 In Story 3, how did the boyfriend propose?
6 How did she accept?

C Which stories do the sentences 1–6 come from? Work in pairs and use the sentences to help you re-tell the stories.

1 We were at a restaurant.
2 I didn't say anything. I just gave her the ring.
3 We met at art school.
4 Luckily, she smiled.
5 I accepted, but I didn't tell him.
6 He tried to stop me.

D Discuss. Which do you think is the best story? Why?

got along well — got on well

GRAMMAR
PAST SIMPLE

4 A Underline examples of verbs in the past simple in Exercise 3C.

B Complete the tables below with the correct form of the verbs in the past simple.

Past Simple			
regular		**irregular**	
appear	*appeared*	go	______
like	______	fall	______
decide	______	get	______
try	______	say	______

negative	I ______ tell him.
question	______ they get married?
short answer	No, they ______ ./Yes, they did.

5 A PAST SIMPLE VERBS: *-ed* endings Listen to three pronunciations of regular past simple verbs.

1 /d/ **lived** They lived in Africa.
2 /t/ **asked** He asked her to marry him.
3 /ɪd/ **started** They started a family.

B Listen and put the words in the box in the correct columns in the table below.

worked wanted stopped smiled walked
needed talked studied helped decided

/d/	/t/	/ɪd/
lived	*asked*	*started*

▶ page 128 LANGUAGEBANK

6 A Complete the sentences with the correct form of the past simple.

go stay see cook spend

1 I ______ my best friend three months ago.
2 I ______ to a wedding last summer.
3 I ______ up all night.
4 I ______ a meal for some friends last night.
5 I ______ the day with my sister on Monday.

B Make *When did you last …?* questions for each sentence in Exercise 6A.

When did you last see your best friend?

C In pairs, ask and answer the questions.

A: When did you last go on vacation?
B: It was a few months ago. I went to …

SPEAKING

7 A Write down five important dates in your life. Prepare to talk about them.

B Work in pairs and take turns. Ask and answer questions about the dates. Try to guess what happened.

A: July 19, 2006.
B: Did you get married?
A: No, I didn't.
B: Did you start work?
A: Yes, I did.

WRITING
LINKING WORDS

8 A Match 1–4 with a)–d) to make sentences. Link the phrases with a word from the box below.

and so but because

1 In 1998, I finished my degree …
2 I moved in 2002 …
3 I wanted to learn Italian …
4 They wanted to buy a house, …
a) they didn't have enough money.
b) I could travel around the country.
c) started my first job.
d) I didn't like my roommate.

B Complete the web comment with linking words (*and*, *but*, *so*, *because*).

2011 was an important year [1]______ I met my wife, Ania. We met in an Internet chatroom, [2]______ we got along immediately. We started to chat and send emails, [3]______ we lived in different countries, [4]______ it was difficult for us to be together. Now we live in the U.K. with our two children.

C Write about an important year in your life. Use linking words (*and*, *but*, *so*, *because*).

I moved / roommate — I moved house / flat-mate

1.3 NICE DAY, ISN'T IT?

F making conversation
P linking
V conversation topics

VOCABULARY
CONVERSATION TOPICS

1 **Work in pairs. Discuss the questions.**

1 Do you enjoy **having conversations** with people you don't know?
2 What topics do you usually **talk about**?
3 What do you **say** when somebody **interrupts** you?
4 Do you ever **gossip** about celebrities?
5 Are you good at **telling jokes**?
6 Can you think of any **bad conversation habits**?

2 A **Complete the article with the words in the box.**

joke gossip saying conversation talk interrupt tells

B **Work in pairs. What problem does the article describe? Which tips do you think are good advice?**

C **Cover the article. How many tips can you remember?**

Top Conversation Killers

Do you ever find that you're having an interesting [1] ______, and then suddenly everything goes really quiet and you're not sure why? Next time, watch out for these conversation killers.

"You look tired"
There's nothing worse than when a friend who hasn't seen you for a while [2] ______ you that you're looking tired or stressed.

Me, Me, Me
This is one of the biggest conversation killers. Don't [3] ______ people to talk about yourself. It's a great idea to talk about things you have in common, but just remember to take turns.

"Sorry, what were you [4] ______?"
It's always easier to talk than to listen, but learning to listen and being interested in the response is an important conversation skill.

"Have you heard what people are saying about … ?"
Don't [5] ______ or say rude things about people you know, even if it's only a [6] ______.

Don't be too negative
Try not to [7] ______ about too many negative topics. As they say, "Laugh, and the world laughs with you; cry, and you cry alone."

FUNCTION

MAKING CONVERSATION

3 A Listen to two conversations. Which conversation (Conversation 1 or Conversation 2) do you think is better? Why?

1.5

B Listen again and complete the responses.

Conversation 1

A: Hi, David. This is my friend, Rachel.
B: Hi, Rachel. [1]_______ to meet you.
B: Would you like a drink, Rachel?
C: I'd [2]_______ a coffee, thank you.
B: Where exactly do you come from?
C: I'm [3]_______ Huntington, near L.A.

Conversation 2

A: Hi, Felicia. Nice day, isn't it?
B: Yes, it's [4]_______.
A: Did you have a good weekend?
B: Yes, it was [5]_______. I didn't do much.
A: Did you watch the game last night?
B: Yes, it was [6]_______.
A: I'll see you later.
B: Yes, see you [7]_______.

4 Work in pairs and take turns. Student A: look at page 160. Student B: look at page 162.

▶ page 128 LANGUAGEBANK

LEARN TO

SOUND NATURAL

1.6

5 A LINKING Listen to these phrases again. Notice how words are linked.

1 Would‿you like‿a drink?
2 Did‿you have‿a good weekend?
3 This‿is my friend, Rachel.
4 I'd love‿a coffee, thank‿you.
5 Yes,‿it was‿OK.
6 Nice‿to meet‿you.

B Listen again and repeat.

SPEAKING

American Speak out TIP

Use *so* to help a conversation when you ask another question. *Poland? So, where exactly in Poland do you come from?* You can also use it when you want to change the topic. *So, did you watch the game last night?* Can you add *so* to any questions in Exercise 3B? Practice saying the questions.

6 A Look at the topics in the box below. Think of five questions related to the topics that you can ask people.

movies	home	next vacation
food/drinks	free time	family
weather	work/studies	weekend

B Talk to as many different people as possible in the class. Start conversations with them. Try to ask at least three of your questions and then end the conversation. Be careful not to kill the conversation too quickly.

So, what kind of movies do you enjoy?
Where exactly do you live?
So, what do you do in your free time?

game / Practice / movies — match / Practise / films

1.4 SOMEONE SPECIAL

DVD PREVIEW

1 A Work in pairs and discuss the questions.

1 What kinds of programs do you enjoy watching on television?

2 Which TV shows are popular in your country at the moment?

3 Do you enjoy watching situation comedies (sitcoms)? Why/Why not?

B Read the program information and answer the questions.

1 What is Miranda's problem?

2 Why do you think she finds it difficult to answer Mike?

Miranda

Whatever Miranda tries to do in life, something always goes wrong. Now, she has a boyfriend called Mike, but, every time he says the words "I love you," Miranda panics and doesn't know how to respond. What's the real problem? Is it something to do with her old college friend Gary? And can her best friend, Stevie, help her to work it out?

DVD VIEW

2 A Watch the DVD. Why can't Miranda say "I love you" to Mike? What's the problem?

B Watch again. Number the sentences in the order you hear them.

a) "What was your first love?" "Doughnuts."

b) "You love him, but you're not in love with him."

c) "When he tells me he loves me, I freak out. Can't say it back." *1*

d) "I wouldn't laugh. It's one of the reasons I love you."

e) "You're not in love with your boyfriend. It's only fair you split up with him."

f) "What truly makes your heart skip?" "Gary."

3 A Who says sentences 1–6: Miranda, Mike, the man, Stevie or Gary? Whom are they talking to?

1 "I'm gonna to have to dash. I will see you later."

2 "What springs to mind when I say, 'What do you love?'"

3 "Now we need to work out how you'll end it."

4 "I'm going to have to write Mike a letter. It's the only way."

5 "Listen, I really really need your help. Do you think you could spare a few hours this afternoon?"

6 "I'm in love with Gary!"

B Watch again to check your answers.

4 Work in pairs and answer the questions.

1 What do you think Miranda should do now?

2 What do you think will happen next?

programs / have to run | programmes / have to dash

American Speakout a special person

5 A Think about people you know. Who is the best person to:

- go on vacation with?
- talk to about your problems?
- borrow money from?
- go out for dinner with?
- invite to your house for dinner?
- work/live with?
- go to a concert/art gallery with?

B Work in pairs and discuss your answers.

6 You are going to talk about an important person in your life. Think about questions 1–6.

1 Who is this person?
2 What is their relationship to you?
3 How did you meet?
4 How often do you see them?
5 What kind of things do you do together?
6 Why is this person important to you?

1.7

7 A Listen to someone describing a friend and answer the questions.

1 When did they meet?
2 Why are they good friends?
3 Does she say anything negative about her friend?

B Listen again and check (✓) the key phrases you hear.

KEYPHRASES

I've known [name] for …
We met …
We get along really well [because …] …
We have lots of things in common …
We both enjoy …
One thing I like about [name] is …
The only problem with [name] is …
He/She is one of those people who …
He/She's a great person.

C Work in pairs and take turns. Student A: tell your partner about your special person. Use the key phrases to help. Student B: ask questions to find out more information about him/her.

writeback a competition entry

8 A Read the competition entry below. Underline three reasons Julie is the writer's best friend.

Is your friend the "best friend in the world"? Tell us why.

Julie is the best friend in the world because she is always there for me. Julie is the person I call when I have a problem or if I need to borrow money. She has helped me through some difficult times. We have known each other for nearly twenty years, so we know everything there is to know about each other. We argue sometimes. But, we have the same sense of humor, so our arguments don't last very long. I can talk to Julie about anything, and I know she will be a friend forever.

B Write an entry for the competition about your best friend or someone special. Use the questions in Exercise 5 to help you.

check / humor | tick / humour

V FREE TIME

1 A Complete the questions with the missing word.

1 How often do you ______ a barbecue?
2 What do you usually do when you have time ______ work/from your studies?
3 How do you usually ______ time with your family?
4 What kind of things do you hate ______ money on?
5 Where is your favorite place to ______ out?
6 Where do you like to ______ shopping?

B Work in pairs. Ask and answer the questions.

V QUESTION FORMS

2 Work in pairs. Complete the application form for your partner. Ask and answer questions using the words in parentheses.

A: What is your name?
B: Pedro Gonzales

APPLICATION FORM

Name: (what)
Pedro Gonzales

Age: (what)

Place of birth: (where)

Address: (what)

Telephone number: (what)

Cell phone number: (what)

Email address: (what)

Occupation: (do)

Hobbies: (have)

3 A Choose some of the topics in the boxes below. Write five questions to ask other students.

B Work in groups. Ask and answer the questions.

V RELATIONSHIPS

4 A Find five mistakes in this paragraph.

I met Layla at a market. She was selling bread. We started chatting and got well along. At the time, I didn't keep a girlfriend, so I asked her on a date. We went to a local bakery! We soon fell to love, and I proposed at her after a month. I hid the ring in a piece of cake. Fortunately, she accepted, and she didn't eat the ring! It was a good way to get engaged. A week later we became married.

B In pairs, check your answers. Close your books. Student A: re-tell the story. Change two details. Student B: guess the changes.

G PAST SIMPLE

5 A Put the words in the correct order to make questions.

On your last vacation:

1 did / go / where / you?
2 why / there / did / go / you?
3 in / you / a / stay / did / hotel?
4 do / day / during / did / you / the / what?
5 evenings / out / the / you / go / in / did?
6 the / weather / hot / was?
7 you / language / speak / what / did?
8 you / friends / make / new / any / did?

B Work in pairs. Ask and answer the questions in Exercise 5A.

6 A Write a list of ten verbs you learned in Unit 1. What are the past simple forms?

B Work in pairs and take turns. Student A: say a verb. Student B: say the past simple form.

A: meet
B: met

C Now use the verbs from Exercise 6A to make questions.

D Ask and answer the questions.

A: When did you meet your partner?
B: We met in 2006.

V MAKING CONVERSATION

7 A Complete the conversations.

Conversation 1
A: Hi, (name) ______. ______ day, isn't it?
B: Yes, it's ______.

Conversation 2
A: This is my ______ (name) ______.
B: Hi. ______ to meet you.

Conversation 3
A: So, ______ you work here?
B: No, I'm a ______.

Conversation 4
A: Where exactly do you ______ from?
B: I'm ______ (place) ______.

Conversation 5
A: Did you have a ______ weekend?
B: Yes, it was ______. I didn't do ______.

Conversation 6
A: Did you ______ the game last night?
B: Yes, it ______ terrible.

Conversation 7
A: We lost 3–0.
B: Oh, ______! I'm ______ to hear that.

Conversation 8
A: I'll ______ you later.
B: Yes, see you ______.

B Work in pairs and practice the conversations.

favorite / parentheses / cell (phone) / learned — favourite / brackets /mobile (phone) / learnt

2 Work

SPEAKING
2.1 Talk about what motivates you at work
2.2 Talk about dangerous jobs
2.3 Talk about your perfect job
2.4 Describe your work/life balance

LISTENING
2.1 Listen to interviews about jobs
2.3 Listen to a man talking about his job
2.4 Watch an extract from a documentary about commuting

READING
2.2 Read a newspaper article about dangerous jobs
2.4 Read the results of a survey about work/life balance

WRITING
2.1 Write an email about work experience
2.4 Write a web comment about work/life balance

What do you do?

INTERVIEWS

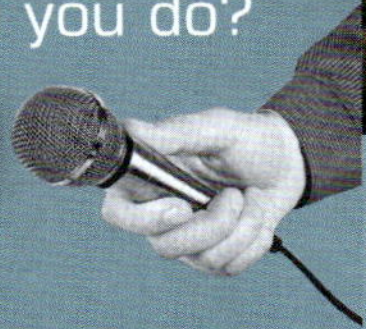

2.1 THE COMPANY 4 U?

G present simple and continuous
P word stress
V work

VOCABULARY

WORK

1 **Discuss the questions.**

1 What are the people doing in the second photo?
2 What kind of company is it?
3 Would you like to work for a company like this? Why/Why not?

2 **A** **Work in pairs. Match the words in the box with definitions 1–10.**

~~company~~	employee	salary	office	customer
employer	staff	task	boss	bonus

1 a business that makes or sells things or provides services *company*
2 a person who buys products or uses services
3 extra money given to a worker (often for especially good work)
4 a place where many people work at desks
5 a worker
6 a job you need to do
7 a person who manages the workers in the company
8 everyone who works in the company
9 a fixed, regular sum of money given to someone for doing a job
10 a person or business that pays workers to do a job

2.1 **B** **WORD STRESS** **Listen to the words and repeat.**

SPEAKING

3 **A** **Work in pairs. Discuss. What are the most important things for people who work? Number the items below in order of importance. 1 = very important. 8 = not important at all.**

- flexible hours/long vacations
- a big salary
- big bonuses for good work
- good relationships with other employees/customers
- working for a big company
- a friendly boss
- a chance to develop your skills
- interesting tasks

B **Compare your ideas with other students.**

LISTENING

2.2 **4** **A** **Listen to someone talking about how companies motivate their staff. How are the pictures (A–D) connected to the ideas?**

> **M** **mo.ti.vate** /ˈməʊtəveɪt $ ˈmoʊt̬əˌveɪt/ verb to make someone want to do something: *Teachers should motivate students to stay in school.*

from Longman WordWise Dictionary

B **Listen and check. Which other ideas do they talk about? Which ideas do you think are the best?**

2.3 **5** **A** **Listen to three employees describe what they are doing. Check (✓) the activities they mention.**

watching a movie	choosing a CD	fishing
studying	waiting for a customer	making coffee
getting a massage	checking emails	

B **Listen again. Answer the questions.**

1 What is the "agreement" between the two stores?
2 What does the company pay for?
3 Why can the woman start work at 1 p.m.?

GRAMMAR

PRESENT SIMPLE AND CONTINUOUS

6 A Read sentences a) and b). Answer the questions.

a) This is the clothing store.

b) I'm taking a break.

1 Which sentence describes something that is always true?

2 Which sentence describes a temporary situation?

3 Which sentence uses the present simple?

4 Which sentence uses the present continuous?

B Read sentences a)–d). Answer the questions.

a) I'm choosing my free CD for the week.

b) I'm checking my emails.

c) I'm studying history.

d) Six of us are taking online courses.

1 Which two sentences refer to this exact moment?

2 Which two sentences refer to the general present, but not to this moment?

▶ page 130 LANGUAGEBANK

7 Make two sentences or questions with the prompts. Use the present simple and present continuous.

1	**you / work**	on a special task at the moment? on Saturdays?

Are you working on a special task at the moment?

Do you work on Saturdays?

2	**I / look**	for a job at the moment at my emails when I get to work
3	**I / not / use**	English for my job the photocopier at the moment
4	**you / watch**	the news on TV every day? TV right now?
5	**I / not / read**	any good books at the moment a newspaper every morning
6	**you / have**	a good time at this party? a company car?

8 A Make *you* questions with the prompts. Use the present simple or present continuous.

1 think / your salary / good?

Do you think your salary is good?

2 speak / any other languages?

3 why / learn English?

4 study for / an exam / now?

5 work on / a special project / at the moment?

6 have / your own / office?

B Work in pairs. Choose four or five questions to ask your partner. Find similarities and differences between you and your partner.

WRITING

STARTING/ENDING AN EMAIL

9 A Look at the phrases below. Which are formal (F) and which are informal (I)?

Starting an email:

Dear colleagues *F*
Dear Sir Hi Dear Dr. Bryce Hello
Dear all Hi everyone

Introducing the main topic:

I am writing about … It's about … Regarding …

Ending an email:

See you soon Best wishes Bye for now
I look forward to hearing from you Best
Talk to you soon Take care Bye Love
Sincerely

B Read the email. What work does Vanessa do?

Dear Mr. Shaw,

I am writing to apply for the position at your company advertised in JSI. I believe my personal qualities and my experience make me a good candidate for this job.

I worked for Seng Tech for three years, producing designs for apps. Our customers included Sherring Inc. and BTZ Co. I am currently developing cell phone apps for two other companies.

I am very motivated by interesting tasks, and I am looking for a chance to develop my skills in a bigger company.

I look forward to hearing from you.

Sincerely,

Vanessa Chiarollo

C Read the ad and write to BES. Use the prompts below and phrases from Exercise 9A.

1 Say why you're writing and introduce yourself.

2 Say what you're doing now (studying English, etc.).

3 Ask for information about BES's work experience program.

4 End the email.

BES is an international furniture design company. Based in Ankara, we design and produce household furniture in 15 countries.
We are looking for people who want work experience in design, sales and other areas.
Write to Hakan Balik at hbalik@BES.nett.

Dr. / ad, advertisement — Dr / advert, advertisement

2.2 A RISKY BUSINESS

G adverbs of frequency
P stressed syllables
V jobs

VOCABULARY

JOBS

1 A Work in pairs. Discuss. Which are the best/worst jobs? Think about:

- meeting people
- opportunities to travel
- problems to deal with
- tasks
- hours of work
- salary

B Match the jobs with photos A–G.

sales rep	fashion designer	IT consultant
foreign correspondent	personal trainer	
rescue worker	courier	

2.5

C STRESSED SYLLABLES Listen and repeat. Underline the stressed syllables.

sales rep

American Speakout TIP
The stressed part of a word or phrase sounds l o n g e r, LOUDER and higher than the other parts. Practice saying new vocabulary, focusing on the stressed parts.

▶ page 152 PHOTOBANK

2 A Complete the phrases with the words in the box.

work	deal with	risk	get

1 ______ a good salary/long vacations
2 ______ on a team/under pressure
3 ______ their lives/your health
4 ______ problems/customers

B Use the phrases to talk about the jobs in Exercise 1.

An IT consultant gets a good salary.

3 A Complete sentences 1–6 with the words in the box.

get	team	under	deal	vacations	risk

1 People are more motivated when they ______ a good salary.
2 People work better ______ a lot of pressure.
3 It's important that employees get long ______.
4 People who ______ their lives at work should get more money.
5 It's more enjoyable to work on a ______ than alone.
6 These days, people usually ______ with their own IT problems.

B Work in pairs. Discuss. Which of the sentences above do you agree/disagree with? Why?

READING

4 A Work in pairs. Discuss. Which of the jobs in Exercise 1 do you think is the best paid, most interesting or most dangerous? Why?

B Work in groups. Student A: read the text below. Student B: read the text on page 160. Student C: read the text on page 162. Make notes on:

- job
- country
- people interviewed
- why the job is dangerous
- special memories/stories

C Tell your group about your text using the notes.

Danger Rating 6/10

Mountain rescue worker, Austria

Up in the mountains, the view is beautiful, but not for emergency doctor Martin Schmidt, paramedic Marius Adler and helicopter pilot Klaus Hartmann. Their job is to find and rescue people in trouble: climbers caught in an avalanche, injured skiers, even lost walkers. Reporter Lucy Rose met the team members and asked them about their work.

Adler says they love their jobs, but they sometimes get angry with the people they rescue. "Climbers always risk their lives, but, when they get into trouble, they also risk ours."

What exactly are the dangers? Hartmann says that, although the sun is shining today, they usually fly in much worse weather conditions, which can be very dangerous. Another problem is that, often, the people they rescue are frightened. They panic, and this makes it difficult for the team.

And what are the best things about the job? Hartmann says, "Saving lives is its own reward." And occasionally they get a surprise. "One time we rescued a woman after a skiing accident. She was badly hurt. Later her husband brought us a huge box of chocolates." The people they rescue, Schmidt explains, hardly ever say thank you!

GRAMMAR

ADVERBS OF FREQUENCY

5 A Look at sentences 1–9. Put the words in bold in the correct place on the line.

1 He **never** worries.
2 **Often** the people they rescue are frightened.
3 The mountain rescuers **sometimes** get angry.
4 It **usually** involves a few broken bones.
5 Life as a jockey is **rarely** safe.
6 These people **always** risk their lives.
7 The people they rescue **hardly ever** say thank you.
8 **Once in a while** jockeys even die during a race.
9 **Occasionally** they get a surprise.

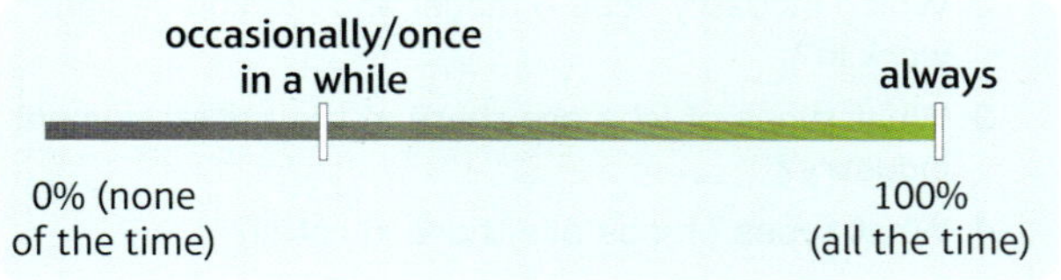

B Read your text again. Underline all the adverbs or expressions of frequency. Look at the other texts to find more examples.

▶ page 130 LANGUAGEBANK

6 A Find and correct the mistakes in sentences 1–6. There is one mistake in each sentence.

1 I work always at night.
2 Once on a while, I study on weekends.
3 I ever hardly study alone.
4 I work at home occasional.
5 It is sometime difficult to study and work at the same time.
6 I don't usual miss classes because of work.

B Write four sentences about your job or studies.

I deal with customers once in a while.

C Compare with a partner.

SPEAKING

7 A Work in groups. You are making a TV program about dangerous jobs. Discuss the questions and choose three jobs for your program.

1 Which jobs are dangerous? Why? How often are the people in dangerous situations?
2 Which jobs are the most interesting for your TV audience?
3 Whom will you interview for the program? What questions will you ask them?

B Work with another group and compare your ideas.

on weekends — at weekends

2.3 I LIKE WORKING OUTSIDE

F expressing likes/dislikes
P intonation: sound interested
V types of work

VOCABULARY
TYPES OF WORK

1 A Work in pairs. Look at the types of work below. Answer the questions.

education | the fashion industry | sales and marketing | retail | the tourist industry | accounting | the entertainment industry | the food industry

1 Which industry does a chef, cook and waiter work in?
2 Which industry does a model and fashion designer work in?
3 What types of jobs are there in the entertainment industry?
4 What types of jobs are there in retail?

B Look at photos A–D. Which industries are the people working in?

FUNCTION
EXPRESSING LIKES/DISLIKES

S2.5

2 A Listen to an interview with someone about his job. What job is it? What does he like about it?

B Listen again and complete the sentences.

1 I **like** ______ outside.
2 I **can't stand** ______ at a desk all day.
3 I **absolutely love** ______.
4 I **don't like** ______ on a team. I prefer working alone.
5 I **don't mind** ______ my hands dirty.
6 I **like** ______ new things.
7 I **hate** ______ under pressure.
8 **I don't really like** ______ for a company. I want to be my own boss.

C Read the sentences. Which phrases in bold are very positive (+ +), positive (+), negative (–), or very negative (– –)? Which are not positive or negative (*)?

3 A Which of the statements in Exercise 2B is true for you?

B Work in pairs. Find out three things that your partner loves/likes/hates and write sentences about them. Use the phrases in Exercise 2B to help.

Maria can't stand smoking.

▶ page 130 LANGUAGEBANK

LEARN TO
RESPOND AND ASK MORE QUESTIONS

S2.6

4 A Read and listen to the extracts from the audio script. Notice how the listener responds and complete the phrases. The first has been done for you.

M: One good thing about my job is that I like working outside.
W: I [1] *see*.
M: I travel a lot, and I absolutely love traveling, particularly in South America and Australia.
W: And what [2] ______ **your colleagues,** people you work with?
M: I don't like working on a team. I prefer working alone.
W: [3] ______ **? And what about the type of work?**
M: You're always discovering new things.
W: That's great. It [4] ______ **wonderful.**

S2.7

B INTONATION: sound interested Listen and repeat the phrases in bold. Notice the intonation. Copy the intonation to sound interested.

C Look at audio script S2.6 in Exercise 4A. Underline other examples of comments and questions. Write them in the table.

comments	*I see.*
questions	*And what about ...?*

I like, am interested in / I don't really like, am not really interested in / traveling

I'm keen on / I'm not very keen on / travelling

5 A **Work in pairs. Student A: complete sentences 1–4. Student B: complete sentences 5–8.**

1 I got a new job as a ______.
2 Yesterday I bought a new ______.
3 I'm going on vacation to ______.
4 Last night I saw ______.
5 I've always wanted to ______.
6 Yesterday I learned how to ______.
7 I watched a great movie about ______.
8 This morning I met ______.

B **Work in pairs and take turns. Student A: read a sentence. Student B: respond and ask a follow-up question.**

A: I just got a new job as a ski instructor!
B: Really? When do you start?

SPEAKING

6 A **Work in pairs. What is the perfect job for you? Think about your job now or a job you'd like to have in the future. Make notes on the:**

- industry (entertainment, tourism, medical ...)
- type of work (creative, manual, IT-based ...)
- skills (networking, writing, planning ...)
- hours (9-5, flexible ...)
- location (outside, in an office, traveling ...)
- people (work alone, on a team, in a large corporation ...)

B **Work with other students. Talk about your perfect job. As you listen, respond and ask questions.**

My perfect job is in the tourist industry. I like meeting new people, and I absolutely love showing people around my city.

2.4 DREAM COMMUTERS

DVD PREVIEW

1 Work in pairs. Discuss the questions.

1 How do you get to school/work?

2 How long would you be prepared to travel to school/work (one hour/three hours)?

2 A Read the program information and answer the questions.

1 What was Justin unhappy about before?

2 What did he decide to do?

The Money Programme: Dream Commuters

The Money Programme is a documentary series. Dream Commuters tells the story of a man who was **fed up with** his **commute** to work and his lifestyle. Every day there was a lot of **traffic** on the roads, and the commute to work took a long time. He wasn't happy with his work/life balance. So he bought a **property** in France and took his family to live there. He now takes cheap **flights** to work. He is one of a growing number of **commuters** who live in another country. He says it has **transformed** his life.

B Match the words in bold in Exercise 2A with meanings 1–7.

1 completely changed

2 trips in a plane

3 people who travel to work

4 cars, motorcycles, etc. on the road

5 trip to work

6 a building or land that you own

7 unhappy with something, so you want to change it

DVD VIEW

3 A Watch the DVD. Do you think Justin's life is better now? Why/Why not?

B Are the sentences below True (T) or False (F)?

1 More and more people are choosing to live abroad and commute to their jobs in the U.K.

2 Justin is manager of an online business based in the U.K.

3 Justin's commute costs him hundreds of pounds every week.

4 Justin's commute home is about 70 miles.

5 Justin's wife and children stay in France while he travels to the U.K. every week.

4 Watch the DVD again. What exactly do they say? Underline the correct alternative.

1 "We were fed up with *waiting in the airport/the traffic*."

2 "He's one of a group of *travelers/commuters* who take the same flight to Toulouse every week."

3 "We looked on the Internet, and we saw properties available *much cheaper/more expensive* than in Britain."

4 "That's the house down there. With the *swimming pool/terrace*."

5 "We've just transformed our *house/lifestyle*."

5 Work in pairs. Discuss the questions.

1 Could you be a "dream commuter" with your present job/studies?

2 Where would you choose to live, and how would you get to work?

The dollar is the currency used in the U.S. and other countries like Canada. The pound is the currency used in Britain. Euros are used in most of the rest of Europe.

trips / motorcycles | journeys / motorbikes

American Speakout work/life balance

6 Read the text and discuss the questions.

In the U.K., people work 43.5 hours per week on average. Men work 46.9 hours. In France, the average working week is 35 hours. Research also shows that 16 percent of U.K. workers work over 60 hours per week. At home in the U.K., working parents play with their children for only 25 minutes per day. 1 out of 8 (12.5 percent) fathers see their children only on the weekend.

1 Is the work/life balance the same in your country?
2 Do you think people work too much? What problems can this cause?
3 Are you happy with your work/life or study/life balance? Why/Why not?

S2.8

7 Listen to an interview with a student. Does she have a good work/life balance? Check (✓) the key phrases you hear.

KEYPHRASES

How much time do you spend ... (sleeping/ relaxing/ commuting)?

I spend a lot of time ... (working/exercising).

Do you ever ... (take a vacation)?

What about your ... (social life/weekends)?

How do you spend your weekends?

8 A Write some questions about work/life balance. Use the things in the box to help you.

exercise/sports   social life   family
weekends   enjoyable hobbies   vacations
work/study habits

How much time do you spend with your family?

B Work in groups and take turns. Ask and answer your questions. Find someone who has a similar work/life balance to yours.

writeback a web comment

9 A Read the entry to www.worklife247.nett. Answer the questions.

1 Is this a stressful job? Why/Why not?
2 Would you like a job like this?

22-10-16 Posting 1

I'm a personal trainer. I eat well, and I exercise a lot. I spend about five hours a day working with clients. In general, I think my work/life balance is good. I take time off every few months just to relax, and I rarely get stressed. Once in a while, I go out partying. For me, a balanced lifestyle is really important. When I was younger, I worried if I missed a day of exercise. These days I don't worry about it.

My only problem is the one-hour commute. I hate taking the train every day, and it's expensive. I'm planning to move so I can live near the gym where I work and walk to work every morning.

Comment

B Think about your work/life balance and write a comment for www.worklife247.nett.

exercising | doing exercise

G PRESENT SIMPLE AND CONTINUOUS

1 Work in pairs. Which verb can you use for a) and b)? Put each verb into the present simple or present continuous.

1 a) Don't switch off the TV! I *'m watching* it.
b) I love that program! I *watch* it every week.

2 a) Can you call me back later? I ______ my homework.
b) I try to stay in shape. I ______ yoga and aerobics every day.

3 a) I love tennis, but I ______ badly.
b) Sorry, I can't hear you because Matthew ______ the piano.

4 a) I ______ about twenty text messages a day, usually to friends.
b) She ______ a book. It will be published next year.

5 a) Daddy can't come home now. He ______ late at the office.
b) Usually he ______ from 9 a.m. to 5 p.m., Monday to Friday.

6 a) I like to spend time with friends. That's what ______ me happy.
b) I ______ some coffee. Do you want some?

7 a) She loves the school. She ______ a lot of friends there.
b) Jill ______ some problems with her phone. Can you check it?

8 a) He only met his real father last month. They ______ to know each other now.
b) In the U.K., about 50 percent of married couples ______ divorced.

9 a) She always ______ a book to her son before he goes to sleep.
b) I ______ his new book at the moment. It's really good.

10 a) Hi Tim! I'm in town for a week. I ______ an old friend.
b) When we go to New York, we usually ______ at the Metropolitan Museum of Art.

2 A Make six true sentences about your life/job. Use a word/phrase from each box.

at home | my friends | in bed | on the weekend | in the shower | on Friday evenings | my family | during my vacation | at my desk

work | drink | play | do | sing | eat | write | talk | call | visit

often | sometimes | rarely | never | always | usually | once in a while | occasionally | hardly ever

B Work in pairs and compare your sentences.

A: I rarely work at my desk.
B: Do you often work at home?

G ADVERBS OF FREQUENCY

3 A Match questions 1–7 with answers a)–g).

1 How often do you play sports?
2 Do you usually get up before 7 a.m.?
3 How often do you call your mother?
4 Do you eat a lot of meat?
5 How many texts do you send in a week?
6 Do you ever go camping?
7 How often do you read a newspaper?

a) Yes, my children wake me up at 5:30 a.m.
b) I don't know. Maybe twenty.
c) Very rarely. I watch the news on television.
d) I play tennis once in a while.
e) No, hardly ever. I prefer fish.
f) Once a week. We always speak on Sundays.
g) Yes, occasionally. But it usually rains.

B Work in pairs and take turns. Ask and answer questions 1–7.

V WORK AND JOBS

4 Work in pairs and take turns. Student A: choose a word/phrase from the box. Student B: choose another word/phrase and explain the connection between them.

IT consultant | office | staff | work on a team | foreign correspondent | sales rep | risk their lives | fashion designer | boss | deal with customers | task | courier | company | get a good salary | opportunity | rescue worker | personal trainer | deal with problems

A: IT consultant
B: An IT consultant deals with problems related to technology.

F EXPRESSING LIKES/DISLIKES

5 A Work in pairs. How well do you know your partner? Think of questions for answers 1–6.

1 I absolutely love it.
2 I can't stand it.
3 I don't like it very much.
4 I don't mind it.
5 I'm not very interested in it.
6 I like it.

B Ask your partner the questions. Ask follow-up questions to find out more.

A: Do you like Italian food?
B: I absolutely love it.
A: What's your favorite dish?
B: Spaghetti Bolognese.
A: Really? How often do you eat it?

3 time out

FREE IN NYC p28

RELAX! p30

CAN I TAKE A MESSAGE? p32

RIO DE JANEIRO p34

SPEAKING
3.1 Talk about your future plans
3.2 Discuss how you spend your free time
3.3 Make and receive phone calls
3.4 Plan a perfect day out

LISTENING
3.1 Listen to a radio program about going out in New York
3.3 Understand some problem phone calls
3.4 Watch an extract from a travel program about visiting Rio de Janeiro

READING
3.2 Read about how people spend their free time around the world

WRITING
3.1 Write an email invitation
3.4 Write an invitation for a day out

What do you like doing in your free time?

INTERVIEWS

3.1)) FREE IN NYC

- **G** present continuous/*be going to* for future
- **P** fast speech: *going to*
- **V** time out

VOCABULARY

TIME OUT

1 A Complete the word webs with the verbs in the box.

have go get see go to

1 ______: a bar, a club, a concert, a restaurant, a museum, an art gallery, the theater, a market

2 ______: an exhibition, a comedy show, a band, some live music

3 ______: a snack, the bus, some tickets

4 ______: sightseeing, dancing, shopping

5 ______: dinner, a free meal, an evening out, a drink

B Work in pairs and take turns. Ask and answer questions using the phrases in Exercise 1A.

A: *How often do you go to a museum?*
B: *Not very often.*

▶ page 153 PHOTOBANK

LISTENING

2 A Work in pairs. Discuss the questions.

1 What kinds of things do you like to do when you visit a city?
2 Where can you go/what things can you do for free or very cheaply where you live?

S3.1

B Listen to a radio program. Answer the questions.

1 Is New York an expensive city to live in?
2 Are there lots of free things to do there?
3 How much money do the journalists have to spend?
4 What do they have to do?

3 A Complete the information about Rafael and Carmen's plans.

Rafael

1 He plans to start the day with a delicious bagel and then to spend the morning in ______.
2 He's going to the ______ of American Finance.
3 He's taking the Staten Island Ferry to see ______ of New York.
4 In the evening, he's going to see some ______ music.

Carmen

5 She's going to see a free ______ exhibition.
6 She's going to Times ______ because she likes the atmosphere.
7 She's going to an ______ restaurant near there.
8 In the evening, she's going to a ______ class.

B Listen to the program again to check your answers. Which places in the photos do the speakers talk about?

C Work in pairs. Discuss. What do you think of the two plans? Which things would you like/not like to do?

> If you say you're going to the theater in American English, you probably mean you're going to see a play. You might go to a movie theater to see a movie though.

SPEAKING

6 A Think about your future plans. Make notes about:

- places/people you plan to visit
- a movie you want to see
- something delicious you want to eat

	You	Your Partner
tonight	*visit friend*	
this weekend		
next week/month		
later this year/next year		

B Work in pairs and take turns. Ask and answer questions about your plans (What? Where? With whom? Why?). Add notes to the table.

A: What are you going to do tonight?
B: I'm going to visit an old friend.

WRITING
INVITATIONS

7 A Put the emails in the correct order.

To
Hi Sonia—I'm going to be in New York next week. Sue and I are meeting for a drink on Tuesday evening at 6:30 p.m. Would you like to come?
Annabel ☐

To
I'd love to. Sounds great! See you there.
S ☐

To
We're going out for a meal. Do you want to meet us for dinner? We're having a pizza at Mario's at 8 p.m.
A ☐

To
Great to hear from you. I'm sorry, but I'm busy. I'm going to an exercise class from 6 p.m. to 7:30 p.m. What are you doing afterward?
Sonia ☐

B Look at the emails in Exercise 7A. Underline two phrases for inviting and two responses.

C Write emails with the prompts.

To
Hi Matt
What / you / do / tonight? A few people / come / watch / soccer / my house. Want / come?
Ali

To
Tilly
What / do / weekend? Would / like / dancing / Saturday night?
Frank

To
Ali
Great / hear. Love / to. Time / everyone / come?
Matt

To
Sorry / busy / Saturday evening. Want / go movies / Sunday?
T

To
That / great / idea. Love / to. What / want / see?
Frank

afterward — afterwards

GRAMMAR
PRESENT CONTINUOUS/*BE GOING TO* FOR FUTURE

4 A Read sentences a)–d) and answer the questions.

a) I'm going to see a free art exhibition.
b) I'm meeting a friend.
c) I'm going to see some live music.
d) I'm not going running.

1 Do the sentences refer to the present or the future?
2 Is there a definite time and place for the plans?
3 What tenses do the sentences use?

S3.2

B FAST SPEECH: *going to* Listen to the pronunciation of *going to* in fast speech /'gʌnə/. Listen and repeat the sentences.

▶ page 132 LANGUAGEBANK

5 A Make sentences or questions with the prompts. Use the present continuous or *be going to*.

1 we / go / the movies / Friday
2 you / go / stay / at / home / this evening?
3 she / not / work / this weekend
4 what time / we / meet / tomorrow?
5 I / go / watch / the football game / later
6 they / go out / for a pizza / on Saturday

B Change two sentences so they are true for you.

C Work in pairs and compare ideas.

3.2 RELAX!

- G questions without auxiliaries
- P stress in compound nouns
- V places to visit

VOCABULARY
PLACES TO VISIT

1 A Look at the words in the box and answer the questions.

1 Are they usually indoors or outdoors?

2 What free time activities do we usually do in these places?

concert hall	countryside	sports field
nightclub	street market	shopping mall
nature trail	waterfront	

B Write the words in the correct place and add as many other places as you can in one minute. Compare with other students.

indoors

outdoors

2 A STRESS IN COMPOUND NOUNS Listen to the words in the box in Exercise 1A. Underline the stressed syllables. Which word is usually stressed in compound nouns (nouns made of two words)?

<u>con</u>cert hall

B Listen again and repeat.

READING

3 A Work in pairs. Read the questions about how different nationalities spend their free time and guess the answers.

1 Who spends the most time on the Internet?

2 What is the world's most popular sport?

3 Who spends the most time outdoors?

4 Which country has the most bars per person?

5 Which country has the most popular galleries and museums?

6 Which nation watches the most TV?

7 Which country parties the most?

8 Who exercises the most?

B Read the magazine article to find the answers.

C Work in pairs. Discuss the questions.

1 Is there any information in the text that surprises you? Why?

2 How do people spend their free time in your country? Are the activities in 1–8 popular?

ocean | sea

How the World Spends Its Free Time

1 Internet
People from Canada spend, on average, 43.5 hours per week online, 8 hours longer than people in the U.S., who come in second. One reason: Canada has long, cold winters, so people spend lots of time indoors.

2 Sports
Soccer is king. In second place, surprisingly, is cricket. Only a few nations play the game seriously, but it's very popular in India, which has 1.2 billion people.

3 Outdoors
New Zealanders spend the most time outdoors. The countryside is perfect for hiking, mountain climbing and water sports. If you live in New Zealand, you're never more than two hours' drive from the ocean. And then there is the rugby, too …

4 Bars
Spain has six bars per 1,000 inhabitants, easily the highest number. In Spain, a bar is for families, not just drinkers. It's a meeting place and often an eating place (try the tapas!).

5 Galleries and Museums
The U.K. has six of the top 20 most visited art galleries/museums in the world, including the National Gallery, the British Museum and Tate Modern.

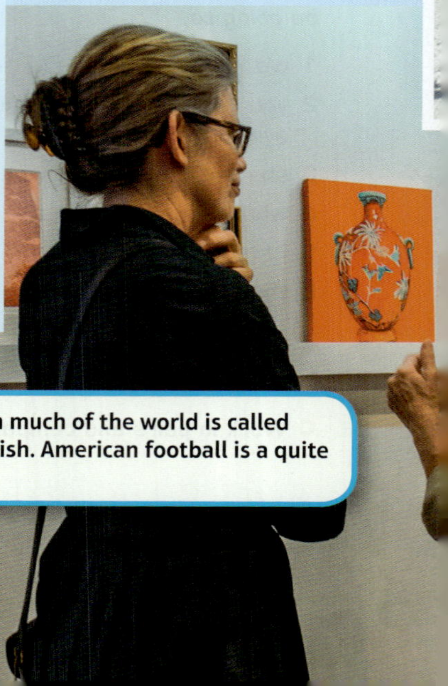

What's called "football" in much of the world is called "soccer" in American English. American football is a quite different game!

6 TV

The biggest TV-watchers are in Thailand. They spend 22.4 hours a week watching TV. In second place comes the Philippines (21 hours) and, in third place, Egypt (20.9 hours), famous for its never-ending soap operas!

7 Party!

It's impossible to say who parties the most, but Brazil's annual carnival makes it a good choice. Some of the best cities for partying include Bangkok (friendly people, great nightclubs), Berlin (live music scene) and the island of Ibiza (dance music).

8 Exercising

The biggest exercisers are people from Greece and Estonia. Over 80 percent of people in those countries exercise regularly. In both countries, soccer and the Olympic sports are the most popular, but Estonia has one very special game: ice cricket!

GRAMMAR

QUESTIONS WITHOUT AUXILIARIES

4 **Read the examples and answer questions 1–3.**

a) Subject questions

Question: ***Who*** *exercises the most?*

Answer: ***Greeks*** *exercise the most.*

b) Object questions

Question: What did ***you*** *do last night?*

Answer: ***I*** *went to a party.*

1 Which question asks us to name the subject (the people who do the action): a) or b)?

2 Which question asks for other information about the subject: a) or b)?

3 Which type of question uses the auxiliary?

▶ page 132 LANGUAGEBANK

5 **Complete the questions for the answers in italics with the words in the box.**

makes	did	Who (x 2)	Which	do	is

1 ______ invented basketball?
A Canadian called James Naismith invented basketball.

2 ______ country makes the most movies?
India makes the most movies.

3 What ______ people do when it's too cold to go out?
They watch TV or read!

4 ______ exercises more: the Japanese or the Germans?
The Germans exercise more.

5 Which sport ______ Brazil famous for?
Brazil is famous for soccer.

6 Which country ______ the most cars?
China makes the most cars.

7 What ______ you do last night?
I stayed at home.

SPEAKING

6 **A** **Ask other students questions to find out:**

1 who listens to music the most frequently
How often do you listen to music?

2 who exercises the most
Do you exercise a lot?

3 who spends the most time on the Internet

4 who regularly goes to art galleries and/or museums

5 who has been to the theater or movies in the last four months

6 who goes to the most parties

7 who watches the most TV

8 who is the biggest sports fan

B **As a whole class, answer the questions in Exercise 6A.**

Juan listens to music most frequently. He listens to music on the way to and from work and for two hours every evening!

3.3)) CAN I TAKE A MESSAGE?

- **F** making a phone call
- **P** linking: *can*
- **V** collocations

SPEAKING

1 Work in pairs. Discuss the questions.

1 Do you prefer speaking on the phone or in person?

2 Have you ever made a call or taken a message in English? What happened?

VOCABULARY
COLLOCATIONS

2 A Look at phrases 1–7 below. Have you done any of these on the phone recently? Have you done any in English?

1 reserve a table
2 arrange to meet friends
3 have a chat
4 cancel a reservation
5 check train times
6 change a ticket
7 talk business

B Work in pairs and compare your answers.

A: Have you reserved a table on the phone recently?
B: Yes, I reserved a table at a restaurant last week.

FUNCTION
MAKING A PHONE CALL

3.5

3 A Listen to four people making phone calls. Why are they calling?

B Listen again and complete the notes.

Conversation 1

Sun. May 16: Jack Hopper, table for ______ people.
Time: ______.

Como's
RESTAURANT

Conversation 2

RSA THEATER

2 tickets for James ______.
New date: ______.

Conversation 3

Dinner with Mary and the gang,
Pauly's at ______ on ______ night.

Conversation 4

Witherton's Ltd

Date: August 22. Time: 2:20.
To: Ally Sanders. Caller: Kim Brower.
Message: Cancel ______. Please call back.

4 Complete the sentences with the words in the box.

it's	back	for	leave	here	take	can

Start the call.

Caller: Hello, this is Andy./Hello, [1] ______ Andy. (NOT ~~*I am Andy*~~)

Receiver: Hello, Paul speaking.

Ask to speak to someone …

Caller: [2] ______ I speak to … ?

Receiver: Who's calling?

When the person the caller wants isn't there …

Caller: Can I [3] ______ a message?

Receiver: I'm afraid she's not [4] ______ at the moment. Can I [5] ______ a message? I'll ask her to call you [6] ______.

Finish the call.

Caller: See you soon. Goodbye.

Receiver: Thanks [7] ______ calling. See you soon. Goodbye.

calling | phoning

5 A Underline the correct alternative to complete the phone conversations.

Conversation 1

Sasha: Hello. Sasha [1]*here/speaks*.
Mustafa: Hi, [2]*I'm/it's* Mustafa.
Sasha: Hi, Mustafa. How are you?
Mustafa: I'm fine, thanks. How about you?
Sasha: Good, thanks.
Mustafa: Are you busy? Do you want to have lunch at that Turkish place on Broad Street?
Sasha: That sounds good. What time?
Mustafa: One o'clock?
Sasha: Great.
Mustafa: OK. [3]*Talk/See* you soon.
Sasha: OK. Bye.

Conversation 2

Receptionist: Anderson Products.
Sasha: Hello. Can I [4]*connect/speak* to the HR Manager?
Receptionist: One moment. Who's [5]*called/calling*?
Sasha: It's Sasha Barnes here.
Receptionist: I'm afraid he [6]*isn't/not* here at the moment. Can I take a [7]*message/call*?
Sasha: Please tell him to call me [8]*return/back*. I'm waiting in the Turkish restaurant!

B Work in pairs and practice the conversations. Take turns changing roles.

▶ page 132 LANGUAGEBANK

LEARN TO
MANAGE PHONE PROBLEMS

6 A Look at the phrases in bold in the extracts below and match them to problems a)–e).

a) we need to hear something again *2, 6*
b) the speaker is speaking too fast
c) the speaker is speaking too quietly
d) when we are not sure the information is correct
e) the speaker isn't sure the listener heard anything

In the U.S., phone numbers are typically written and spoken as a three-digit (area code) plus three-digit prefix and then the remaining four digits, (415) 235-7898.

Extract 1

C: OK, one moment. [1]**Can I just check?** What's the name, please?
D: The tickets are reserved in the name of James King.
C: [2]**Sorry, I didn't catch that**. Did you say King?
D: James King.
C: OK, yes. Two tickets for July tenth. What date would you like to change to?
D: What dates do you still have seats for?
C: There's nothing on the twelfth or thirteenth. There are two seats for the eleventh, but they're separate. We have ...
D: [3]**Sorry, can you slow down, please?**

Extract 2

E: Hello?
F: Hello, it's Mary here. Hello? [4]**Can you hear me OK?** It's Mary here.

Extract 3

F: Are you doing anything on Saturday? A few of us are going out for dinner.
E: Sorry, Mary, [5]**can you speak up, please?** I'm at the station, and I can't hear a thing.

Extract 4

H: It's (415) 823 2766.
G: [6]**Can you repeat that, please?**

S3.5 **B LINKING: *can* Listen and repeat the phrases. Notice how *can* and *you* are linked in connected speech: /kənju:/**

S3.6 **7 A Listen and write an appropriate response.**

S3.7 **B Listen to check.**

American Speak out TIP: Before you make a phone call, think carefully about the words you will use. How will you start the conversation? What information do you want? Write down some key words that you will use and expect to hear.

SPEAKING

8 Work in pairs. Student A: turn to page 160. Student B: turn to page 162.

3.4 RIO DE JANEIRO

DVD PREVIEW

1 Work in pairs and discuss.

1 When you visit a new city, what kind of things do you like to do?

2 Do you like to see and do the things a tourist would do, or do you prefer to spend time with the local people? Why?

2 A Work in pairs and discuss.

1 What do you know about Rio de Janeiro in Brazil?

2 Would you like to go there? Why/Why not?

B Read the program information. What kind of things do you think the locals will do in Rio?

Going Local: Rio

Going Local takes its hosts to fantastic cities around the world and asks them to explore the city by doing a series of challenges. However, to complete the challenges, they need to throw away the guidebook and ask the people who know best—the locals. In this episode, Rafael Estophania travels to Rio de Janeiro, the city of sand and samba, to find out how the *cariocas* (locals) spend their time.

DVD VIEW

3 A Which of these activities do you think the host tries to do?

1 find somewhere good to eat

2 use public transportation with good views

3 eat exotic fruit

4 play a game with the locals

5 dance samba

6 play music

B Watch the DVD to find out.

4 A Correct the information in the sentences.

1 Rio is the home of sunshine, ~~*salsa*~~ and Sugarloaf Mountain. *samba*

2 You can view all the *favelas* from the train.

3 The locals tell him to go to the supermarket to find exotic fruit.

4 The cashew nut tastes like a mixture of strawberries and lemons.

5 The men like to play frescoball in the park.

6 They play music with a local band on the street.

B Watch the DVD again to check your answers.

5 Work in pairs. Discuss the questions.

1 Would you enjoy any of the things the host does? Which ones?

2 When did you last do any of these things? Where were you?

American Speakout a day in your city

6 A Listen to Alessandro talking about his plans for a day out in Pisa. Number the activities in the order he talks about them.

a) have a pizza ______
b) go to a market ______
c) have a coffee __1__
d) walk through the old city ______
e) have lunch in a restaurant ______
f) go to a park ______

B Listen again and use the key phrases to complete sentences 1–6.

KEYPHRASES

We're starting the day …
We're going to …
Afterward, for lunch we're …
In the afternoon, we're planning to …
In the evening, we're …
It's going to be …

1 … spend the morning walking through the market.
2 … a day to remember.
3 … with a coffee and a fresh pastry.
4 … go a little outside Pisa.
5 … going to one of the best restaurants I know.
6 … going back toward the Leaning Tower.

7 A Work in groups. You are going to plan 24 hours in a city of your choice. Plan your day in detail. Try to include areas that only locals would know about. Use questions 1–6 to help you.

1 Which city are you planning to visit?
2 What are you going to do there?
3 How are you going to get around?
4 What are you going to eat/drink? Where?
5 What are you planning for the evening?
6 What is going to make the day special?

B Work with other students and tell them about your plans. Which plans do you think are the best?

writeback an invitation

8 Write an invitation. Describe the day you have planned and give it to someone in another group. Use the emails on page 29 to help you.

toward | towards

V TIME OUT

1 Cross out one phrase that is not possible in each sentence.

1 I went to *a bar/sightseeing/the market*.
2 Do you want to get *the bus/a snack/an art gallery*?
3 They went to *the art gallery/the museum/a snack*.
4 She has gone *a bar/sightseeing/dancing*.
5 Can we have *a club/dinner/a drink*?

G PRESENT CONTINUOUS/*BE GOING TO* FOR FUTURE

2 A Put the words in the correct order to make questions.

1 are / what / doing / tonight / you?
2 you / weekend / are / this / doing / special / anything?
3 dinner / evening / is / this / your / who / cooking?
4 you / vacation / are / on / going / when?
5 are / going / city / you / to / visit / which / next?
6 after / to / are / class / going / what / do / you?

B Work in pairs and take turns. Ask and answer the questions.

V PLACES TO VISIT

3 Work in pairs and take turns. Student A: choose a word from the box and describe it. Student B: guess the word.

concert hall	countryside
sports field	nightclub
street market	shopping mall
nature trail	waterfront

It's a place where …

A: It's a place where people play outdoor sports.
B: A sports field.

G QUESTIONS WITHOUT AUXILIARIES

4 A Make questions with the prompts. Add a question word and put the verb into the correct form.

1 famous works / include / *Romeo and Juliet* and *Hamlet*?
Whose famous works include Romeo and Juliet and Hamlet?
2 be / an actor / before / he became U.S. President?
3 1975 Queen album / include / the song "Bohemian Rhapsody"?
4 be / a fourth great Renaissance painter, besides Leonardo, Michelangelo and Titian?
5 "John" / win / an Oscar for his song "Can You Feel the Love Tonight"
6 Bob Marley song / include / the words "Let's get together and feel alright"?
7 watery Italian city / have / an international art exhibition every two years?
8 member of the Dion family sell / 200 million records before 2007?
9 hit songs / include / "I'm like a Bird," "Promiscuous" and "Maneater"?

B Do the quiz above. Each answer begins with the last two letters of the previous answer.

1 Shakespeare
2 Re _ _ _ _
3 _ _ight at the Ope_ _
4 _ _pha_ _
5 _ _t_ _
6 "_ _e Lo_ _"
7 _ _ni_ _
8 _ _ li _ _
9 _ _ lly Furtado

C Check your answers on page 160.

F MAKING A PHONE CALL

5 A Complete the phone call with the words in the box.

here	it's	back	like	can

A: Hello there, [1]______ Billy Blue.
B: Hello, Billy. How are you?
A: I'm really good, thanks.
B: So, Bill, what [2]______ I do for you?
A: I'd [3]______ to speak to Mrs. Chow.
B: Sorry, she's not [4]______ right now.
A: Any idea when she'll be [5]______?
B: Never. Today she got the sack.

B Complete the message with the words in the box.

call	leave	this
message	busy	

Hello, [1]______ is Pete and Paul.
Sorry, there's no one here at all.
We're probably [2]______, in a meeting,
Or maybe in a restaurant, eating,
Or maybe in a bar watching a game,
But [3]______ a [4]______ and your name.
We'll [5]______ you back sometime soon,
And pigs might fly* around the Moon.

**Pigs might fly* is an idiom that means "it will never happen."

C Work in pairs and take turns. Read the conversation in Exercise 5A and the message in Exercise 5B. Concentrate on the rhythm.

got fired — got the sack

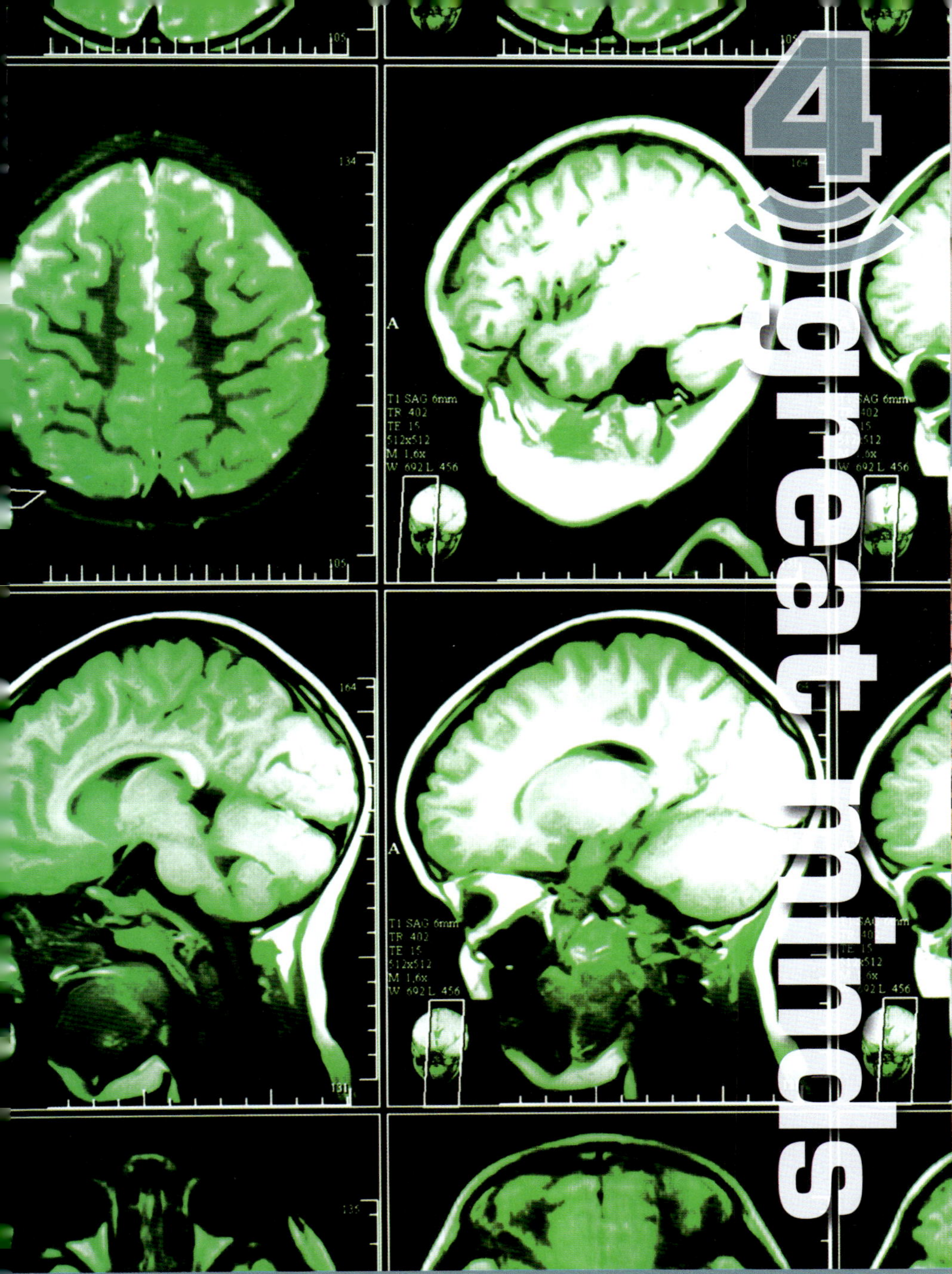

4 great minds

SPEAKING

4.1 Talk about hidden talents
4.2 Talk about rules in schools
4.3 Give advice and make suggestions for language learners
4.4 Talk about inventions

LISTENING

4.1 Listen to someone describing how he used his hidden talent
4.4 Watch an extract from a documentary about developments that have changed the world

READING

4.2 Read an article about different schools

WRITING

4.1 Check your work and correct mistakes
4.4 Write a forum post about inventions

Are you learning anything at the moment?

INTERVIEWS

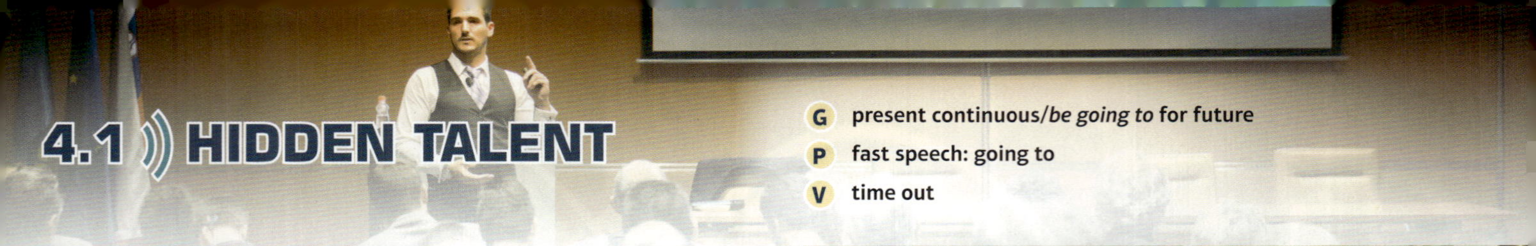

4.1 HIDDEN TALENT

G present continuous/*be going to* for future
P fast speech: going to
V time out

VOCABULARY

MAKE AND *DO*

1 A Work in pairs. Which of the phrases in bold below can you see in the pictures?

Make ...

a **speech** in front of more than fifty people

a **meal** for more than eight people

a **phone call** in a foreign language

a **decision** that changed your life for the better

Do ...

a **project** with a big team

business in another language

well/badly on an test

your homework on the way to school

B Which of the activities in Exercise 1A have you done: a) in the last 24 hours? b) in the last week? c) in the last month? Which have you never done? Compare your answers with other students.

GRAMMAR

PRESENT PERFECT + *EVER/NEVER*

S4.1

2 A Listen and read the conversation below. Which tenses do the speakers use?

A: Have you ever given a speech in public?
B: No, never. Have you?
A: Yes, I have. I gave a speech at work.
B: Really? When did you do that?
A: At a conference last year. I was really nervous.
B: I'm not surprised. OK, have you ever made friends with someone from another country?
A: No, I haven't, but my brother has. He met a woman from Chile in 2014. In fact, they got married a week ago!

B Answer the questions about the conversation.

1 Underline two questions about general experiences (where the exact time is not important). How are they formed?

____ *you* (*ever*) + past participle ... ?

2 Find two sentences that say <u>when</u> the actions happened in the past. Which verb tense is used?

3 Circle the three short answers to *Have you ... ?* questions.

C WEAK FORMS: *have* Listen again. Notice how *have* is pronounced in the questions. How is it different in the short answers?

▶ page 134 LANGUAGEBANK

3 A Underline the correct alternative.

1 She *has been/was* on TV yesterday.
2 *Have you ever written/Did you ever write* a speech?
3 I*'ve never eaten/never ate* snails.
4 Last night I *have finished/finished* the book.
5 *Have you ever been/Did you ever go* to the U.S.?
6 He *has finished/finished* the project this morning.

B Complete the sentences.

1 I've ...
2 Yesterday,
3 I've never ...
4 I've always ...
5 When I was a child, I ...

C Work in pairs and compare your answers.

4 **A** **Write the past participles in the table below. Check your answers on page 127.**

catch	*caught*	give	______
keep	______	swim	______
make	______	sleep	______
drive	______	lose	______
do	______	win	______
fly	______	buy	*bought*
come	______	pay	______
cross	______	grow	______

B **Match the verbs that have rhyming past participles. Then listen and check.**

caught /kɔːt/— bought /bɔːt/

C **Work in pairs. Use the verbs above to make six *Have you ever ...?* questions. Use the ideas in the box to help you.**

fish	anything expensive	a bus	a prize
all day	a plane	plants	in a river

D **Work in pairs and take turns. Ask and answer the questions.**

A: Have you ever caught a fish?
B: Yes, I have. I caught three last weekend!

LISTENING

5 **A** **Look at the pictures and listen to an interview with Mario, the boy in the story. As you listen, answer questions 1–3.**

1 What was Mario's hidden talent?
2 When did he start to use his talent?
3 How did he use his talent to change his job?

B **Listen again and complete the extracts.**

1 I've always ______ cooking.
2 Then in my twenties, I started to ______ meals for my friends.
3 I had the idea to ______ my food at work.
4 I wanted to ______ something more interesting.
5 ______ you ever thought, "Oh, I prefer my old office job"?
6 It's the best decision I ever ______.

SPEAKING

6 **A** **Think about your hidden talent or something you love doing. Write notes about the following questions.**

1 What is the talent?
2 Have you ever done it in public?
3 Do you practice? When/Where?
4 Is it/Will it be useful in your job/future job?

B **Work in groups and take turns. Describe your hidden talent.**

I am good with numbers. I can do difficult calculations in my head without using a calculator.

WRITING

CORRECTING MISTAKES

7 **A** **Read the paragraph below. Find nine mistakes and correct them. Use these symbols:**

gr = grammar   p = punctuation
sp = spelling

My Hidden Talent

My talent is that I can sing really well. I've always like music I sing all kinds of songs, including rock, pop and classical music I first discovered this abillity when I was young. I often listened to music and sang at the same time. I've doing it many times at parties, in front of my freinds, and in karaoke bars. There is no magic secret I just listen carefuly and am practicing on my own.

American Speak out TIP
Don't make the same mistake twice! Look through your corrected written work. Do you repeat your mistakes? Write down the correct form in a different color.

B **Write a paragraph about your hidden talent or about someone you think is very talented (an athlete, actor, singer, writer, etc.).**

C **Work in groups. Read the paragraphs and correct any mistakes.**

color / athlete   colour / sportsperson

4.2)) SCHOOLS OF THOUGHT

G *can, have to, must*
P weak forms: *have to*
V education

VOCABULARY
EDUCATION

1 Work in pairs. Discuss the subjects in the box. Which subjects did you like at school? Were there any subjects you didn't like? Why/Why not?

math science history literature art languages IT (information technology)

▶ page 154 PHOTOBANK

2 A Complete the phrases with the verbs in the box.

make wear take give play study

1 ______ art/music
a foreign language
online
2 ______ sports
games
a musical instrument
3 ______ mistakes
friends
4 ______ a test
exams
5 ______ a performance
6 ______ a school uniform

B Which of the things above did you do at school? Did you enjoy them? Write (+), (–) or (?) (no experience) next to each one.

C Work in pairs and compare your answers. Who enjoyed their school experience more?

READING

3 A Work in pairs. Discuss. Who was your favorite/least favorite teacher at school? Why? Were your teachers traditional in their approach to teaching? Do you think this was good or bad?

B Read the text. Match paragraphs 1–3 with topics a)–c) below.

a) making mistakes is OK
b) a school where students make the decisions
c) children watch videos outside class

C Read the text again. Discuss. Which of the ideas in the text do you think is the best? Which is the worst? Would these methods work in your country?

ARE TRADITIONAL WAYS OF LEARNING *the best?*

Read about some alternative schools of thought . . .

1 THE ALTERNATIVE SCHOOL

The Alternative School, in Lancashire, U.K., offers a different type of schooling for young people who are having problems in mainstream education. The school offers an innovative and interesting educational program, which is designed specifically for the individual. Students can decide when they come to school and which subjects they want to study. They don't have to come to school every day. They can choose to start with just a few hours a week. The school uses an "open door" policy where students are allowed to leave classes if they are bored or unhappy.

2 THE FLIPPED CLASSROOM

Many classrooms around the world are adopting a flipped classroom approach. This learning model switches classroom learning and homework. In a traditional classroom, the teacher explains the lesson to the students in the classroom, and the students do homework outside class, where they have to work on their own and can't ask anyone for help. So, in a flipped classroom, children can watch a video of their teacher giving a lecture on the subject at home. They don't have to do any written work. When they come back to the classroom, they have to do the more traditional exercises, but they can ask the teacher or their classmates for help if they don't understand.

3 STARTING YOUNG

A child learning music with the Suzuki method has to start as young as possible. Even two-year-old children can learn to play difficult pieces of classical music, often on the violin. They do this by watching and listening. They learn by copying, just like they learn their mother tongue. The child has to join in, but doesn't have to get it right. "They soon learn that they don't have to stop every time they make a mistake. They just carry on," said one Suzuki trainer. The children have to practice for several hours every day, and they give performances once a week, so they learn quickly. "The parents must be involved, too," said the trainer, "or it just doesn't work."

math — maths

GRAMMAR

CAN, HAVE TO, MUST

4 **Read sentences 1–6 and put the verbs in bold in the correct place in the table.**

1 Students **can** decide when they come to school.
2 (The students) **can't** ask anyone for help.
3 They **have to** do the more traditional exercises.
4 At The Alternative School, you **don't have to** come to school every day.
5 They **don't have to** stop every time they make a mistake.
6 The parents **must** be involved, too.

possible/allowed	not possible/not allowed
can	
necessary	not necessary

▶ page 134 LANGUAGEBANK

5 **A** **Complete the text with *have to/don't have to, must/mustn't, can/can't*. There may be more than one possible answer.**

Do I have to go to school today?

They [1]______ (not necessary) wear a uniform, and they [2]______ (not necessary) wait for the school bus. These are two of the advantages of being home-schooled. But there are more. "You [3]______ (possible) choose which subjects you want to study," says Jasmin, aged fourteen. "You [4]______ (necessary) work hard, but you [5]______ (possible) choose to work when you feel like it." Jasmin is one of 55,000 children in the U.K. who doesn't go to school. She stays at home for her education, and she's much happier. "School is all about rules: you [6]______ (necessary) be at school at 8:30 a.m.; you [7]______ (not allowed) wear sneakers; you [8]______ (not allowed) use your cell phone in class; etc. I prefer being at home." Jasmin's mother, Terry, educates her four children at home. "Some people think that children who study at home [9]______ (not allowed) go to the exams and get the same qualifications, but they [10]______ (allowed), and they do!"

B **WEAK FORMS: *have to*** **Listen and check.**

C **Listen and notice the pronunciation of have to** /həv tuː/.

D **Listen again and repeat.**

6 **Work in pairs. Discuss two or three similarities and differences between home-schooling and going to a normal school. Do you think home-schooling is a good idea? Why/Why not?**

SPEAKING

7 **Work in pairs. Read the statements. Are the rules the same or different in your country? Do you think this is a good or a bad idea? Discuss.**

1 In the U.K., children have to learn a foreign language at school.
2 In the U.K., you can take exams in art, cooking and sports at school.
3 Children in Thailand have to sing the national anthem in the morning.
4 In Singapore, children have to learn most subjects (math and science) in English.
5 In France, children don't have to wear uniforms to school.
6 In Japan, children can't be late for school, or they can't get in.
7 In Spain, children don't have to eat at school. They can go home for lunch.
8 In the U.K., children can eat a vegetarian meal at lunch.
9 Children in Poland have to repeat the year if they fail their exams.

sneakers, tennis shoes / cell phone   trainers / mobile phone

4.3)) WHAT SHOULD I DO?

F giving advice
P silent letters
V language learning

SPEAKING

1 A **Read the quotes about learning. Do you agree with any of them? Why/Why not?**

"We learn by doing.

A little knowledge is a dangerous thing.

Anyone who stops learning is old, whether at twenty or eighty.

The best way to learn is to teach."

B **Compare your ideas with other students.**

VOCABULARY
LANGUAGE LEARNING

2 A **Read sentences 1–7. Then match the words in bold with definitions a)–g).**

1 I **re-read** articles we use in class.
2 I **look up** new words in a dictionary.
3 I watch films with **subtitles.**
4 I **go online** to read the news in English.
5 I **chat** with other learners.
6 I **write down** new phrases in my notebook.
7 I listen to English songs, and I try to **memorize** them.

a) find information in a book/on a computer
b) read again
c) talk (possibly on the Internet)
d) study until you remember
e) words on a screen that translate what a character says
f) write
g) use the Internet

B **Work in pairs. Discuss the questions.**

1 Which of the activities above do you do? How often?
2 Which do you think are the most important/useful for learning English?
3 Do you have any other ideas on how to improve your English?

FUNCTION
GIVING ADVICE

3 A **Read the website message below and think of three things Zeynep can do to improve her English.**

Hello everyone. In two months, I'll start work at an international company. The only problem is I need to improve my English quickly. I did well on my recent English exam, but I need to do business in English. I know it'll be more difficult. Do you have any good ideas?
Zeynep

B **Work in pairs and compare your answers.**

4 **Read the replies and discuss. Which ideas have you tried? Which do you think are the most useful ideas?**

Hi Zeynep. I think you should use message boards to make new friends. Then you can chat with them online in English, and it doesn't matter if you make mistakes.
Ahmed L

Zeynep, go online and find a business website you like. When you don't understand some words, you should look them up and write them in a notebook.
Ruby 335

You shouldn't worry. They gave you the job, so you're good enough. Relax and just watch some movies in English.
Marie 98

Why don't you use leveled readers? They're enjoyable, and they'll help you learn new words.
Ana Kosicka

Zeynep, I think it's a good idea to use language learning apps because these help you measure your progress.
Jung-sun Huang

memorize / did well on / because — memorise / did well in / as

5 **A** **Look at the replies in Exercise 4 again. Complete phrases 1–6 below.**

1 I ______ you should …
2 Find ______
3 You should ______
4 You shouldn't ______
5 Why ______ you ______ …?
6 I (don't) think it's a good ______ to …

B **Discuss. Which phrases have the same meaning?**

C **SILENT LETTERS** **How is *should* pronounced? Which letter is silent? Listen and repeat.**

6 **A** **Listen to two teachers discussing language learning. What problems do they mention?**

B **Work in pairs. Complete the notes in the table.**

Problem	Advice
Students too shy to speak. Worry about [1] ______ ______.	Give students time to [2] ______. Let them practice in [3] ______.
Students have problems [4] ______.	Watch movie clips on YouTube. Watch the mouth, [5] ______, body language. Use [6] ______ the second time.

C **Listen again to check.**

D **Work in pairs. Discuss the questions.**

1 Do you have the problems mentioned in the recording?
2 What do you think of the advice?
3 Can you add any other advice?

LEARN TO
RESPOND TO ADVICE

7 **A** **Read the extracts below. How did the listener respond? Listen again and write the response.**

1 They can take notes first.
2 Let them practice in groups before they speak in front of everyone. This will give them confidence.
3 And using subtitles? Some teachers say we shouldn't use them. Ever!
4 They can see which words are swallowed.

B **Read the responses. Mark them (✓) I agree, (✗) I disagree or (?) I agree, but not completely.**

1 That's a good idea.
2 I suppose so.
3 You're right.
4 I'm not sure that's a good idea.

▶ page 134 LANGUAGEBANK

8 **A** **Look at pictures A–D below. What do you think the problems are?**

A

1
A: I think ______ in the food industry. (you / work)
B: That's ______ idea. (good)

B

2
A: You ______ so much time watching TV. (not / spend)
B: ______ right.

C

3
A: ______ we find you a personal trainer? (why)
B: I ______ a good idea. (not sure)

D

4
A: I think ______ idea to start going shopping together. (good)
B: I ______. (suppose)

B **Complete the conversations in pictures A–D using the words in parentheses.**

9 **Work with two other students. Take turns to ask for and respond to advice. Student A: turn to page 160. Student B: turn to page 162. Student C: turn to page 164. Read your situation and explain it to the others.**

I have this problem …

4.4 INVENTIONS

DVD PREVIEW

1 Work in groups. Discuss the questions.

1 Do you ever travel by airplane? How frequently?

2 Have you ever flown a long distance? If so, did you enjoy the experience?

3 What do you know about the invention of the airplane? (Who? Where? When?)

2 Read the program information. Why does Dallas Campbell go to the U.S.A.?

Supersized Earth: The Way We Move

Supersized Earth looks at amazing developments that have changed the modern world. This program shows the start of airplane travel. Dallas Campbell goes to the U.S.A., where the Wright brothers first flew a glider, an early type of airplane without an engine, in 1902. Campbell tries out a replica (a perfect copy) of the glider to see if he can fly it.

3 A Read the sentences. What do you think the words and phrases in bold mean?

1 The brothers' first journey **triggered a whole century of innovation**.

2 The **invention** the Wright brothers are known for is the airplane.

3 They began to **conquer** the skies.

4 The brothers **achieved** this in a simple way.

5 The first plane **launched a revolution** in the way we travel.

B Match the words/phrases in bold in Exercise 3A with meanings a)–e) below.

a) were successful at something

b) caused one hundred years of new ideas

c) started something that changed society

d) a new creation

e) become the master of (something)

DVD VIEW

4 A Watch the DVD and answer the questions.

1 What does Dallas Campbell tell us about the Wright brothers' first flight?

2 Does Dallas Campbell fly the glider successfully?

B Which words complete the notes? Choose the correct alternative. Watch the DVD again to check.

1 On 17 December, *1903/1913* the Wright brothers made a journey.

2 They traveled *120 miles/120 feet*.

3 A year before flying a plane, the brothers built *a glider/a plane engine*.

4 Dallas Campbell says the plane "helped transform our *travel/planet*."

5 Work in pairs. Discuss. What new information did you learn from the program?

airplane | aeroplane

American Speakout inventions

6 A Look at the list of inventors and their inventions. What do you know about these people? What other famous inventors do you know?

Johannes Gutenberg (1395–1468): the printing press

Alexander Graham Bell (1847–1922): the telephone

Thomas Edison (1847–1931): the light bulb

Tim Berners-Lee (b. 1955): the Internet

4.7

B Listen to two people talking about important inventions. Which inventions do they mention?

1 Which idea do they think is very good?
2 Which idea do they disagree about?
3 What is the third idea they talk about?

C Listen again and check (✔) the key phrases you hear.

KEYPHRASES

I think the most important …
For me, …
That's true, but …
In my opinion, …
Another invention that I see as really important is …
Definitely.
That's right.
I agree.

7 A Work in pairs. Which three inventions do you think are the most important? Use the ideas in Exercise 6A or choose your own ideas.

B Tell the rest of the class about your choices. Do you all agree?

writeback a forum post

8 A Read about an online survey and then read a post by a commenter. What is the survey about, and what does the person think of it?

World Changers

We asked 15,000 people from 15 countries to name the most important inventions in history. Here are the top ten:

1 wheel	6 electricity
2 telephone	7 refrigerator
3 antibiotics	8 Internet
4 language	9 engine
5 airplane	10 iPhone

I think the list includes some very important inventions, but, in my opinion, there are also some strange choices. Some of them, e.g., language and electricity, aren't inventions at all. These are discoveries of natural things and shouldn't be on this list. I'm also surprised that the toilet and the printing press aren't in the top ten. For me, these are essential. Without the toilet, there would be a lot more disease, and, without the printing press, modern communications would be very different: we would have fewer books, magazines and newspapers. Also, I'm amazed that the iPhone is number ten! How many people in the world actually have an iPhone? It seems strange to include it in a list of basic needs like the wheel and antibiotics.

Nick G

B Write a post saying what you think of the top ten inventions. Explain your reasons. You can also add other suggestions for inventions you think should be included.

The Wright brothers

V MAKE AND DO

1 A Complete the questions with *makes* or *does*.

Who in your family …

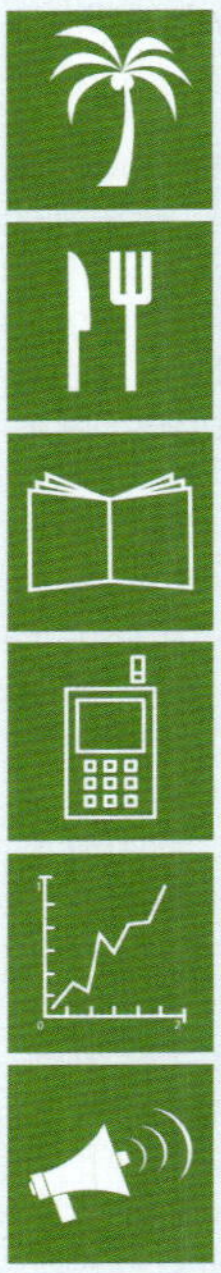

1 makes decisions about where you go on vacation?

2 ______ most of the meals?

3 ______ a lot of homework?

4 ______ the most phone calls?

5 ______ projects at work?

6 ______ speeches?

B Work in pairs and take turns. Ask and answer the questions.

G PAST SIMPLE OR PRESENT PERFECT + *EVER/NEVER*

2 A Complete the sentences with the correct form of the verb in parentheses.

Questions

1 ______ in the ocean? (you / ever swim)

2 ______ on vacation last year? (you / go)

Negatives

3 ______ Africa. (I / never visit)

4 ______ last night. (I / not go out)

Affirmatives

5 ______ in more than one country. (I / live)

6 ______ in a restaurant last weekend. (I / eat)

B Work in pairs and take turns. Guess your partner's answers to questions 1–2.

C Are sentences 3–6 true for your partner? Ask and answer questions to find out.

V EDUCATION

3 A Match 1–7 with a)–g) to make questions.

1 Do you play
2 When you take
3 How do you feel when you make
4 At school, did you
5 Have you ever given a
6 Do you ever study
7 Did you study

a) online?
b) performance of anything?
c) tests, do you get nervous?
d) study art?
e) any sports particularly well?
f) a foreign language at school?
g) mistakes?

B Work in pairs and take turns. Ask and answer the questions.

G *CAN, HAVE TO, MUST*

4 A Underline the correct alternative to complete the sentences.

1 In Australia, you *must/can/don't have to* drive on the left.

2 In the U.K., you *have to/can/can't* smoke in bars and restaurants.

3 You *can't/have to/must* talk on your cell phone during an examination.

4 Children are lucky. They *don't have to/must/can* worry about paying bills!

5 In the U.K., you *have to/can't/mustn't* be 17 years old before you can ride a motorcycle.

B Write down one thing:

- you can/can't do in your country
- you have to do next week
- you can't do during a test
- you don't have to do on the weekend
- you have to do when learning a language
- you shouldn't do while driving
- you have to do every day
- you don't have to do when you are a child

C Work in pairs and compare your ideas.

V LANGUAGE LEARNING

5 A Complete the questions.

1 Do you r______ - r______ articles to help you understand them?

2 When was the last time you went o______ to study English?

3 Do you like watching movies with sub______? Why/Why not?

4 Have you ever used a ch______ room in English?

5 Which words from this unit are you going to mem______?

B Work in pairs and take turns. Ask and answer the questions.

F GIVING ADVICE

6 A Complete the tables below with phrases for giving/responding to advice.

Giving Advice

Responding to Advice

B Work in pairs. Complete the conversation in different ways.

A: Why don't we ______?
B: That's a ______.
A: I think/don't think ______.
B: OK. Let's ______.

C Practice and act out your conversation.

In the U.S., you're more likely to say you have to take a test than an exam, although you'd say *exam* for a big test, e.g., at the end of a semester. The latter is actually short for *examination*.

on the weekend — at the weekend

5 travel

SPEAKING
- 5.1 Tell a travel anecdote
- 5.2 Discuss travel
- 5.3 Ask for and give directions
- 5.4 Present ideas for an award

LISTENING
- 5.2 Understand travel advice
- 5.3 Understand and follow directions in a city
- 5.4 Watch an extract from a travel program

READING
- 5.1 Read about amazing journeys in movies
- 5.3 Read a text about a man who works in three countries every day

WRITING
- 5.2 Write an email describing a trip or weekend away
- 5.4 Write an application for an award

Do you enjoy traveling to different countries?

INTERVIEWS

5.1 FANTASTIC FILM TRIPS

G past simple and past continuous
P weak forms: *was / were*
V transportation

A *Kon-Tiki*

B *Into the Wild*

VOCABULARY
TRANSPORTATION

1 Work in pairs and answer the questions.

1 How many types of transportation can you think of in two minutes? Make a list.

2 What do you think is the best way to travel? Why?

▶ page 155 PHOTOBANK

READING

2 Work in pairs. Look at photos A–C and discuss the questions.

1 What types of transportation do you think appear in the movies above?

2 Where do you think the people are going?

3 Work in groups. Student A: read the text on this page. Student B: read the text on page 161. Student C: read the text on page 163. As you read, make notes about your text.

1 Who made the journey?

2 Why did they want to go?

3 Where did they go?

4 Take turns to tell your group about your text. Which story do you think sounds the most interesting?

KON-TIKI

In the middle of the twentieth century, the Norwegian explorer and writer Thor Heyerdahl developed a theory. He believed that people from South America traveled to Polynesia 1,500 years ago and settled there. At the time, very few others believed his theory. They thought the journey was too difficult without modern technology. While others were discussing the theory, Heyerdahl decided to test it.

Using only materials and technology available to the people of that time, Heyerdahl and his team of five sailors (and a parrot) built a wooden raft.* On April 28, 1947, they left from Peru and crossed the Pacific.

While they were sailing, huge waves crashed into the raft, and whales and sharks came close. 101 days and 4,300 miles later, they arrived in Polynesia. At the time, no one knew this type of journey was possible. But perhaps the most amazing thing about the journey was that Thor Heyerdahl didn't know how to swim!

Heyerdahl later wrote a book about the journey, and, in 2012, a Norwegian movie called *Kon-Tiki* came out, based on the trip.

***raft**: a flat boat usually made of wood

American Speakout TIP

Make short notes. Don't write full sentences. Choose only important information. Try to use your own words. *The sun was shining when they began their journey that Friday morning.* → *Sunny when they left.* Find a sentence in one of the texts. Make a note of the main idea in three or four words.

5 Discuss the questions.

1 Which (parts of the) journeys sound enjoyable/terrible/frightening?

2 Why do you think the stories were made into movies?

3 Can you think of any other journeys that have been made into movies?

transportation — transport

Rabbit-Proof Fence

GRAMMAR
PAST SIMPLE AND PAST CONTINUOUS

6 **A** Look at sentences a)–c) and answer the questions.

a) While they **were sailing**, huge waves **crashed** into the raft.
b) While he **was living** in the wild, he **wrote** a journal.
c) When it **was raining**, the girls **decided** to escape.

1 What are the tenses of the verbs in bold?
2 Which action started first in each sentence (*sail* or *crash*, etc.)?
3 Which action took a longer period of time?
4 Which actions are background information and which are main events?

B Underline the correct alternative to complete the rules.

> **RULES**
> 1 Use the *past simple/past continuous* for background actions that continue for a long time.
> 2 Use the *past simple/past continuous* for shorter actions that move the story forward.

C Find one more example of the past simple and the past continuous in the same sentence in your text.

▶ page 136 **LANGUAGE**BANK

7 **A** Make sentences with the prompts.

1 I / run / start to snow. So …
I was running when it started to snow. So I went home!
2 I / wait for a bus / meet my boss. So …
3 I / watch TV / recognize my best friend! So …
4 I / walk home / find $5,000 in a bag. So …
5 We / travel by plane / a man with a gun stand up. So …
6 We / ride our bicycles / a cow walk across the road. So …
7 We / eat in a restaurant / see a mouse. So …
8 I / study in my room / hear loud music next door. So …

B Work in pairs and compare your ideas.

8 **A** Listen to some ideas for Exercise 7A. Are they similar to yours?

B **WEAK FORMS:** *was/were* Listen again. Notice how *was* /wəz/ and *were* /wɜːr/ are pronounced. Then listen and repeat the first part of the sentences.

9 Work in pairs and take turns. Student A: make sentences with the past simple and the past continuous. Use a prompt from A and a prompt from B. Student B: respond with another sentence beginning with *So* … .

A: *I was sleeping in my bed when I heard a strange noise.*
B: *So I called the police.*

A
- sleep
- ride my motorcycle
- deal with a problem
- go for a drink
- feel sick
- go to a concert
- make a call
- sit on a train
- take some time off
- watch a movie

B
- get hungry
- buy a speedboat
- crash
- decide to change jobs
- start to feel tired
- fall asleep
- see the love of my life
- check my voicemail
- read your email
- hear a strange noise

SPEAKING

10 **A** Describe something that happened to you on a trip or journey. Think about questions 1–8 and make notes.

1 Where and when did you go?
2 Whom were you with?
3 What was the form of transportation?
4 How long did the trip take?
5 What places did you see during the journey?
6 Did anything go wrong during the journey?
7 What happened while you were traveling?
8 How did you feel?

Last summer, I went on vacation to Turkey. I stayed in Istanbul for two days and then went to the coast. One day, while I was traveling by boat, I dropped my bag into the water. I lost my camera and my passport. It was a disaster!

B Work in groups. Tell your stories. Which were the most interesting and/or funniest stories you heard?

recognize   recognise

5.2 TRAVEL TIPS

G verb patterns
P stressed syllables
V travel items

VOCABULARY
TRAVEL ITEMS

1 **Work in pairs. Discuss the questions.**

1 Do you travel light?
2 What do you usually pack when you go away for a short trip/long vacation?

2 **A** **Work in pairs. Look at the words in the box and choose two things for travelers 1–3 below.**

suitcase notebook digital camera souvenirs waterproof clothes dictionary walking shoes sun hat backpack money belt binoculars map umbrella

1 a grandmother visiting her grandchildren in Australia
2 a student traveling around the world
3 a tourist visiting the sights in New York

B **STRESSED SYLLABLES** **Listen and repeat the words. Underline the stressed syllables.**

C **Work in pairs. Discuss. Which of the things in Exercise 2A do you take on vacation with you?**

▶ page 155 PHOTOBANK

LISTENING

3 **A** **Listen to people describing what they take on vacation. Which of the items in Exercise 2A do the travelers mention?**

B **Work in pairs and complete the notes.**

1 I try to learn ______.
2 I love ______.
3 I take a lot of ______.
4 I usually spend my vacations in ______.
5 I sometimes travel in ______ places.
6 I don't carry too much ______.
7 I write things down because I like to ______ them.

C **Listen again to check.**

GRAMMAR
VERB PATTERNS

4 **A** **Look at sentences 1–9 below and underline the verb + verb combinations.**

1 We always expect to hear English.
2 I always want to talk to local people.
3 I love walking when I go on vacation.
4 I always seem to take hundreds and hundreds of photos.
5 I usually choose to go to a warm place.
6 I enjoy traveling in the wilderness.
7 If you decide to go walking, a backpack is easier to carry.
8 It's best to avoid carrying too much money.
9 I need to write things down.

B **Complete the table below with the verbs in the box.**

~~expect~~ want seem choose enjoy decide avoid need

verb + *-ing*	verb + infinitive with *to*
	expect

C **Work in pairs. Add the verbs in the box below to the table above. Which two verbs can go in both columns?**

hope finish imagine hate would like love

▶ page 136 LANGUAGEBANK

5 **Cross out the verb combination that is not possible in each sentence.**

1 I *hope/~~enjoy~~/expect* to get a free plane ticket.
2 I *want/would like/imagine* to visit Australia.
3 She *loves/avoids/needs* traveling.
4 Where did you *like/decide/choose* to go on your next vacation?
5 They *hate/want/love* working with tourists.
6 He doesn't *seem/need/enjoy* to know this area well.
7 Do you *like/expect/love* going to different countries?
8 Why did you *avoid/decide/hope* to become a travel writer?

6 A **Complete the sentences and make them true for you. The next word has to be either the infinitive with *to* or the *-ing* form of a verb.**

1 When I travel:
I always avoid …
I hate …
I love …

2 On my last vacation:
I chose …
I decided …
I enjoyed …

3 For my next vacation:
I want …
I hope …
I would like …

B **Work in pairs and compare your ideas.**

SPEAKING

7 **Work in pairs. Discuss the questions.**

1 What type of vacations can you see in the photos? Which do you prefer? Why?
2 Is there anything that you really love doing when you are on vacation?
3 When you travel, do you try to learn about the place, its customs and its language? Why/Why not?
4 Do you enjoy visiting tourist areas, old cities, new cities or none of these?

A: I really like sightseeing vacations. I love spending time looking at beautiful old buildings.
B: I love taking photos. I put them on my Facebook page when I get back.
A: Me, too.

WRITING
USING SEQUENCERS

8 A **Work in pairs. Read an email describing a trip and discuss. What were the good/bad things about the trip?**

To paolo.moncello@flu.edi
From igonzalez@ab.esp
inbox 12

Hi Paolo,

I hope you're well. I've just got back from my trip to Poland. It was wonderful. First, we flew to Warsaw. We were only there for two days, but we managed to see lots of interesting sights like the Royal Castle and the National Museum. Then, we had a day in Kraków, which was beautiful, especially the huge square in the Old Town. Unfortunately, after a while, it started raining, so we spent the afternoon chatting with locals in a bar. After that, we took a train to Łódź. I loved it. We visited various museums and walked along the famous Piotrkowska Street. Finally, we caught the plane back home. It was a great trip, and we met lots of really friendly Poles, who promised to visit us in Spain!

Love,

Irina

B **Underline five words/phrases that help us to understand the order of events. The first one has been done for you.**

C **Write an email to a friend about a trip or a weekend away. Use the words you underlined.**

5.3 YOU CAN'T MISS IT

F asking for/giving directions
P intonation: questions
V tourism

VOCABULARY
TOURISM

1 Work in pairs. Look at the words in the box. Which things can you see in the photos?

tour guide   boat trip   bus tour   tourists
sightseeing   natural wonder   duty-free shopping

2 A Look at the title of the text below. Discuss. What do you think the man does? Why do you think he works in three countries every day?

B Read the text to find out.

C Discuss. Would you like Juan's job? Why/Why not?

THE MAN WHO WORKS IN THREE COUNTRIES EVERY DAY

JUAN OLIVEIRA was born in Argentina, grew up in Paraguay and now lives in Brazil. He says he loves the three countries equally, and he works in all three of them every day.

Juan is a tour guide in Foz do Iguaçu, a Brazilian town that is close to the borders of both Argentina and Paraguay. He takes tourists around the Iguaçu Falls, one of the great natural wonders of the world.

First, he shows tourists the waterfall from the Brazilian side. Then, they cross the border to see the water from the Argentinian side. After that, they go on a boat trip that takes them under the waterfall. Finally, he takes them on the short journey to Ciudad del Este in Paraguay to do some duty-free shopping.

He says the Falls are amazing, especially in the rainy season. He sees them every day, and he never gets tired of them.

FUNCTION
ASKING FOR/GIVING DIRECTIONS

3 A Look at the map. Where is the tourist? Now listen and follow the routes on the map. For each route, write the destination (the country) on the map.

B Listen again and read audio script S5.4 on page 171. Underline useful phrases for giving directions.

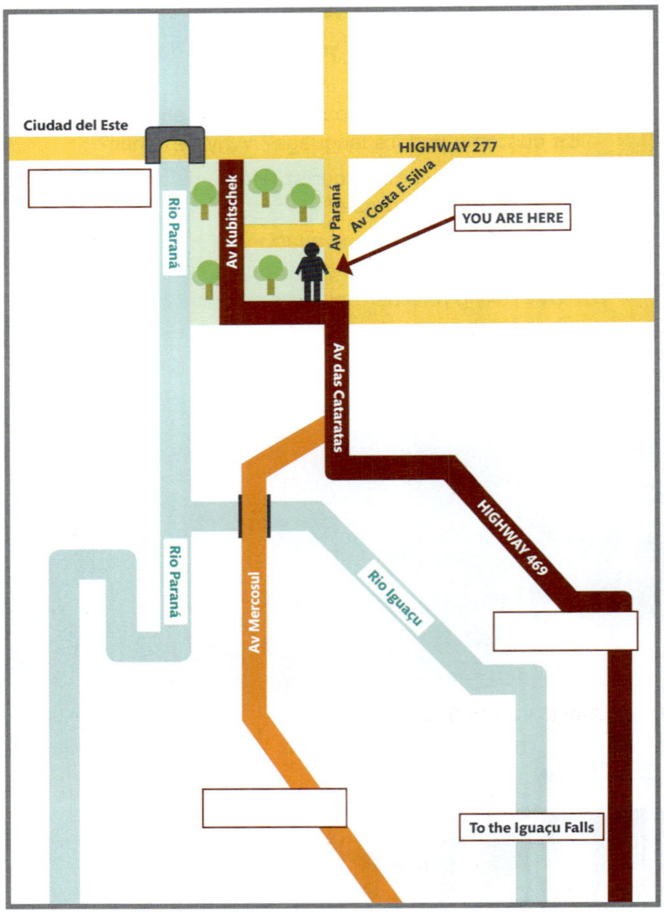

bus tour, bus trip / duty-free — coach tour / tax-free

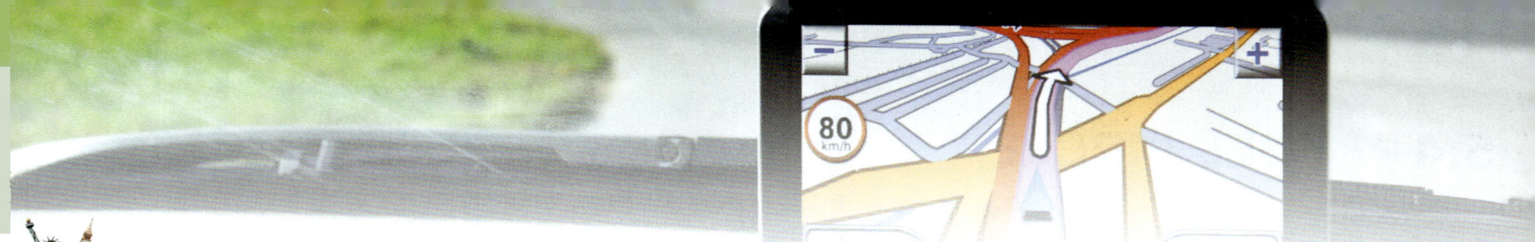

LEARN TO
SHOW/CHECK UNDERSTANDING

4 Label pictures A–J with the phrases in the box.

go along the main road go straight ahead in front of you go past the turn ~~go left~~ take the first right at the corner cross a bridge keep going until you reach (the border) go through the (center of town)

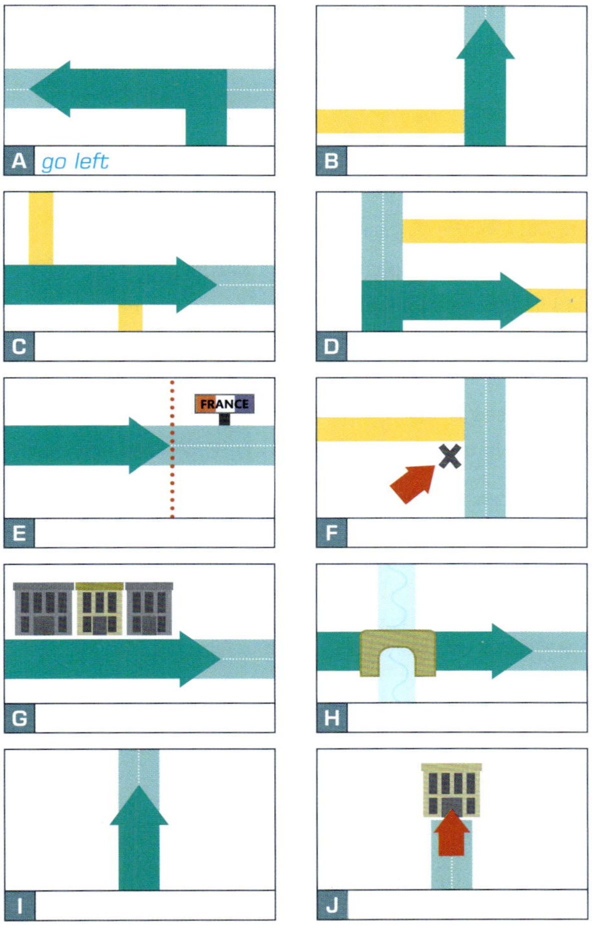

5 A Listen to three conversations. Are the statements true (T) or false (F)?

1 Speaker 1 takes the bus.
2 Speaker 2 has a map.
3 Speaker 3 will see a restaurant before arriving at The Grand Motel.

B Complete the notes. Listen again to check.

Conversation 1 Carnival

It takes ______ minutes. Go straight ahead. You'll hear the ______!

Conversation 2 Plaza Hotel

Go past the movie theater. Take the first ______. Keep going for ______ minutes. You'll see the ______.

Conversation 3 The Grand Motel

Go to the end of this street. Go ______ and go past the ______. It's on the ______.

▶ page 136 LANGUAGEBANK

6 A Read and listen to the extracts from the audio script. Are the phrases in bold asking for information (A), explaining directions (E) or showing understanding (U)?

Extract 1

A: Can we walk? *A*

B: Yes, **it takes about ten minutes** from here. *E*

Extract 2

C: Excuse me, can you help me? I'm looking for the Plaza Hotel. **Is this the right way?**

D: Um ... Plaza Hotel, Plaza Hotel. Yes, **keep going**, past the movie theater and take the first left.

C: OK.

D: Then keep going for about fifteen minutes until you reach the end of the road. And **you'll see** the sign for the hotel. **You can't miss it.**

C: OK. **Can you show me on the map?**

D: Sure.

Extract 3

E: Excuse me, we want to get to The Grand Motel. **Is it far?**

F: Umm ... sorry, I have no idea. Jim, do you know?

G: What?

F: The Grand Motel?

G: The Grand Motel? Yeah, it's just over there. Just go to the end of this street. Go left and go past the ... um ... there's a restaurant. Go past the restaurant, and it's on the left.

E: On the left. **So I need to** go to the end of the street, turn left, go past the restaurant, and it's on the left.

B Which phrases mean:

1 Am I going in the right direction?
2 Continue.
3 It's easy to see it.

C INTONATION: questions Listen to five questions. Which words are said louder and with a higher voice: words at the beginning (*is, can*) or near the end of the question? Listen again to check.

7 Work in pairs. Look at audio script S5.5 on page 171 and practice the first two conversations.

SPEAKING

8 Work in pairs. Student A: look at the map on page 161. Student B: look at the map on page 163. Ask for and give directions.

A: How do I get to the station?
B: Go straight ahead until you reach the Greek restaurant. Then turn right.

go straight ahead | go straight on

5.4 FULL CIRCLE

DVD PREVIEW

1 A Have you ever been on a long and/or difficult journey? What can you remember about it? Tell other students.

B Read the program information and answer the questions.

1 What does Michael Palin do?
2 Where does he travel to in *Full Circle*?
3 How does he travel in this episode?

Full Circle

Michael Palin is an actor and travel writer. In Full Circle, he went on a journey through the seventeen countries along the Pacific coast. While traveling 50,000 miles in ten months, he saw and discovered things beyond his dreams. He learned how to cook eggs in a volcano and how to make music with horses' bones in Chile! In this episode, Michael travels across the Andes from Arica in Chile to La Paz in Bolivia in a small train.

DVD VIEW

2 Watch the DVD. Was it an enjoyable journey? Which of the problems below do the people mention?

- the food is terrible
- the train gets very hot
- the air is thin, and it's difficult to breathe
- the train is very noisy
- the train stops a lot because of animals/cars on the track
- the train is very slow

3 A Work in pairs. What do you think the words/phrases in bold mean?

a) **Twice a week**, a railway service leaves Arica. _1_
b) We've **reached** the Bolivian border. ___
c) It's going to **take two hours**. ___
d) Some passengers are **local**. ___
e) Is it the **journey of a lifetime**? ___
f) It's the **journey of (everyone's) dreams**. ___
g) We've **crossed** the Andes at 16.4 miles an hour. ___

B Watch the DVD again. Number the sentences in Exercise 3A in the order you hear them.

4 Work in groups. Discuss the questions.

1 What do you think of this trip?
2 Would you like to do it? Why/Why not?

a train | railway service

American Speakout an award

5 A Read the text and answer the questions.

1 What is the award?

2 What will the winner do?

My Dream Trip is an award of $5,000 for the best idea for an original and inspiring trip anywhere in the world. The winner will receive training in film-making and will record their experiences for a future program.

5.8

B Listen to someone describing her journey.

1 Where does she want to go?

2 What does she want to do there?

C Listen again and check (✔) the key phrases you hear.

KEYPHRASES

We would like to go to …

The trip is going to take …

Some of the problems we're going to face include …

We want to experience the local culture …

Our plan is to speak to the local people …

We hope to find out about their traditions …

It should be an inspiring trip.

This is the my/our dream trip.

6 A You are going to apply for the award. Work in pairs. Decide:

- where/how you are going to travel
- what you would like to experience/see/do
- which people you are going to stay/work with
- why you deserve the award

B Present your ideas to the class. Use the key phrases to help you. Who should win the award?

writeback an application

7 A Read the application. Match paragraphs 1–3 with headings a)–c).

a) Goals and Objectives

b) Details of the Plan

c) Introduction

APPLICATION FORM

1 ______

We would like to go to Easter Island to live with the local people for three months. Easter Island is one of the great mysteries of the world. It has many famous stone statues of heads, but no one knows who made them or why.

2 ______

Our plan is to talk to the islanders about their history and about their present and future. We will ask them about their lives and what they think of the statues. We want to learn how the world's most isolated people live: what they eat, what they do for entertainment and what they think of the modern world of computers and other technology.

3 ______

We will record all of the interviews on film. We will also keep a journal about our own experiences on the island. Eventually, we hope to make a TV documentary and write a book about our time on the island.

B Write your application for the award. Use the model in Exercise 7A to help you.

V TRANSPORTATION

1 A Choose four types of transportation from the box below. Write sentences about each type. Don't mention the name.

train streetcar minibus
taxi motorcycle ferry
speedboat bus truck
helicopter

It travels through water and is very fast.

B Work in pairs and take turns. Student A: read your sentences. Student B: guess which type of transportation it is.

A: It's a fast type of transportation. It goes on the road. It has two wheels.
B: A motorcycle.

G PAST SIMPLE AND PAST CONTINUOUS

2 A Put the verbs in parentheses into the past simple or past continuous.

1 While they (walk), they (see) a fence.

While they were walking, they saw a fence.

2 While they (cross) the ocean, a terrible storm nearly (destroy) the raft.
3 They (run) away one night while it (rain).
4 While he (wander) in the wilderness, he (meet) some people who helped him.
5 When the men (sail) on the ocean, they (see) many sea creatures.
6 While he (live) in an abandoned bus, he (realize) he might die.

B Work in pairs. Discuss. Which movies from Lesson 5.1 do the sentences go with?

3 Work in pairs and take turns. Ask and answer the question.

Where were you and what were you doing at these times yesterday?

6:00	10:00	1:00
4:00	7:00	10:00

In the United States, it's more common to use a 12-hour clock than a 24-hour clock.

V TRAVEL ITEMS

4 A Add the vowels.

1 stcs *suitcase*
2 bckpck
3 wtrprf clths
4 hkng bts
5 sn ht
6 svnrs
7 bnclrs
8 ntbk
9 dgtl cmr
10 mny blt

B Work in pairs. Decide which of the items above are important for the vacations below.

A sun hat is important for a beach holiday.

G VERB PATTERNS

5 A Complete the sentences with the correct form of the verbs in parentheses.

1 I sometimes choose ______ (go) somewhere on vacation because a friend recommends it.
2 I hope ______ (visit) more cities in my own country this year.
3 I seem ______ (have) good luck with the weather when I go on vacation. It never rains!
4 I want ______ (travel) to places where tourists never go.
5 I always avoid ______ (travel) by boat because I get sick.
6 I don't enjoy ______ (fly) very much.
7 I can't imagine ______ (go) on a camping trip—I prefer hotels!
8 I wouldn't like ______ (go) on vacation with a big group of people.

B Work in pairs. Discuss. Are sentences 1–8 true for you? Why/Why not?

truck lorry

F ASKING FOR/GIVING DIRECTIONS

6 A Find and correct the mistakes. There are two mistakes in each conversation.

Conversation 1

A: Excuse me. I'm looking for the Natural History Museum. Is this right way?
B: Keep going until you reach the intersection. It's in the right.

Conversation 2

A: Hello. We want to go to the Italian Embassy. Is far?
B: No. Just turn left, and you'll see the sign for it. You can't miss.

Conversation 3

A: Excuse me, do you know where is the college?
B: Keep going long the main road. Then you'll see a sign, and it'll be in front to you.

B Work in pairs and practice the conversations.

C Work in pairs and take turns.

Student A: ask for directions:

- from a well-known place in the town to Student B's house
- from Student B's house to the school

Student B: ask for directions:

- from the school to a nearby restaurant
- from a nearby restaurant to a well-known place in the town

A: OK. How do I get from the station to your house?
B: Well, you take the first right ...

6 fitness

SPEAKING
6.1 Talk about your lifestyle
6.2 Discuss food preferences
6.3 Explain health problems
6.4 Talk about healthy habits

LISTENING
6.2 Listen to a radio interview with a food expert
6.3 Listen to conversations between a doctor and her patients
6.4 Watch an extract from a documentary about health

READING
6.1 Identify specific information in an article about types of exercise

WRITING
6.2 Write about food
6.4 Write a blog post about health advice

What do you do to stay in shape?

INTERVIEWS

6.1 STAYING IN SHAPE

G present perfect + *for/since*
P sentence stress
V health

Get moving!

A lot of us spend most of our working day sitting at the computer. If you add this to the seven hours we spend sleeping, we could easily find that we spend nearly two thirds of our day without moving at all. We all know that exercise is good for both the body and the brain. Even a small amount of exercise every day can help us to feel happier and more relaxed. So, how does the world stay in shape? We've looked at some of the latest exercise trends from around the world.

TOWERRUNNING China

Have you ever worked in an office building and wondered how you can stay in shape? Perhaps you should try towerrunning. It's a sport you can do in the skyscrapers of almost any big city, but Asian cities can be particularly good. All you need to do is start at the bottom of an office tower and run up all the stairs until you get to the top. Towerrunning has become popular all around the world with important races taking place in some of the world's tallest towers, like Taipei 101, the Empire State Building in New York, and the China World Trade Center, Beijing.

PILOXING® USA

If you enjoy dance classes like Zumba, but you also want to get rid of your anger, then PILOXING® might be for you. PILOXING® started in the U.S., but has traveled quickly to countries like the U.K. The sport is a mixture of boxing, pilates and dance. PILOXING® uses the power and speed of boxing while building your muscles and strength with pilates. All of this happens to non-stop loud music, and you learn some great dance moves, too.

PADDLEBOARDING Brazil

When it comes to the end of a long day, what could be better than a paddleboard on the ocean? It might look easy, but paddleboarding is a tough sport. You need to be strong to keep your balance. However, if you bring your board down to the water at "golden hour" just before sunset, the water is calm and the ocean will make you forget all your problems.

VOCABULARY

HEALTH

1 A Look at the words/phrases in the box. Are these things good (+) or bad (–) for your health?

junk food	exercise classes	sodas		
fresh fruit/vegetables	stress/worrying			
alcohol	vitamins	running	caffeine	relaxing

B Work in pairs and compare your ideas. Group the vocabulary under the following headings: *food/drinks, exercise, general habits.* Can you add any more words/phrases to each group?

C Work in pairs and take turns. Ask and answer the questions.

1 What do you do to stay in shape and healthy?
2 Do you do anything that is not healthy?

A: What do you do to stay in shape and healthy?
B: I eat lots of fruit. How about you?
A: I ride my bike to work every day.

▶ page 156 PHOTOBANK

READING

2 A Discuss. What sports can you see in the pictures? Do you know anything about these sports?

B Read the text to find out more information about each sport. Which of the sports would you like to try? Why?/Why not?

C Work in pairs. Answer the questions.

1 According to the article, why is exercise good for you?
2 Why is towerrunning popular in Asian cities?
3 How is Piloxing® similar to other sports?
4 When is a good time to go paddleboarding? Why?

office building /while / sodas / ride my bike — office block / whilst / fizzy drinks / cycle

GRAMMAR

PRESENT PERFECT + *FOR/SINCE*

3 A Read sentences a) and b) and answer questions 1–4 below.

a) I've done paddleboarding *since* 2014.
b) He's lived in Asia *for* five years.

1 When did the speaker in a) start paddleboarding?
2 Is she still paddleboarding now?
3 When did the person in b) move to Asia?
4 Does he still live in Asia?

B Underline the correct alternative to complete the rules.

RULES

1 Use the present perfect to look back at something that started in the past and *finished/continues now*.

2 Use *for/since* to talk about a period of time (how long) and use *for/since* to talk about a point in time (when something started).

C Complete the table with the phrases in the box.

~~2005~~ ~~ages~~ July a long time Saturday
I left college two weeks/months/years 2 p.m.
last night an hour or two I was a child/teenager

for	since
ages	*2005*

▶ page 156 LANGUAGEBANK

4 A Complete the sentences using the verbs in parentheses and adding *for/since* as appropriate.

1 I ______ (do) karate ______ I was a child.
2 I ______ (have) this phone ______ two months.
3 I ______ (know) Marcia ______ I was at school.
4 We ______ (live) in this town/city ______ ten years.
5 I ______ (want) to buy a new car ______ a long time.

B Change two or three of the sentences so they are true for you. Compare your sentences with a partner.

6.1 **5 A Listen to the questions and write short answers with *for* and *since*. Don't write the questions.**

1 by the ocean
2 for five years/since 2005

B Work in pairs and compare your answers. Try to remember the questions.

6.2 **6 SENTENCE STRESS Listen and write the questions. Listen again and underline the stressed words.**

1 How long have you lived there?

SPEAKING

7 A Write questions for each topic beginning *Do you ...?* and *How long have you ...?*

Home

Do you ...?
live downtown?

How long have you ...?
lived there?

Hobbies/Sports

Do you ...?
______

How long have you ...?
______

Things You Have (Possessions)

Do you ...?
______

How long have you ...?
______

Work/Study/School

Do you ...?
______

How long have you ...?
______

B Work in groups. Ask and answer the questions. Try to find out more information.

A: Do you have a car?
B: Yes, I do.
A: How long have you had it?
B: It's very old. I've had it for about ten years.
A: What kind of car is it?
B: It's a four-door.

C Tell the class about the students in your group.

6.2 THE FUTURE OF FOOD

G *may, might, will*
P intonation: certainty/uncertainty
V food

VOCABULARY
FOOD

1 A Work in pairs. How many types of food can you think of for each of the categories below? Make a list.

vegetables desserts
meat fruit

B Compare your lists with other students.

▶ page 157 PHOTOBANK

C Work in pairs. Discuss the questions.

1 What is your favorite food?
2 Do you ever eat food from other countries/cultures? If so, what?
3 Which of the dishes in the photos do you often/sometimes/never eat? Would you like to try any of them?

falafel

sushi

paella

burrito

LISTENING

2 A Work in pairs. Look at the pictures and read the sentences about food of the future. Do you think they are true (T) or false (F)?

1 In the future, more people might eat insects.

2 In the future, we will be able to make food from mud, wood and seaweed.

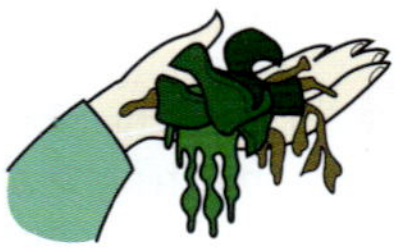

3 In the future, kitchen tools (e.g., knives) might give us information about the food in the kitchen.

6.3

B Listen to an interview with a food expert and check your answers.

C Complete sentences 1–6. Then listen again to check.

1 We may see some changes, things that you might not understand as food g______.
2 Insects are rich in protein, low in fat and easy to f______.
3 Scientists have already found ways to create meat in the l______.
4 We're also looking at ways to make proteins out of things like mud and wood and also s______.
5 Other developments on your kitchen table include an intelligent k______.
6 It will really give people more i______ about their food.

American Speak out TIP

When we aren't sure of a word we hear, we can often guess: What letter does the word begin with? How many syllables does it have? Do we recognize the ending of the word (e.g., *-tion*, *-y*, *-ed*)? Does the context tell us the type of word (e.g., noun, verb, adjective)? After guessing, check with a friend, your teacher or the audio script.

GRAMMAR

MAY, MIGHT, WILL

3 A Read sentences a)–d) and answer the questions about the phrases in bold.

a) We **might see** them (insects) on menus.

b) We **may see** some changes.

c) An intelligent knife **will tell** you about what it's cutting.

d) It tastes awful now, but … it **won't** in the future.

1 Which one is negative?

2 Which ones mean "probably, but we don't know"?

3 Which one is a strong prediction about the future?

▶ page 138 LANGUAGEBANK

6.5

B INTONATION: CERTAINTY/UNCERTAINTY Listen to four sentences. In which sentences are the speakers uncertain?

C Listen again. Notice how the speakers say *will*, *might*, *may* and *won't*. When the speaker is not sure, do *will*, *might*, *may* and *won't* sound longer or shorter?

4 A Write responses to sentences 1–7. Use the prompts in parentheses with *might/might not*, *may/may not* or *will/won't*.

1 We're having a picnic. (rain) *It might rain.*

2 I'm becoming a vegetarian. (lose / weight)

3 Let's go to the best restaurant in town. (be / expensive)

4 I want to stop eating junk food. (feel / healthier)

5 Let's go to the café for breakfast. (not / be / open)

6 I want to try eating octopus. (not / like / it)

7 I'm going to take a cooking class. (enjoy / it)

B Work in pairs and take turns. Student A: say something is going to happen. Student B: respond using *may*, *might*, *will* or *won't*. Continue the conversation.

A: We're having a picnic.
B: It might rain.
A: Don't be so negative! The sun's shining.
B: That's true, but you should take an umbrella.

SPEAKING

5 A Work in pairs. Do you agree with sentences 1–6 below? Check (✔) the four most interesting sentences.

1 In the future, nobody will be hungry for long.

2 People won't eat animals in the future.

3 More people might grow food to save money.

4 Families won't have time to eat together.

5 The next generation may not know how to cook; people will order food on the Internet.

6 I might learn how to cook in the future.

B Compare your ideas with other students.

A: Number 1 might happen, but it won't happen soon.
B: I agree. There is enough food in the world, but it is not reaching the people who need it.

WRITING

SENTENCE STRUCTURE

6 A Work in pairs. Read the extract from a blog below and discuss the questions.

1 When and why did Fernanda move from her home city?

2 What does she say about Colombian food and Colombian cooking?

3 What food did she try in the U.S., and who made it?

How important *is* food *in* your life?

Fernanda Huerta-Gonzalez, from Colombia, talks about food.

In my late twenties, I moved from my home in Medellin, Colombia, to the United States to continue my studies. It was a good move, but I missed my family and friends. I also missed Colombian food. In my country, we have a lot of special dishes like *mondongo* and *peto*, and we take our time preparing food. People say we cook with love!

While in the U.S., I met other international students, and, twice a month, we got together and cooked for one another. It was wonderful, and I tasted food from many countries: Libya, Poland, Tunisia, Peru and Japan. I also made many good friends. My time in the U.S. taught me the importance of food as a part of culture and a way to bring people together.

B Compare the two examples below. What do you notice about the length of the sentences?

I was in my late twenties. I went to the United States. I went to continue my studies.

I was in my late twenties when I went to the United States to continue my studies.

American Speak out TIP

Short sentences may sound unconnected. Long sentences can be difficult to understand. Try to use *and* only once in a sentence. In the next sentence, use *also*. Look at your last piece of writing. Can you use this tip to improve sentence structure?

C Find two examples of the *and/also* pattern in the blog.

D Choose one of the topics in the box below and write a paragraph. Use different sentence lengths.

cooking	restaurants	favorite food	family meals

I love cooking.

One of my favorite restaurants is …

6.3 HOW ARE YOU FEELING?

F seeing the doctor
P difficult words: spelling v. pronunciation
V illness

SPEAKING

1 A Work in pairs. Answer the questions.

1 Do you think men or women go to the doctor more often?
2 Why do you think this is?
3 What reasons do you think people give for not going to see a doctor?

B Read the text to check your answers.

C Work in pairs. Discuss. Do you think any of the excuses in the text are good reasons to avoid seeing the doctor?

Five Reasons You Don't Go to the Doctor

Did you know that men are five times less likely to visit a doctor than women? The reason: they don't like waiting. In fact, 58 percent of men will choose not to go to the doctor, even when they should. Here are the top reasons people give for why they don't go to the doctor.

1 I'm fine.
2 I hate waiting.
3 Nobody told me to go (like my wife/girlfriend/mother).
4 I don't want to talk about it.
5 I don't have time.

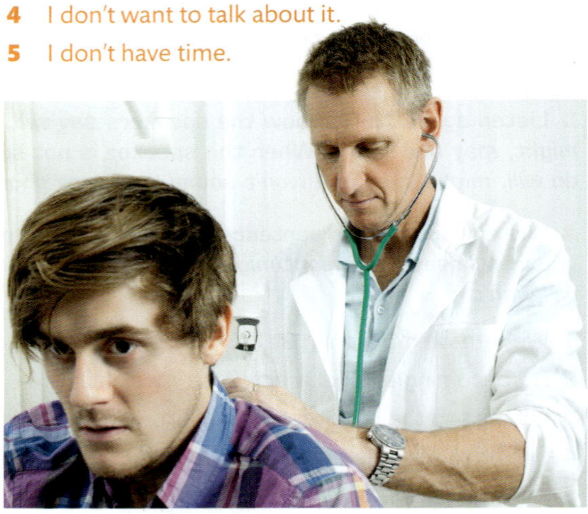

VOCABULARY
ILLNESS

2 A Match problems 1–4 below with advice a)–d).

1 You **have** a **headache/backache**.
2 You have **caught a cold/the flu**.
3 You have **broken your arm/leg**.
4 You have a **sore throat** and a **bad cough**. You also have a **high fever**.

a) Take some **medicine/antibiotics**.
b) Go to the hospital for an **X-ray**.
c) **Get some rest**, and **drink lots of hot liquids**.
d) Take some **painkillers/pills**.

6.5 **B DIFFICULT WORDS: spelling versus pronunciation**
Check your pronunciation. Listen and repeat.

C Work in pairs. Discuss. What do you do when you have a cold/headache/the flu to make yourself feel better?

A: I usually go to bed with a hot drink. How about you?
B: I don't do anything. I just keep on working.

FUNCTION
SEEING THE DOCTOR

6.6 **3 A Listen to two conversations between a doctor and her patients. Answer the questions.**

1 What problem(s) does the patient have?
2 What does the doctor suggest?

B Complete sentences 1–6 below with the words in the box.

~~matter~~	problem	hurt	look	worry	painkillers

1 What's the *matter*?
2 How long have you had this ______?
3 I'll give you some ______.
4 Can I have a ______?
5 Where does it ______?
6 It's nothing to ______ about.

you have / fever — you have got / temperature

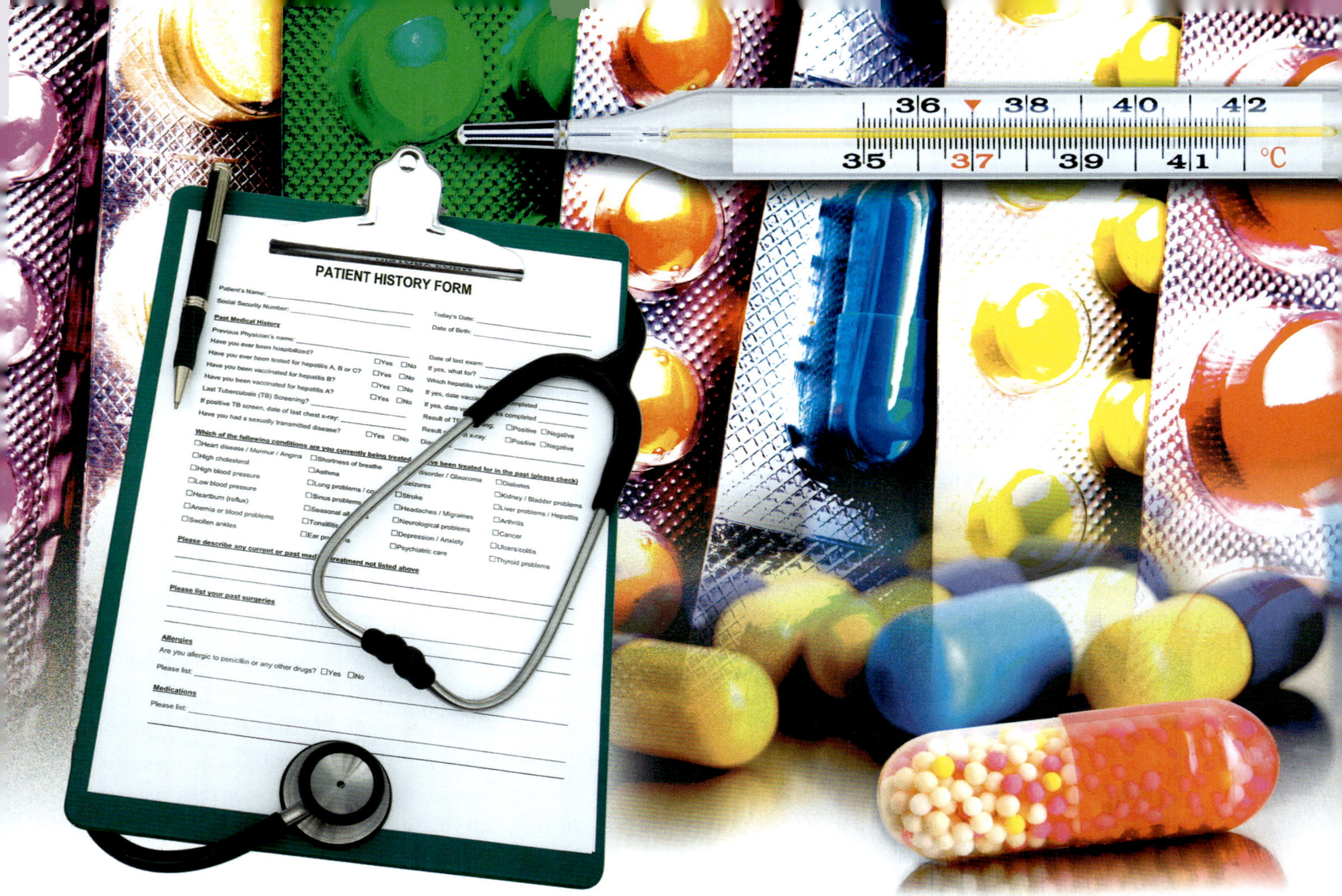

C **Complete sentences 1–5 below with the words in the box.**

painful	sleep	sick	hurts	worried

1 I feel ______ /terrible.

2 I can't ______.

3 I'm ______ about …

4 It ______ when I walk.

5 It's very ______.

D **Listen to the conversations again to check your answers.**

▶ page 138 LANGUAGEBANK

4 **Underline the correct alternative.**

1 My head *hurts/pain/sore*.

2 I have a really bad *flu/cold/sick*.

3 She feels *cough/sick/a temperature*.

4 I think I've *broken/sore/hurting* my arm.

5 Where does it *hurt/pain/sore*?

6 It's nothing to *problem/matter/worry about*.

7 I'll *give/take/look* you some pills.

8 How long have you had this *ill/matter/problem*?

LEARN TO

PREDICT INFORMATION

5 **A** **Work in pairs. Look at the conversation. What do you think the missing words are?**

Doctor: What's the [1]______?

Patient: I've got a really bad [2]______. I feel [3]______.

Doctor: How long have you had the [4]______?

Patient: About a [5]______.

Doctor: Can I have a [6]______?

Patient: It's very [7]______.

Doctor: I'll give you some [8]______.

B **Listen to check your answers.**

C **Listen again and practice saying the phrases.**

American Speakout TIP

When you are going into a situation that you can plan for (a visit to the doctor, a trip to a restaurant, etc.), first try to predict the conversation. This will help you to understand words/phrases when you hear them.

6 **Work in pairs. Student A: turn to page 161. Student B: turn to page 163. Role-play the conversations. Before you start, try to predict what the other person will say.**

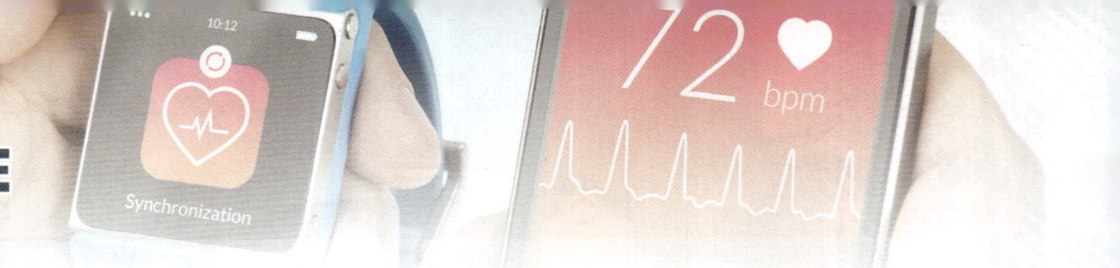

6.4 MONITOR ME

DVD PREVIEW

1 A **Read the program information about *Horizon: Monitor Me*. What type of things will you learn from watching the program?**

Horizon: Monitor Me

Horizon is a documentary series. In this program, Dr. Kevin Fong looks at new **apps** that are changing people's lives. He shows how technology can now **measure** our exercise, sleep, food, drink, etc. When we use this information to **monitor** ourselves, it can improve our health and help us live longer. Dr. Fong thinks the new technology might be a revolution in **healthcare**.

B **Match the words in bold with meanings 1–4.**

1 find out the size or quantity of something
2 carefully watch something to see how it changes over time
3 a small, special program that you download onto a cell phone
4 the service that looks after people when they are sick

DVD VIEW

2 A **Watch the DVD. What did you learn from the program about changes in healthcare and self-monitoring?**

B **Work in pairs. Read the questions and check (✔) the correct options. There may be more than one answer.**

1 You might be healthier if you knew how much/many:
a) steps you took.
b) books you read.
c) food you ate.
d) people you met.
e) hours you slept.

2 Dr. Fong goes to a sports store to:
a) see some apps.
b) look at how bicycles can improve health.

3 Blaine Price shows Dr. Fong apps that measure:
a) steps you take.
b) your sleep.
c) your food.
d) information about your heart.

4 The program also mentions apps that can measure:
a) your blood-alcohol level.
b) how high you can jump.
c) your telephone use.

C **Watch the DVD again to check your answers.**

3 **Work in pairs. Discuss with other students.**

1 What do you think of this "revolution in healthcare"? Is it a good thing for society?
2 Have you ever used an app? Do you think apps help/could help you in your daily life?

American Speakout create a health regimen

4 A Read the notes on the health of three people and answer the questions.

1 What health problems do they have now?

2 What problems might they have in the future?

Marcin, 44, machine operator, 6 ft., 238 lbs

Diet: eats mainly junk food, no vegetables, 6 cups of coffee daily

Exercise/Sleep: no exercise, sleeps 7 hours a night

Social Life: goes out with friends 3 nights a week

Goal: lose 30 lbs and get in shape for soccer

Paulina, 22, student, 5 ft. 8 in., 110 lbs

Diet: eats fresh fruit/vegetables, no meat, vitamins

Exercise/Sleep: does yoga, sleeps 6 hours a night

Social Life: has few friends, stresses about studies

Goal: gain 14 lbs., have more energy

Alvaro, 68, retired bank manager, 5 ft. 9 in., 209 lbs

Diet: eats meat twice a day

Exercise/Sleep: has back pain (takes painkillers), no exercise, sleeps 8 hours

Social Life: many friends, watches TV 6 hours a day

Goal: be fit enough to play with grandchildren

In the U.S., heights are typically measured in feet (ft.) and inches (in.) and weights in pounds (lbs.) and ounces (oz.), whereas in much of the rest of the world, heights are measured in meters (m) and centimeters (cm) and weights in grams (g) and kilograms (kg).

B Listen to a health expert saying how one of the three people can improve their health. Which person is the expert talking about?

C Listen again. Check (✓) the key phrases you hear.

KEYPHRASES

To get healthy, you need …

There are some changes he can make.

For example, he needs to [exercise/stop eating junk food] …

He could try [going for walks/cycling/taking exercise classes] …

He should spend time [exercising/seeing friends] …

He has to lose weight.

Maybe he could [eat less meat/stop drinking sodas] …

It's a good idea to …

5 A Work with other students. Plan health regimens for the other two people in Exercise 4. Think about how they can become healthier if they exercise and change their diet and lifestyle.

B Work with another group and compare your ideas.

writeback health advice

6 A Read the problem below and answer the questions.

1 What health problems does Ahmed have?

2 Why is he writing?

I'm worried about my health. Every winter I get sick. I get a cough or a sore throat, and sometimes I have a high fever. I also get really bad headaches. Generally, I try to live healthily. I don't eat much junk food, and I exercise at least once a week. The problem is, I have a stressful job and never sleep for more than six hours. Winter is coming, and I don't want to spend it lying in bed and taking antibiotics. I've heard it's a good idea to monitor my food and exercise, but I'm not sure about this. What can I do?

Ahmed al Muntari

Hi Ahmed, Sorry to hear you have health problems during the winter. That sounds tough! I have a few ideas that might help you. First, …

B Complete the blog post replying to Ahmed. Try to include advice about some of the following: diet, sleep, exercise, using apps to monitor your health.

6.5 LOOKBACK

V HEALTH

1 A Make questions with the prompts below for a class survey.

1 go / exercise classes
2 eat / junk food / drink / sodas
3 time / relaxing
4 take / vitamins
5 go / running
6 stress / worrying
7 drink / caffeine
8 eat / fresh fruit / vegetables

B Work in groups and take turns. Ask and answer the questions.

C Tell the class what you found out.

G PRESENT PERFECT + *FOR/SINCE*

2 A Write the name of:

1 a place you haven't been to since you were a child
2 something you have only had for a few months
3 someone you have known since you were a teenager
4 something you haven't done since you left school
5 something you have wanted to do for a long time
6 a sport/hobby you have done for more than five years

B Work in pairs and compare your ideas. Ask and answer questions about each thing.

A: I haven't played tennis since I left school. Have you?
B: Yes, I love tennis.

V FOOD

3 Find twelve types of food in the word snake.

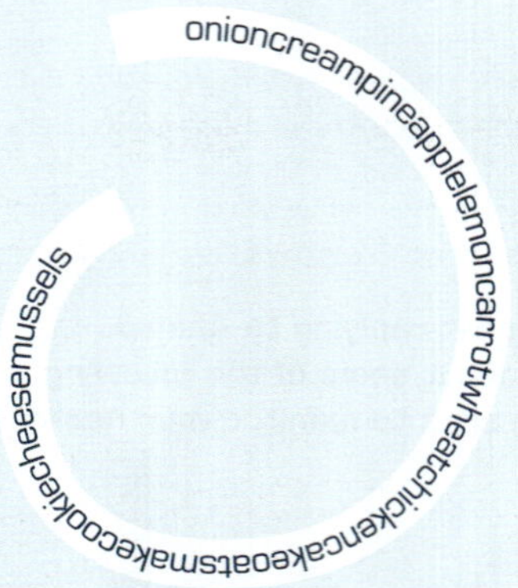

4 A Work in pairs. Divide the food in Exercise 3 into these categories. There are two words for each category.

Desserts	Dairy
Fruit	**Vegetables**
Grains	**Meat/Seafood**

B Add words to each category.

G *MAY, MIGHT, WILL*

5 A Match statements 1–6 to responses a)–f).

1 I've drunk eight cups of coffee.
2 I've started buying fresh vegetables.
3 I've stopped smoking.
4 I've stopped taking vitamins.
5 I've started doing yoga.
6 I've decided to run a marathon.

a) You won't cough all the time.
b) You might feel less stressed.
c) You may get more colds.
d) You may not be in good enough shape.
e) You will taste the difference.
f) You might not sleep well tonight.

B Work in pairs and take turns. Student A: use the prompts in the box to make statements with *I've decided to … .* Student B: respond using *may/may not, might/might not, will/won't*.

buy a house in Florida
give up eating meat
write a book join a boxing club
get a pet tiger live in Hawaii
become a dancer
get a degree in physics
marry an astronaut
go into politics

A: I've decided to buy a house in Florida.
B: It might be expensive!

6 Work in groups and take turns. Ask and answer the questions.

1 What do you think will happen to your country in a few years' time?
2 Who do you think will win the next World Cup?
3 Where might you be in five years' time?
4 What job will you do in the future?
5 What will you do on your next birthday?
6 Where will you go on your next vacation?

F SEEING THE DOCTOR

7 A Complete the questions with the correct form of the verbs in the box.

catch feel give break
cannot have

1 Have you (or anyone in your family) ever ______ your arm/leg? Where? How?
2 Do you often ______ colds or the flu? What do you do to get better?
3 Is there any food that makes you ______ sick?
4 Do you ever find you ______ sleep? What do you do?
5 When was the last time the doctor ______ you some pills?
6 What do you do when you ______ a headache?

B Work in pairs and take turns. Ask and answer the questions.

7 changes

SPEAKING
7.1 Talk about a life change
7.2 Talk about why people tell lies
7.3 Learn to check and confirm information
7.4 Talk about new experiences

LISTENING
7.1 Listen to a radio program about a woman who changed her life
7.3 Understand short, predictable conversations
7.4 Watch an extract from the beginning of a movie about a family that moves to Greece

READING
7.1 Read about living the dream
7.2 Read and predict information in a story
7.3 Read about studying abroad

WRITING
7.1 Use paragraphs to write about a change
7.4 Write a blog/diary

How has your life changed in the last ten years?

INTERVIEWS

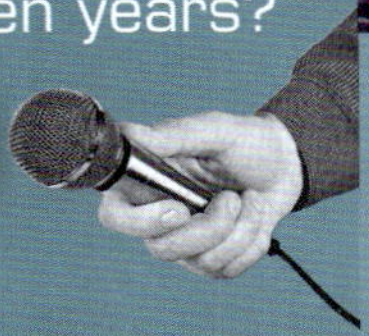

7.1 LIVING THE DREAM

G *used to*
P weak forms: *used to*
V verbs + prepositions

VOCABULARY
VERBS + PREPOSITIONS

1 A **Work in pairs. Discuss. Would you like to change anything in your life? What would you change? Why?**

B **Read the text. Why do you think many people do not manage to live their dreams?**

> **Living the Dream**
>
> Are you bored with your life or your job? Do you do the same thing every day? Perhaps it's time to **look for** something new.
>
> Every year, thousands of people **dream about** changing their lives. Many want to give up their jobs and start a new career, or move or learn a new skill. Lots of people say they'd like to do something different, like **travel around** the world or **move to** a new country. But only a few people actually follow their dreams. Around vacation time, a quarter of the people in the U.K. **think about** changing jobs, but when the vacation finishes, they just **go back** to work as normal. Others **wait for** an opportunity their whole lives, but it never comes.
>
> The BBC talked to Jessica Fox, who wanted to **get away** from her life in the California sunshine and move to Scotland and run a second-hand bookstore. She tells us about how she made her dream come true.

2 A **Complete the sentences with the phrases in bold from the text in Exercise 1B.**

1 I sometimes *think about* doing a different job.
2 I really enjoy traveling, but I wouldn't ______ another country to live.
3 I want to give up my job and ______ to studying.
4 I need to speak English for my job. I ______ becoming a famous journalist.
5 I should ______ a raise, before I buy a new car.
6 I would love to ______ different countries.
7 Things have been so busy, I just need to ______ for a few days and relax.
8 Can you help me ______ my bag? I can't find it anywhere.

B **Check (✔) the sentences that are true for you. Work in pairs and compare your ideas.**

> **American Speak out TIP**
> There are many phrases with prepositions in English. Keep a page for phrases with prepositions in your notebook. Write the examples of verbs + prepositions in your notebook. Can you think of any other examples?

LISTENING

3 A **Jessica Fox left her dream job in sunny California to move across the world and live in Scotland. Which place would you prefer to live in? Why do you think she moved?**

S7.1 **B** **Listen to the interview to find out.**

bookstore / raise — bookshop / pay rise

4 A Listen to the interview again and answer the questions.

Part 1

1 Did Jessica enjoy her life in California?

2 What did she dream about?

Part 2

3 What did Jessica do to realize her dream?

4 Did she send a lot of emails?

Part 3

5 How did Jessica feel when she went back to LA?

6 What does she enjoy about her life now?

B Work in pairs. Discuss the questions.

1 Do you think it was a good idea for Jessica to make this life change? Why/Why not?

2 Would you do this kind of thing yourself?

GRAMMAR

USED TO

5 A Read sentences a)–c) and answer the questions.

a) Jessica used to live in California.

b) She didn't use to work in a bookstore.

c) What did she use to dream about?

1 Did Jessica live in California in the past?

2 Does she live in California now?

3 Did Jessica work in a bookstore in the past?

4 Does she work in a bookstore now?

5 Does question c) ask about the past or present?

B Look at your answers to questions 1–5 above and underline the correct alternatives to complete the rules.

RULES

1 *Used to* describes a habit or situation that was true in the past, but it is not the same now. You can also use the *present/past simple* with a similar meaning, but *used to* emphasizes the change.

2 If something *used to* happen, it happened *once/for an extended time*.

▶ page 140 LANGUAGEBANK

6 A Find and correct the mistakes. There are mistakes in four of the sentences.

1 When I was a child, I used to ride my bike to school yesterday.

2 My brother always used listen to heavy metal music.

3 My family used to live in a different city.

4 I used to stay up all night dancing. Now I get tired at 10 p.m.

5 We didn't used to have any pets.

6 We used to go skiing for vacation last year.

S7.2 **B Listen to check.**

S7.3 **C WEAK FORMS: *used to* Notice the pronunciation of used to /juːstə/. Listen and repeat the phrases.**

used_to

D Change the sentences so they are true for you. Compare your sentences with other students.

SPEAKING

7 A Make a note of three things that used to be true about you ten years ago (e.g., appearance, home, work, studies, free time, personality, etc.).

B Work in pairs. Discuss. How have your lives changed? Whose life has changed the most?

WRITING

PARAGRAPHS

8 A Read about Ryan's life-changing decision. Put the sentences in the correct order to complete the paragraphs.

Paragraph 1

One of the best decisions I ever made was to go back to school. 1

I've always thought that being a teacher would be interesting. __

So I went back to college and took a teacher training course. __

Before that, I was working for a company, but I didn't enjoy my job. __

Paragraph 2

Doing the program wasn't easy. 1

Now, I have a teaching degree, and I'm doing the job I've always wanted to do. __

So I used to study in the evenings. __

For example, I had to work to earn money and find time to do the homework. __

B In each paragraph find sentences that:

1 contain the main idea

2 support the idea

3 finish or conclude the paragraph

C Write about a decision that changed your life. Write your story in paragraphs. Use sentences to introduce and support the idea and conclude the paragraph.

One of the best decisions I ever made was ______. I wanted to ______. So I ______. ______ wasn't easy because ______. But ______. Now, I ______.

realize or make her dream come true / emphasizes / degree

realise her dream emphasises / qualification

7.2 THE GREAT IMPOSTOR

G purpose, cause and result
P rhythm in complex sentences
V collocations

1 Ferdinand Waldo Demara was probably the greatest impostor in history. He was born in the U.S.A. in 1921. As a young man, he pretended to be a doctor, an engineer, a lawyer, a college professor, a soldier and a sailor. Demara's greatest adventure was during the Korean War.

What did he do?

a) He pretended to be a doctor on a ship.
b) He worked for the Korean government.
c) He pretended to be a politician.

Read 6 to find out

2 Demara pretended to be a teacher, and the police caught him. He spent six months in prison. After this, he played one more role. He appeared in a 1960 movie (called *The Hypnotic Eye*) to make some money, acting as a doctor. But real fame arrived in 1961 when Hollywood made a movie of Demara's life.

3 The bullet was very close to the soldier's heart. Demara studied from a book so that he could save the man's life. He removed the bullet, and the soldier lived. In fact, while Demara worked as a doctor, none of his patients died. But, in the end, he became too successful.

What happened?

a) He appeared on TV, and his friends recognized him.
b) His photo and false name appeared in a newspaper.
c) He became a movie star.

Read 5 to find out

4 Demara didn't go to prison because people thought he was a hero. Instead the police released him and gave him extra money to say "thank you" for his great work! But later the police arrested him for a different crime.

What did he do?

a) He robbed a bank.
b) He pretended to be a policeman.
c) He pretended to be a teacher.

Read 2 to find out

5 Demara became famous because of his great work as the ship's doctor, and his photo appeared in some newspapers in Canada. The mother of the real Dr. Cyr saw the photo. She knew this was not her son. So she told the police, and they arrested him.

What happened next?

a) He went to prison. **b)** He didn't go to prison. **c)** He escaped to Europe.

Read 4 to find out

6 In 1951, Demara pretended to be Dr. Joseph Cyr (a real doctor) so that he could work on a ship. The soldiers loved him! He cured their illnesses; he pulled out bad teeth; and he performed difficult operations. He had his greatest moments after a soldier was shot.

What did he do?

a) He jumped into the ocean and helped the soldier.
b) He pretended to be the dead soldier.
c) He performed an operation that saved the soldier's life.

Read 3 to find out

READING

1 A Look at the photo of a famous impostor and the tools he used in different jobs. What do you think this man pretended to be?

> **im.pos.tor, imposter** /ɪmˈpɒstə/ /ɪmˈpastə-/ noun someone who pretends to be someone else in order to trick people

from Longman WordWise Dictionary

B Read the story. As you read, stop at each question and, with a partner, guess the answer. Then read to find out.

2 Work in pairs and discuss the questions.

1 Why do you think Demara did these things?
2 Do you think he was a good man?
3 Do you think people like Demara should be punished?

VOCABULARY
COLLOCATIONS

3 A Match 1–7 with a)–g) to make collocations (words that go together).

1 cure	a) successful/famous
2 make a	b) a role/a part in a movie
3 save	c) movie/documentary
4 become	d) a crime/a murder
5 be arrested for	e) a man's life/money
6 spend	f) illnesses/people
7 play	g) six months in prison/time abroad

B Work in pairs. Re-tell the story of Demara's life using the collocations above.

American Speak out TIP: Many words come in pairs, e.g., *cure illnesses*, *become famous*. When you hear or read collocations, write them in your notebook. Think of other words that go with *play* and *make*.

GRAMMAR
PURPOSE, CAUSE AND RESULT

4 A Complete sentences 1–3 with *so*, *to* or *because*.

Purpose (the reason for an action)

1 He appeared in a 1960 movie ______ make some money.

Cause (it makes something happen)

2 Demara didn't go to prison ______ people thought he was a hero.

Result (the consequence of something)

3 She knew this was not her son, ______ she told the police.

B Check your answers in the text in Exercise 1.

C Look again at the text in Exercise 1 and find more examples of *so*, *to* and *because*.

▶ page 140 LANGUAGEBANK

5 A Underline the correct alternative.

1 I'm taking an English class *so/to/because* improve my speaking.
2 I'll do many jobs in the future *so/to/because* I like to try different things.
3 I'd like to become famous, *so/to/because* I'm going to study acting.
4 You need to communicate well *so/to/because* become successful in my job.
5 I'd like to make a movie about my life *so/to/because* I've had many great experiences.
6 I'd love to spend time abroad *so/to/because* experience another culture.
7 I'm going to take a test, *so/to/because* I have to study a lot.
8 It's difficult to be an impostor *so/to/because* you can never relax.

7.4

B RHYTHM IN COMPLEX SENTENCES Listen to the answers. As you listen, follow the words on the page with your finger. Listen again and say the sentences at the same time.

C Are any of the sentences true for you? Work in pairs and compare your ideas.

6 Work in pairs and take turns. Student A: make sentences with phrases from A. Use the past simple. Student B: complete Student A's sentences with phrases from B and *so*, *to* or *because*.

A: I went to the movie theater …
B: … to watch a movie.
A: I studied my notes …
B: … because I had a test.

A	B
go to the movie theater	have a test
study my notes	become a nurse
want to help people	can't drive
go to the doctor	get a Master's degree
like traveling	invite her to a party
go to college	feel sick
call my friend	love listening to music
ride a bike to work	watch a movie
buy an MP3 player	become a pilot

SPEAKING

7 A Discuss the questions below.

1 Why do people tell lies about their lives?
2 When might you tell a lie?

B Work in pairs. Read the situations below and discuss. Would you tell a lie in these situations? Why/Why not?

1 An employee at your company is bad at her job. She tells you a secret: she used false documents (résumé and references) to get her job. The boss asks you about her.
2 Your best friend introduces her new boyfriend to you. You don't like him because he doesn't listen to or care about anyone else. Your friend asks for your opinion of him.
3 A friend buys a designer bag for $50 from a man on the street. She says the bag usually costs $300, so she bought it. You know the bag isn't a real designer bag. She asks if you want one.

taking (a class) / call — doing (a class) / phone

7.3)) CAN YOU TELL ME?

F finding out information
P intonation: checking information
V facilities

"Read 1,000 books and walk 1,000 miles"

... is a Chinese saying about education. And this is exactly what students from the People's Republic of China are doing. Thousands of Chinese students have joined students from Europe, India, the U.S.A., Saudi Arabia and other countries to study at U.K. colleges. So, how do they feel about coming to the U.K.? "It's difficult at first," says Yi Lina, a student at Bristol University. "Everything is very different: the food, the people. But it gets easier. You open a bank account, get a cell phone contract, and start talking to people. It has been a great experience."

SPEAKING

1 **Work in pairs. Discuss the questions.**

1 Is there a college in your town? What can you study there?

2 Would you like to study in another country? Why/Why not?

2 **Read the text. What do the students think about studying abroad?**

VOCABULARY
FACILITIES

3 **A** **Match 1–5 with the places in the box.**

reading room	bookstore	cafeteria	library
stationery store	main office	classroom	
photocopy room	lecture hall		
student services office	registration desk		

1 borrow a book
2 buy pens, paper and notebooks
3 register for a new class
4 buy a snack
5 find information about where you are staying

B **Work in pairs and take turns. Student A: say a place. Student B: say what you can do there.**

A: What can you do in a photocopy room?
B: You can make photocopies.

C **Discuss. Which of these facilities can you find in your language school/college? Where are they? Which of them do you often/never use?**

FUNCTION
FINDING OUT INFORMATION

4 **A** **Make questions with the prompts below.**

a) where / register for my class _1_
Where do I register for my class?
b) where / the reading room __
c) what time / the library open __
d) can / help / find my classroom __
e) where / use the Internet __
f) where / buy a notebook __
g) where / get a new student card __
h) can / tell me / where / go (for information about ...) __

S7.5

B **Listen to the situations. Number the questions above in the order you hear them.**

main office — main reception
student services department or office — accommodation/welfare office

5 **Listen again. Are the statements true (T) or false (F)?**

1 The registration desk is in the main office.
2 The reading room is next to the cafeteria.
3 There is Internet in the library.
4 The library is open from ten until five every day.
5 You can get a new student card from the main office.
6 Room 301 is on the third floor on the right.
7 The stationery store is upstairs.
8 The student services office is next to the stationery store.

6 **A Complete the phrases with the words in the box.**

can	excuse	have	need	help	time	kind

Getting attention
[1]______ me, …
Could you [2]______ me?
Can you tell me where/what … ?
Asking for information
Where [3]______ I get/find/buy … ?
When can I use/start … ?
What [4]______ is the library open?
What time do the classes start?
Can I … ?
Do I [5]______ to … ?
Is it free/open/near?
I [6]______ to find out about/speak to …
Thanking someone
Thank you so much.
That's very [7]______.

B Read audio script S7.5 on page 172–173 to check your answers.

▶ page 140 LANGUAGEBANK

7 **Find and correct the mistakes. There are two mistakes in each conversation.**

1 **A:** Excuse to me, where's the bookstore?
B: There's one around corner.

2 **A:** What time do the swimming pool open?
B: During the week, it opens on eight o'clock. On the weekend, it opens at nine.

3 **A:** Can tell me where to get a student card, please?
B: You need going to the main office.

4 **A:** Where I can get a coffee?
B: There's a cafeteria over there, next the library.

8 **Work in pairs. Student A: turn to page 165. Student B: turn to page 166.**

LEARN TO
CHECK AND CONFIRM INFORMATION

S7.6

9 **A Read and listen to the different ways of checking information in bold below.**

Extract 1
B: Do you know where the main office is?
A: **Sorry**?

Extract 2
C: It's next to the cafeteria.
A: **The cafeteria?** Where's that?

Extract 3
A: Do I have to pay?
D: No.
A: **So, it's free for students.**

Extract 4
E: It's open every day, from 9 a.m. until 6 p.m.
A: **Did you say "every day"?**

Extract 5
A: I need to find out about my housing. Can you tell me where to go?
I: **Housing**? I think you have to go to the student services office.

B What are the speakers doing in each conversation?

a) repeating the key words/phrases as a question
b) asking a checking question/asking for repetition
c) rephrasing

S7.7

C INTONATION: checking information Listen and repeat the phrases in bold in Exercise 9A. How does the intonation change?

10 **Work in pairs. Role-play the situation below. Student A: you are a student. You have lost your bag. Student B: you work at the main office.**

Student | **Receptionist**

Explain the situation.
→ Find out exactly what happened.
Ask what you need to do.
→ Explain that he/she needs to go to the student services office and complete a form.
Ask where the student services office is.
→ Give directions.
Check that you understand what you have to do/ask for repetition.
→ Repeat any information.
Thank the receptionist.

7.4 A GREEK ADVENTURE

DVD PREVIEW

1 Work in pairs. Discuss. Do you ever have problems trying to communicate with people who can't speak your language? Where? What happens? What can you do to help make yourself understood in situations like this?

2 Read the program information. Where does the family move to? Why?

My Family and Other Animals

My Family and Other Animals is a movie based on Gerald Durrell's book. It tells the story of the Durrells, a rather unusual family: Gerry – a twelve-year-old who loves animals, his sister Margo, his brother Leslie, his eldest brother, the writer Lawrence, and their mother. One wet gray day in the 1930s, the family decides to escape the English weather. They sell their house and move to the sunny island of Corfu in Greece. Here they experience a new life of freedom and adventure. But the beginning isn't easy, so they are delighted when they make a new friend, Spiro.

DVD VIEW

3 **A** **What kind of problems do you think the family might have? Do you think life will be better or worse for the family? Why? Watch the DVD to find out.**

B **Number the scenes in the correct order.**

a) The family is at home in London. It's August, but no one feels well. *1*

b) The family looks for a house to live in, but cannot find one with a bathroom.

c) The family meets Spiro, and he finds the family a beautiful house (villa).

d) The family members decide to look by themselves, so they try to get a taxi.

e) They arrive on a boat, and the customs officer checks their suitcases.

4 **A** **What do they say? Use the words in the box to complete the sentences.**

sunshine	bathroom	Greek	tourists
language	place		

1 "It's August. We need ______ ... Why don't we pack up and go?"

2 "You've shown us ten houses, and none of them has a ______."

3 "They must have bathrooms. We'll find a ______ ourselves."

4 "We don't actually speak ______."

5 "You need someone who talks your ______?"

6 "All the English ________, they ask for me when they come to the island ... There. Villa with bathrooms." "We'll ______ it."

B **Watch the DVD again to check.**

5 **Work in pairs and discuss the questions.**

1 Which character do you like best? Why?

2 Where do tourists like to go when they visit your country? What problems do they have?

family decides, is, looks / gray — family decide, are, look / grey

American Speakout a new experience

6 A Listen to Agata talking about when she moved to the U.S. Answer the questions.

1 What was the problem?
2 How did she feel?
3 What happened in the end?

B Listen again and check (✔) the key phrases you hear.

KEYPHRASES

It was my first day at ...
The biggest problem was ...
I felt very (nervous/shy/excited/...) when ...
I couldn't ...
I didn't know ...
I wasn't ...
Luckily, I met/made friends with ...
In the end, ...

7 A Talk about a new experience (e.g., when you moved to a new place/started a new class/job). Before you speak, think about the questions below. Make some notes.

1 Where were you?
2 How did you feel?
3 Did you have any problems?
4 What did you do about them?
5 Did you meet anyone who helped you?
6 What happened in the end?

B Work in groups and take turns. Tell each other about your experiences.

writeback a blog/diary

8 A Read part of a web diary about Sadie's first year at college and answer the questions.

1 Is she enjoying college life?
2 Did she have any problems? What were they?

Search

POST ARCHIVE REGISTER CONTACT US

So Far ... So Good

I moved to Turkey in July to go to Bilkent University, and I am really enjoying the experience so far. It's been a fantastic year. I've really enjoyed living somewhere so new and exciting, but I miss my family and friends at home. I've met lots of people, and I love living in this big city. There is always so much to see and do, and Turkish people are so friendly. It's very different from living at home. When I first arrived, I used to get lost around the city. Now, I enjoy exploring and finding out about new places.

B Write a blog/diary about a new experience. Use the questions in Exercise 7A and the structure below to help you.

One thing that has really changed in my life is ______.
I decided to ______ so that/to ______.
Before that, I used to ______. At first, ______ because ______, but ______.
In the end, ______.

V VERBS + PREPOSITIONS

1 A Complete the phrases with a suitable preposition.

1 What do you dream ______ doing in the future?
2 Would you like to travel ______ the world? Which countries would you like to visit?
3 Would you like to get ______ from work/school for a few days? Where would you go?
4 Would you ever move ______ a different town/city? Why/Why not?
5 Are you thinking ______ making any changes to your life at the moment? What are they?
6 Would you like to go ______ to your last school for a day?

B Work in pairs and take turns. Ask and answer the questions.

G *USED TO*

2 A Make questions with the prompts. Begin with *Did you use to ... ?*

When you were a child:

1 you / work / hard / school?
2 you / eat / fast food?
3 you / spend / time / your grandparents?
4 you / get / sick / often?
5 you / have / special friend?
6 you / play any sports?
7 you / go to school / public transportation?
8 you / live / different place?

B Choose two or three of the questions above and write two more related questions.

C Work in pairs and take turns. Ask and answer the questions.

A: Did you use to work hard at school?
B: Yes, I did.
A: What subjects did you use to enjoy?
B: I used to enjoy art and drama.
A: Really? Did you use to get good grades on your tests?
B: Well, most of the time ...

V COLLOCATIONS

3 A Underline the correct alternative in sentences 1–8 below.

1 The doctor *cured/cared* me.
2 This hero *rescued/saved* my life!
3 Sometimes businesses can *become/develop* very successful.
4 My friend Jack *spends/goes* most of his time watching TV.
5 She lost her job after being arrested *by/for* a crime.
6 The criminal *spent/passed* ten months in prison.
7 I *played/was* the role of Hamlet.
8 I would like to *build/make* a movie.

B Work in pairs. Add another sentence to each sentence above.

The doctor cured me. Then I married him!

G PURPOSE, CAUSE AND RESULT

4 A Match 1–8 with a)–h) to make sentences.

1 I went to the library last week
2 I helped my friend
3 I wanted to eat out,
4 I studied
5 I put my feet up and watched TV so
6 I called some old friends to
7 I went to bed late because
8 I went to a meeting

a) to improve my English.
b) I was at a party.
c) to discuss business.
d) hear their news.
e) I could relax.
f) to find a book.
g) because she had a problem.
h) so I went to a restaurant.

B Work in pairs. Choose four phrases from 1–8 above. Make questions to ask what your partner did last week.

A: Did you go to the library?
B: Yes, I did.
A: Why?
B: To find a book.

F FINDING OUT INFORMATION

5 A Put the sentences in the correct order to complete the conversations.

Conversation 1

a) Excuse me, could you help me? 1
b) Thank you. And what's your last name? __
c) Do you have a registration form? __
d) Your class? OK. Do you have a registration form? __
e) I need to find out about my class. __
f) Sorry? __
g) Oh, yes. In my bag. Here it is. __
h) It's Gorski. __
i) Yes, of course. What can I do for you? __

Conversation 2

a) At the main office? __
b) The swimming pool opens at eight o'clock. __
c) OK, thanks. Is it free for students? __
d) Yes, that's right. __
e) Thanks very much. __
f) No, it's not free, but it's cheaper if you have a student card. __
g) Yes, show your card at the main office when you come in. __
h) Eight. OK. So, do I have to bring my student card? __
i) Excuse me, could you tell me what time the swimming pool opens? __

B Work in pairs and practice the conversations.

last name | surname

8 money

SPEAKING
8.1 Talk about a product that people should invest in
8.2 Talk about why you should earn more
8.3 Describe items; go shopping
8.4 Present a money-making idea

LISTENING
8.2 Listen to a discussion about salaries
8.4 Watch an extract from the news about an Ethiopian business

READING
8.1 Read a story about a treasure hunt
8.3 Read a questionnaire about shopping

WRITING
8.2 Write an opinion piece
8.4 Write a competition entry for a business investment

How do you feel about shopping?

INTERVIEWS

8.1 TREASURE HUNT

G relative clauses
P pronouncing the letter "s"
V money

VOCABULARY

MONEY

1 A Read the money questionnaire. What do you think the words in bold mean?

B Work in pairs. Ask and answer the questions.

S8.1 **C PRONOUNCING THE LETTER "S" Underline each example of the letter "s" in the words in bold in the questionnaire. How many ways is it pronounced? Listen and check.**

D How do you say the letter "s" in these words: ***measure, earns, tips, profession, credit cards, lends, imposter, souvenir?***

How do you earn, save and spend your money?

1 Do you usually pay with **cash** or by **credit card** when you buy things?
2 Do you ever **lend** money to family or friends? Why/Why not?
3 Have you ever **borrowed** a lot of money? What for?
4 How many **bills** or **coins** do you have in your pocket at the moment?
5 In your country, how much do you **tip** waiters?
6 Which three people do you think **earn** the most money in your country?
7 Have you ever **invested** money **in** something?
8 Who pays the **bills** where you live?
9 Which of your **possessions** is **worth** the most to you?
10 Have you ever thought of **treasure** hunting?

▶ page 158 PHOTOBANK

READING

2 A Discuss the questions.

1 Do you know any true stories or movies that involved treasure hunting?
2 The man in the photo was very rich and very ill. What is his connection with the treasure chest? Guess and tell your partner. Read to find out.

B Discuss in pairs. What are the connections between:

1 1988 … and … Fenn hiding the treasure?

He was diagnosed with cancer in 1988. He wanted to leave something for the world after his death, so he hid the treasure chest.

2 a poem in Fenn's autobiography … and … the treasure chest?
3 new clues … and … tourism in the area?
4 13,000 … and … 18?
5 the Air Force … and … an art gallery?

C What do you think of Fenn's treasure hunt? Do you like the idea? Why/Why not?

Hidden Treasure

In 1988, U.S. millionaire Forrest Fenn was diagnosed with cancer. Thinking that his life was nearly over, he wanted to leave something to the world. Then he had a really interesting idea. He decided to fill a wooden chest with treasure and hide it.

He included old gold coins, ancient animal figures and antique jewelry, all covered in gold dust, and left the chest somewhere in the desert, probably in New Mexico, where he lives. Then he published his autobiography and included in it a poem that contained clues about where the treasure was hidden. Against all expectations, Fenn recovered from cancer, so he has lived to see the success of his plan.

He says his idea was to provide people with an adventure: hunting outside, with the chance of getting rich. He loves stories and adventures. and he clearly enjoys the attention his plan has brought him. Every few months he releases a new clue, which keeps treasure hunters interested. It seems it is working: he has received more than 13,000 emails from people who want more clues, as well as 18 marriage proposals! There are blogs that describe Fenn's treasure hunt, and tourism in the area has increased, thanks to people who want to find the chest.

Fenn was originally from a poor family in Texas. As a child, he spent his summers in Yellowstone National Park, which is where he first discovered his love of the outdoors. After a career in the Air Force, he eventually opened an art gallery in Santa Fe, making his money by buying and selling paintings. He also became known for organizing amazing parties that were attended by all kinds of famous people. Now he lives with his wife, with whom he happily looks on as treasure hunters arrive in his hometown.

bills / treasure hunting / jewelry — notes / hunting for treasure / jewellery

GRAMMAR

RELATIVE CLAUSES

3 Read sentences 1–5 and complete the rules below.

1 He releases a new clue, **which** keeps treasure hunters interested.

2 There are blogs **that** describe Fenn's treasure hunt.

3 Tourism has increased, thanks to people **who** want to find the chest.

4 He lives with his wife, with **whom** he happily looks on as treasure hunters arrive.

5 He probably hid it in New Mexico, **where** he lives.

RULES

Relative clauses tell you:

- which thing, person or place we are talking about.
- what a thing, person or place is or does.

Use 1 *which* or 2_____ for things.

Use 3_____ or 4_____ for people.

Use 5 _____ for places.

▶ page 142 LANGUAGEBANK

4 A Read sentences 1–3 below. Which things in the box do they describe?

~~casino~~	inventor	library	wallet
DVD player	investor	bank	credit card

1 It's a place where you go to win money. *casino*

2 It's a thing that you use when you want to pay without cash.

3 It's a person who creates new things.

B Use the prompts below to write definitions for the other things in the box above.

1 place / people look after / your money

2 thing / use / carry / money and credit cards

3 person / gives money / to a product or business (to make more money)

4 place / you go / borrow books

5 thing / use / watch movies

C Work in pairs. Student A: turn to page 164. Student B: turn to page 167.

SPEAKING

5 A Work in pairs. Read about what some super-rich people do with their money and discuss the questions.

1 Which projects/donations do you think are the most useful for the world?

2 Are there any that you think are not especially useful? Why?

3 Do you know of any other super-rich people who do interesting things with their money?

B If you had billions of dollars to invest in something interesting or useful, what project would you start? Think about whom it would help, where you would do it, and how long it would last.

What interesting things do the super-rich do with their money?

- Amazon boss, Jeff Bezos, is building an enormous clock inside a mountain; the clock is designed to last 10,000 years.
- TV star, Oprah Winfrey, built a school in South Africa to educate girls from poor families.
- Economist, Muhammad Yunus, founded Grameen Bank, which gives small loans to the poor to start businesses.
- Richard Branson is working to send tourists into space. His company, Virgin Galactic, has spent millions developing commercial spaceships for transporting tourists.

8.2)) PAY ME MORE!

G *too much/many, enough, very*
P multi-word verb stress
V multi-word verbs

LISTENING

1 A Look at the infographic about the pay for different jobs. Discuss the questions.

1 Are you surprised by any of these figures?
2 Why do you think the high earners make so much money?

8.2 **B Listen to three people saying why they should be paid more. As you listen, complete the table.**

Speaker	Job	Difficulties with Job	Should Earn More Because …
1	nanny	1 ______	2 ______
2	3 ______	4 ______	save people, buildings, businesses
3	5 ______	hard to get funding	6 ______

C Listen again and discuss the questions.

1 Which speaker (1, 2 or 3) says:
a) he/she doesn't want a bigger salary for him/herself? What does he/she want?
b) some people are "stupid"? Why?
c) he/she does extra work? What type of work?
2 Who do you think makes the best argument for more money?

The symbol € is used for euros, the currency in most of Europe. £ is used for pounds, the currency of the U.K. The symbol for dollars, as well as for some other currencies, is $.

GRAMMAR

TOO MUCH/MANY, ENOUGH, VERY

2 A Read sentences 1–6 from the recording. Match the words in bold with meanings a)–f) below.

1 Scientists spend **too much** time applying for grants. _b_
2 **Too many** of us do extra work like cleaning. __
3 We should earn **enough** just from being a nanny. __
4 Nannies **aren't paid enough**. __
5 It's **too** dangerous **to** be paid so little. __
6 Some of our projects are **very** expensive. __

a) should earn more
b) more (time) than necessary
c) so (dangerous) that they should be paid more
d) really
e) the right amount
f) more (people) than necessary

B Look at the cartoons below. Underline the correct alternative to complete the rule.

RULES

1 Use *too much/too many* with countable nouns.
2 Use *too much/too many* with uncountable nouns.

I have too much work to do.
I have too many jobs to do.

▶ page 142 LANGUAGEBANK

3 Underline the correct alternative.

1 I don't have *enough time/time enough/very many time* to do the things I enjoy.
2 I drink *too many/much/too much* coffee.
3 I do some *too/enough/very* difficult tasks in my work.
4 I am sometimes *very/enough/too* busy to study English.
5 I spend *very much/too many/too much* hours online.
6 Did you have *the enough/enough/too many* to eat, or do you want more?

4 A Complete the sentences so they are true for you.

1 In my work/studies, I worry too much about …
2 One thing that makes me very happy about my work/studies is …
3 During my working day, I don't have enough time to …
4 One thing that is too difficult for me is …
5 These days too many people …

B Work in pairs and compare your sentences.

VOCABULARY
MULTI-WORD VERBS

5 A Look at sentences 1–6. What do you think the multi-word verbs in bold mean? Match the verbs with the definitions a)–f).

1 If you're talented and you want to be famous, you should never **give up**. __
2 Even the best jobs can **turn into** a nightmare if you have a bad boss. __
3 In my country, it's common for men to **take over** their father's job. __
4 You should never **turn down** a dream job even if the salary is bad. __
5 I think rich people should **give back** some of their money to the community. __
6 In many jobs, e.g., teaching, paperwork **takes up** too much time. __

a) stop trying (to do something difficult or important)
b) return something (to someone) or give something to someone because they have done something for you
c) use or fill an amount of time or space
d) become responsible for something (e.g., a job), replacing the person who did it before you
e) refuse an offer
f) become

B Do you agree with sentences 1–6? Compare your ideas with a partner.

58.3

C MULTI-WORD VERB STRESS **Which words are stressed in multi-word verbs? Listen to check.**

6 Answer questions 1–5 and compare your ideas with other students.

1 Would you like to take over your father's or your mother's job?
2 Have you ever done a job/task that turned into a nightmare? What happened?
3 What boring tasks take up your time?
4 Have you ever turned down a good offer?
5 Why do you think so many people give up trying to learn a foreign language?

American Speakout TIP

A multi-word verb is a verb + preposition/adverb, e.g., *wake up*. Multi-word verbs often have a different meaning from the individual words in them. Always write down multi-word verbs in example sentences: *I wake up at 7 a.m.* Write some multi-word verbs that you know. Ask your partner to think of example sentences.

SPEAKING

7 A Think about your answers to questions 1 and 2.

1 What do the people in photos A–F below do? Who should earn the most money? Why?
2 Think of three reasons why you or people in your (future) profession should get more money.

B Compare your ideas with other students.

WRITING
ADDING EMPHASIS

8 A Read the extract from an opinion piece. What is the main idea?

1 The economy is bad.
2 Many nurses are changing profession.
3 Nurses should get a higher salary.

B Look at the words in bold and answer the questions with a partner.

1 What type of word comes after them?
2 Which of the words in bold is the strongest?
3 Which is the weakest?

These are **extremely** difficult times for many professions—the economy is **very** weak—but we need to pay our nurses better. Many nurses cannot retire at 60 the way they used to because they aren't sure they will have enough money to support themselves. This means newly qualified nurses are finding it harder to get jobs. While people used to think the profession was **fairly** secure (the sick and the old will always need care), these days it has become **really** clear that the job is changing. Working conditions are getting harder, but the pay is not increasing.

C Choose a job in Exercise 7 or your own job/future job. Write the first paragraph of an opinion piece saying why the job deserves a higher salary. Include the words in bold above.

8.3 I'M JUST LOOKING

F buying things
P weak forms: *do you/can I*
V shopping

VOCABULARY
SHOPPING

1 A Work in pairs. Which of the words in white below are represented in the photos A–E?

1. Do you enjoy **window shopping**? Why/Why not?
2. Do you prefer to shop in **department stores** or in **markets**?
3. Do you find **prices** better if you **buy online**? What kind of things do you buy?
4. Do you like shopping when there's a **sale**? Why/Why not?
5. Do you like buying particular **brands** of products? Can you give examples?
6. What is the most **expensive** thing you bought recently? Where did you buy it?

B Discuss the questions.

FUNCTION
BUYING THINGS

8.5

2 A Listen to five conversations in stores. What are the people buying? Underline the correct answer.

1 food / we don't know / books
2 a carpet / a computer / clothes
3 clothes / hair products / we don't know
4 a musical instrument / a cell phone / cleaning products
5 a candle / a credit card / we don't know

B Complete the phrases below with the words in the box.

for	here	of	enter	on	cash	me

Customer
Excuse [1]______.
I'm just looking.
Do you sell …?
Do you have one [2]______ these in red/blue/a larger size?
Can I try it/this [3]______?
Where's the fitting room?
It doesn't fit/It fits. I'll take it.

Salesclerk
Can I help (you)?
Are you looking [4]______ anything in particular?
Who's next, please?
Are you paying with [5]______ or by credit card?
Can you [6]______ your PIN, please?
Can you just sign [7]______, please?

C Listen again to check.

D

E

S8.5

3 WEAK FORMS: *do you/can I* **Listen to the questions. Notice how *Do you …?* and *Can I …?* are pronounced. Listen again and repeat the questions.**

Do‿you sell pens? /dujə/

Can‿I try it on? /kənaɪ/

4 **Work in pairs. Look at audio script S8.4 on page 173 and practice the conversations.**

▶ page 142 LANGUAGE**BANK**

5 **Work in pairs. Use the prompts to practice the conversation.**

Student A	Student B
help? *Hello. Can I help you?*	
	look / for / shirt *Hi, I'm looking for a shirt.*
color?	
	white
some / over there	
	larger size?
yes / here you are	
	try / on?
yes / fitting room / there	
	thank you
fit / OK?	
	fine / take it
want / pay / credit card?	
	yes
here's your receipt	
	thank you / bye
bye	

6 **Work in pairs. Student A: turn to page 163. Student B: turn to page 166. Role-play the situations.**

LEARN TO
DESCRIBE THINGS

7 **A** **Look at the phrases in bold. Which are used for countable nouns and which for uncountable nouns?**

1 **A:** Hi there. Are you looking for anything in particular?
B: Yeah, do you sell **those things that** soldiers wear? Er … it's like a jacket.

2 **A:** Hello. I was wondering if you have any of **that stuff you use for** cleaning swimming pools.
B: Um … yeah, we usually sell a liquid cleaner.

B **Put the phrases in bold in the correct place in the conversation.**

1 **It's a type of**
A: What are you looking for?
B: Pen. You use it to write on walls.

2 **It's a kind of**
A: Are you looking for anything in particular?
B: Yes. Oil that you use for cooking.

SPEAKING

8 **A** **Think of an example of a type of clothing, a type of food and something you use in the house.**

B **Work in pairs and take turns. Student A: describe your things. Student B: guess what they are.**

A: It's a type of clothing that you wear around your neck when it's cold.
B: A scarf!

8.4 SOLEREBELS

DVD PREVIEW

1 Work in pairs and discuss the questions.

1 Can you think of any companies that started small?

2 Why do you think such companies became successful? Good products? Great leadership? Other ideas?

2 A Read the program information. What kind of company is soleRebels? Has it been successful?

BBC News: soleRebels

When Ethiopian Bethlehem Tilahun Alemu started her business, she knew she wanted to use local **talent** and help offer **opportunities** to the **unemployed** people living in her neighborhood. She decided to start selling cool, colorful shoes, made of **recycled** materials, including car tires. But, even she didn't realize how successful it would be. Her company, soleRebels, quickly became Africa's fastest growing footwear brand and the first **fair trade** shoe company in the world. Bethlehem was named in a list of the World's 100 Most Powerful Women. BBC reporter George Alagiah meets the **entrepreneur**.

B Match the words/phrases in bold in Exercise 2A with meanings 1–6.

1 without work

2 natural ability to do something well

3 a person who starts a business (or businesses) and hopes to make money

4 chances to do something

5 a business where fair prices are paid to the producers

6 materials or objects that are used again

DVD VIEW

3 A Watch the DVD. What do you think of the shoes made by soleRebels? Would you buy a pair? Why/Why not?

B Complete the fact file for the company.

soleRebels Fact File

1 soleRebels makes shoes using old ______ and homespun cotton.

2 When the company started, there were just ______ workers.

3 soleRebels shoes can be ______ all around the world.

4 soleRebels pays workers ______ times the average wage for the area.

5 The company has stores in Taiwan, Japan, Sweden and Austria and is planning to open in ______ also.

6 The company has helped to reduce the number of people living in ______.

C Watch the DVD again to check your answers.

4 Look at the expressions in bold that the reporter uses and answer the questions.

1 "... an **ancient skill**, but they're using it in a modern way."

Is the skill they are using old or new?

2 "Private sector companies are breathing new life into Ethiopia's once **faltering economy**."

Do you think a "faltering economy" is weak or strong?

3 "The finished product is a rather **funky** shoe."

Are the shoes fashionable or not?

4 "That is a **win-win**."

Do you think this is a situation that is good for everyone?

5 Work in pairs. Discuss. Why do you think Bethlehem's business idea was so successful?

neighborhood / tires neighbourhood / tyres

American Speakout a money-making idea

8.6

6 A Listen to someone talking about a small business idea. Underline the correct alternatives to complete the summary.

Ragbags will make different types of [1]*bags/clothes* out of recycled [2]*newspapers/material*. It plans to make the bags and sell them at [3]*markets/parties*, in local stores and on the Internet. It [4]*needs/doesn't need* a lot of money to start the business, but it does need a beautiful [5]*website/workshop*.

B Listen again. How does the speaker finish the key phrases? Choose the correct ending (1–6) for each key phrase.

KEYPHRASES

Our business is called …

Our idea is to …

We hope to make money by … *1*

To be successful, we need to …

We plan to …

The best thing about the company is …

1 re-using old material and turning it into different types of bags.
2 *Ragbags*.
3 that you will have an amazing bag, and we'll have fun making them, too.
4 make beautiful bags … out of recycled material.
5 make sure the bags are really good quality and look wonderful.
6 sell *Ragbags* at markets, in local stores and also online.

7 A Work in groups. Choose a hobby/interest you have and think about how you could make money from it. Answer the questions.

1 What is the name of the business?
2 What is the product/idea?
3 How will the business make money?
4 Whom will you sell to?
5 What will you need to start/be successful?

B Prepare presenting your ideas to the class. First practice your presentation. Use the notes in Exercise 7A to help you practice.

C Take turns presenting your ideas to the class. Which group has the best idea? Which idea do you think could be the most successful? Why?

writeback a website entry

8 A Read an advertisement for a competition and one of the entries. What is different about the business idea?

Newsfeed Sharing Timezone

Calling All Entrepreneurs

If you have a good business idea and would like some help or investment from us, write and tell us about it. The winner of the "Entrepreneur of the Year Award" will be given up to $10,000 to help start their business.

We plan to open a clothing store called "One World." Our idea is to import handmade clothes from India and sell them in stores and on the Internet. Our business will be different because we will pay fair prices to the people making the clothes in their own country. We need $10,000 to open the store and build the website.

B Write an entry for the competition. Explain what your idea is, how it is different from other ideas and what you would do with the money. Use the model above to help you.

8.5 LOOKBACK

V MONEY

1 A Complete the poem.

Brenda Bones was poor and thin
Until her famous lottery win.
She won a million, paid her [1]b_ _ _ _,
Bought a big house in the hills,
Told her friends it's time to rest,
But decided to [2]in_ _ _ _
In a super-size hot air balloon
And flew from Crete to Cameroon
Forgetting the money she gave or [3]l_ _t,
'Til every penny of her win was spent.
Then one sad day the balloon crashed
And Brenda Bones ran out of [4]c_ _ _.
She [5]borr_ _ed [6]c_ _ ns and took a train
And walked 'til she was home again.
She had no money, had no car.
She found a job in a little bar
And told long stories about her trips
And all the customers gave her [7]t_ _ _.
It took her years to finally learn it,
But money's better when you [8]e_ _ _ it!

B Work in pairs and compare your answers. Then read the poem aloud.

G RELATIVE CLAUSES

2 A Complete the sentences with *that*, *where* or *who*.

1 Monday is the day of the week *that* I like best.
2 Pasta is the food I eat most often.
3 My mother is the person has helped me the most.
4 The town I grew up is really beautiful.
5 My brother and sister are the only people understand me.
6 The restaurant I usually have lunch is expensive.

B Make the sentences true for you.

C Work in pairs and compare your ideas.

A: Sunday is the day of the week that I like best.
B: Really? Why?
A: Because I can relax.

G *TOO MUCH/MANY, ENOUGH, VERY*

3 Look at the pictures. What's the problem in each situation? Make as many sentences as you can using *too*, *very*, *(not) enough*, or *too much/many*.

V MULTI-WORD VERBS

4 Work in pairs and take turns. Ask the questions and complete the responses using the correct multi-word verb.

1 **A:** Are you still trying to become a movie star?
B: No. I *gave up* acting.
2 **A:** How was your dream vacation?
B: It ______ ______ a nightmare: I lost my wallet, and then I got sick!
3 **A:** Do you still have her book?
B: No. I ______ it ______.
4 **A:** Do you still have all those guitars in your living room?
B: No. They ______ ______ too much space.
5 **A:** Did you accept the job offer?
B: No. I ______ it ______.
6 **A:** Did he join another company?
B: No, he ______ ______ this one!

F BUYING THINGS

5 A Put the words in the correct order to make conversations.

Conversation 1
A: I / you / help / can ?
B: looking / just / I'm

Conversation 2
A: I / help / can ?
B: tools / you / gardening / do / sell ?
A: just / I'll / check

Conversation 3
A: you / particular / looking / are / anything / in / for ?
B: you / these / do / red / have / of / in / one ?

Conversation 4
A: it / is / how ?
B: doesn't / it / fit
have / do / in / size / bigger / one / you / a / of / these ?
A: look / I'll / a / take
you / here / are
B: Thanks.
OK / fits / it

Conversation 5
A: next / who's ? are / or / by / credit / paying / with / you / card / cash ?
B: card / credit / please
A: here / just / you / please / can / sign ?

Conversation 6
A: me / excuse
this / try / can / I / on ?
B: certainly / sir / yes
A: room / where's / fitting / the ?
B: left / it's / the / on

B Work in pairs. Practice the conversations.

9 nature

SPEAKING	9.1 Talk about green issues 9.2 Give your views on life in the city or the country 9.3 Talk about different animals 9.4 Talk about amazing places
LISTENING	9.1 Listen to a radio program about green ideas 9.4 Watch an extract from a documentary about the northern lights
READING	9.1 Read about great green ideas 9.2 Understand an article about an experience in the wild
WRITING	9.1 Write about your views on the environment 9.4 Write a travel blog

How do you feel about being in the countryside?

INTERVIEWS

9.1 GREEN LIVING

G comparatives/superlatives
P stressed syllables
V nature

VOCABULARY
NATURE

1 A Work in pairs. Discuss. Have you ever:

- swum in an ocean, a river or a lake?
- walked in a desert or a rainforest?
- climbed a mountain?

B Work in pairs. Think of an example for each thing in the box.

mountain range	lake	waterfall	
river	desert	ocean	rainforest

a mountain range—The Andes

C Work in pairs. Can you think of cities that have access to each of these natural features?

In Sydney, you can swim in the Pacific Ocean.

▶ page 158 PHOTOBANK

LISTENING

2 A Look at photos A–C. What do you think is happening?

9.1 **B Listen to the program to find out.**

C The program talks about three green ideas. What are they?

3 A Read the summary below. Can you find four mistakes?

Great Green Ideas

Hug It Forward is a project that uses plastic boxes to build schools in developing countries. Children and adults work together to build schools using bottles filled with inorganic trash.

Club Surya is an eco-nightclub in Tokyo. It has a special dance floor that uses the people dancing to produce electricity. The club produces 100 percent of its electricity like this. Also, if you walk to the club, you can get in free.

The Seoul River Park was created by Dr. Kee Hwang. His idea was to take down one of the main shopping malls in Seoul and uncover the river that was below. He made the area into a green park in the city center.

B Listen again to check your ideas.

C Work in groups. What do you think of the ideas? Which one do you like best? Why? Do you know of any similar ideas to these?

A

B

C

GRAMMAR
COMPARATIVES/SUPERLATIVES

4 A Read sentences 1–5 and complete the rule.

1 The area was a lot clean**er**, too.
2 People are happ**ier than** before.
3 It gets **more** difficult to find green spaces in cities.
4 **More** communities are building their own schools.
5 There is **less** traffic chaos than before.

RULES
Use comparatives to compare two things, people or situations.
With short adjectives, add ______ or ______ to the end of the adjective (+ *than*)*.
With longer adjectives, use ______ + adjective.
We also use ______ / ______ + noun to compare things.
*For adjectives ending in *-y* (*happy*), the *-y* changes to an *-i* (*happier*).

B Read sentences a)–c) and complete the rule.

a) Seoul is one of **the largest** and **busiest** cities in the world.
b) **The most difficult** thing was filling the bottles.
c) **The least important** problem is …

RULES
Use *the* + superlative to say which is the biggest, the best, etc. in a group.
With short adjectives, use *the* and add ______ to the end of the adjective.*
With longer adjectives, use *the* + ______ / *least* + adjective.
*For adjectives ending in *-y* (*happy*), the *-y* changes to an *-i* (*happiest*).

▶ page 144 LANGUAGEBANK

5 A Complete the table.

Adjective	Comparative	Superlative
long	*longer*	*the longest*
high	______	______
healthy	______	______
difficult	______	______

S9.2 **B Listen and check your answers.**

S9.3 **C STRESSED SYLLABLES Listen and repeat. Underline the stressed syllables.**

1 It's the most beautiful place I've ever been to.
2 It's hotter than I expected.
3 The food is cheaper than at home.
4 It's more dangerous than I thought.

6 A Complete the questions. Use the comparative or superlative form of the adjective in parentheses.

1 What is ______ part of your town? (green)
2 Is your country ______ it used to be? (warm)
3 Where is ______ place you have been to? (nice)
4 Do you think living by the coast is ______ living in the city? Why/Why not? (healthy)
5 What's ______ away from home you've been? (far)
6 Is your country ______ other countries near it? (big)
7 Are people who live by the ocean ______ people who live in the city? Why/Why not? (friendly)
8 What is ______ place you have been to? (polluted)

B Work in pairs and take turns. Ask and answer the questions.

SPEAKING

7 A Work in pairs. Read "The Eco Survey." What can you do to protect the environment? Write two more questions.

THE ECO SURVEY

1 Do you recycle? Why/Why not?
2 Do you usually walk or take the car?
3 Do you grow your own food?
4 Do you think nuclear energy is a good or a bad idea?
5 ______________________
6 ______________________

B Work in groups. Ask and answer the questions. Who is the "greenest" person in your class? Why?

WRITING
SIMILAR SOUNDING WORDS

8 A Underline the correct alternative.

1 Is this *you're/your* umbrella?
2 What are you going to *where/wear* today?
3 I bought *too/two/to* tickets for the concert.
4 I'm going to *write/right* an article about it.
5 I can't *sea/see* why it's so difficult.
6 I can't help. It's *there/their/they're* problem.

B Find and correct six spelling mistakes.

I think everyone should recycle. I've done this since I was a child, and it's not difficult. Children need to be educated about the write way to look after the world we live in. I use a bicycle to get to work every day, and I get very angry when I sea people use a car to drive around the corner to the store. Their are lots of small things we can do to help the environment, like turning off the TV when your not watching it, using plastic bags for you're garbage, and recycling, two.

C Choose one of the topics in Exercise 7A and write your own comment.

around / garbage, trash — round / rubbish

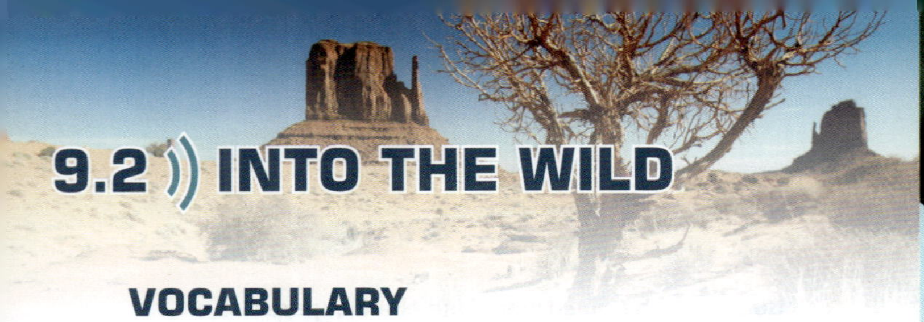

9.2 INTO THE WILD

G articles
P word stress, weak forms: *a* and *the*
V the outdoors

VOCABULARY
THE OUTDOORS

1 Work in groups. Discuss the questions.

1 Do you like wild places?
2 Have you ever slept outdoors or been out in the wild?
3 Which wild places would you like to visit?

2 A Work in pairs and read sentences 1–8. What do you think the words in bold mean?

1 I'd like to live in a **rural area** when I'm older; it's nicer than the city.
2 The north of my country is an area of **natural beauty**; tourists often visit it.
3 Where I live there is a lot of **beautiful scenery**; it's good for walking.
4 I went camping in a **national park**; it was very quiet and peaceful.
5 We visited the **wildlife center**; there were lots of unusual birds.
6 I'd like to visit a **tropical rainforest** and see the trees and insects.
7 My country has interesting **geographical features**, like volcanoes and forests.
8 I like being out in the **fresh air**; it's nice to be out of the city.

B Discuss. Which sentences are true for you?

S9.4 **C WORD STRESS Listen and underline the stressed parts of the words in bold.**

rural area

D Listen and repeat the sentences.

READING

3 A Look at the picture and the title of the story. What do you think happened?

B Read the text to find out.

4 Answer the questions.

1 Where was the writer traveling?
2 What did she plan to do?
3 What did she particularly enjoy about the trip?
4 Why did the tribe want to hold a ceremony?
5 How did she feel when she first saw the snake?
6 What happened at the end of the story?

5 A Work in pairs. Look at words/phrases 1–6. What do you think they mean? Use a dictionary to check your ideas.

1 howling
2 hot and humid
3 a clearing
4 staring
5 froze with fear
6 sink into the ground

B Use the picture and words above to retell the story.

Anaconda!

Anthropology student Marisa Evangelou talks about how she came face to face with an anaconda in the jungle in Peru.

I was traveling in the Amazon in Peru, and my plan was to spend some time with one of the tribes there. They live in simple huts deep in the jungle, and I traveled with a guide on a small boat for hours to get there. As we traveled, the sounds of the jungle grew louder and louder. I could hear monkeys **howling** and laughing and the songs of tropical birds. It was **hot and humid**, and I was covered in mosquitoes.

The days I spent with the tribe were some of the most wonderful days of my life. We spoke very little, but I helped the women prepare meals, played with the children, and learned about the plants they use for medicine. On my last day, one of the men called to me to follow. He spoke a little Spanish and told me the medicine man wanted to thank me for my stay and welcome me into their tribe. They planned a ceremony for me, but I would need to choose between life and death. Was I happy to do that?

I agreed and followed my new friend into **a clearing** in the trees. He asked me to shut my eyes. I could hear feet approaching me. "Are you ready?" he asked. I knew that my answer would probably change my life. "Yes," I whispered, with my eyes still closed. Soon I felt a heavy weight on my shoulders. I slowly opened my eyes to find a huge anaconda snake **staring** me in the face. I **froze with fear**, and the snake moved her head closer to my neck.

I knew that with one move she could kill me, and to make things worse my "friend" smiled and told me the snake was very hungry. "Breathe," he said, "make her your friend." I didn't have a lot of choice, so I took a deep breath and tried not to scream. I could feel my feet **sink into the ground**. I breathed again, and slowly a strange thing started to happen. The snake lowered her head and rested it on my arm. I had passed the test.

GRAMMAR
ARTICLES

6 **Read the rules and put examples 1–6 in the correct place.**

1 with **a guide**
2 **a** huge anaconda **snake**
3 **The snake** was very hungry.
4 in **the Amazon** in Peru
5 **tropical birds**
6 in **Peru**

RULES

1 Use *a/an* before singular nouns: *I traveled on* **a boat.**
Use *a/an* the first time we mention the thing/person: a) ______
Use *a/an* before job titles (in general): b) ______

2 Use *the* before nouns when there's only one: *the moon*
Use *the* before the names of some places: c) _____
Use *the* if we have already mentioned the thing/person (the listener knows which one): d) ______
Use *the* in some phrases with prepositions: *on the first day, in the wild, on the left*

3 Use no article before most cities, countries and continents: *I was on a trip in Argentina.* e) ______
Use no article before plural nouns: *covered in mosquitoes*
Use no article to talk about general types or groups of things: f) ______
Use no article in some phrases with prepositions: *for lunch, for months, on one occasion, at night, in class*

▶ page 144 LANGUAGEBANK

7 **A Find and correct the mistakes below. There is one mistake in each sentence.**

1 I always wanted to be host of nature programs.
2 I was one of many tourists in the South America.
3 A guide met us at the airport. The next day, same guide took us hunting.
4 On second day, the guide took us to a river.
5 I sometimes make a programs in Britain.
6 In my job, I can explain natural world to millions of people.
7 I hate the insects in general, but especially hate mosquitoes.
8 I had camera in my bag.

9.5

B WEAK FORMS: *a* and *the* **Listen to check your answers. Notice how *a* is pronounced /ə/ and *the* is pronounced /ðə/ or /ðiː/.**

9.6

C Listen and write the sentences you hear.

8 **Complete the text with *a, the* or – (no article).**

When I was ten, my father took me camping for the first time in [1]______ Michigan, U.S.A. He wanted to teach me about wild animals, insects and trees.

We enjoyed the first two days together walking and fishing. Then, [2]______ my uncles came with [3]______ bows and arrows to go hunting.

One evening, we were sitting by the fire when [4]______ bird flew over us. Immediately my uncles jumped up and fired their arrows at [5]______ bird. All of them missed. But suddenly the arrows were flying down at us from [6]______ sky. There were arrows everywhere; they looked like rain! We ran to escape them, and fortunately no one was injured.

That day I didn't learn anything about [7]______ animals or insects or trees, but I learned [8]______ great lesson about gravity!

SPEAKING

9 **A Work in pairs. Read two comments about country life and city life. Which is closer to your opinion?**

> I can't stand the countryside or wild places. There are too many flies and animals that either want to eat you or your food. Even worse: there are no movie theaters, no supermarkets, and you can't get a good coffee!

> I get out of the city whenever I can. I love the peace and quiet of the countryside, and the people are much nicer there. I love the wild: animals, trees, mountains, forests—these are the best things in life.

B Discuss the advantages and disadvantages of living in a rural area and a city in your country.

C Work in pairs. Explain where you prefer to live and why.

host, emcee presenter

9.3 IT COULD BE BECAUSE ...

F making guesses
P silent letters
V animals

VOCABULARY
ANIMALS

1 A Work in pairs. Look at the word webs. How many animals can you add to each category?

- wild — *jaguar*
- insect — *bee*
- domestic/farm — *dog*
- reptile — *snake*

B Work in pairs and take turns. Student A: say a letter. Student B: say an animal that begins with it.

▶ page 159 PHOTOBANK

American Speakout **TIP** Get a study buddy. *Buddy* is another word for *friend* in American English. Review vocabulary and take turns testing each other.

LISTENING

2 Discuss the questions below with other students.

1 What can humans do better than animals?
2 What can animals do better than humans?

3 A Work in pairs and take the quiz.

B Compare your answers with other students.

S9.7 **4 A** Listen to two people discussing the questions in the quiz. As you listen, note the correct answers.

B Listen again to check.

QUIZ: Man & Animals

WHY...

1 do we use rats after an earthquake?
2 do some prisons use abandoned dogs?
3 does the army use dolphins?
4 did airport security plan to use gerbils in the 1970s?
5 do we use seals for research in the ocean?

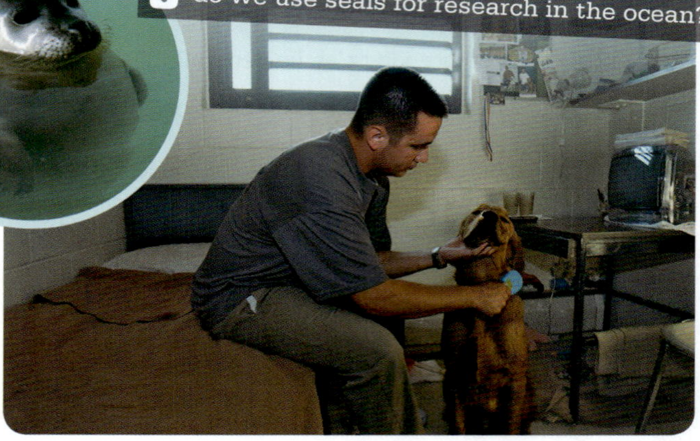

FUNCTION
MAKING GUESSES

5 A Read the sentences from the recording. Complete the table with the phrases in bold.

1 **It could be** as prison guards.
2 **It might be** because they can live in very cold temperatures.
3 **It can't be** that because they'd be trained dogs.
4 **Maybe** they use the dogs to guard the prisoners.
5 **Perhaps** they can smell drugs.
6 **It's definitely not** to attack people.

It's Possible	It's Not Possible
______	______
______	______
______	______

B Which "silent letters" are not pronounced in *could* and *might*?

S9.8 **C** SILENT LETTERS Listen and repeat.

D Now say the phrases below quickly.

1 It could be … It could be you!
2 It might be … It might be us!
3 It can't be … It can't be them!

▶ page 144 LANGUAGEBANK

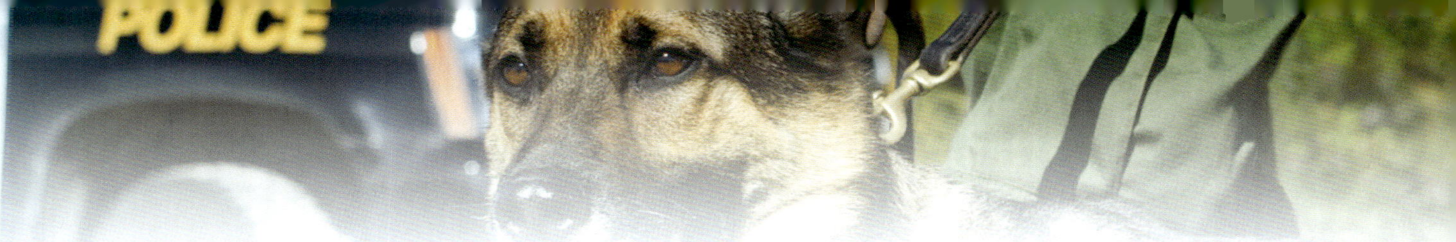

6 A Underline the correct alternative.

1 What's the world's biggest fish?

It *could be/can't be* a whale because whales aren't fish.

2 What's the world's fastest bird?

It *is definitely not/might be* a penguin. They can't fly.

3 What is the largest bird?

It can't be/Maybe it's an ostrich because they are often taller than humans.

4 What's the longest land animal?

Perhaps it's/It can't be a crocodile because some snakes are much longer.

5 What's the world's fastest land animal?

Maybe it's/It can't be a cheetah because they can run at 100 km/hr.

6 Which animal causes the most deaths?

It could be/It's definitely not a shark because they only kill a few people every year.

7 Which animal has the largest brain?

It can't be/Perhaps it's a whale because they are very large and intelligent.

8 Which animal lives the longest?

It *can't be/might be* a tortoise because they can live to 150 years old.

B Work in pairs. Do you know the answers to questions 1–8? Check on page 164.

LEARN TO

GIVE YOURSELF TIME TO THINK

7 Look at the extracts from audio script S9.7. The phrases in bold give the speaker time to think. Complete the phrases by adding a word in each space.

1 Why do we use rats after an earthquake?
I'm not ______.

2 Why do some prisons use abandoned dogs?
Let me ______.

3 It's definitely not to attack people because dolphins are kind of nice. **It's hard to** ______.

4 Why do we use seals for research in the ocean?
______ **a good question.**

8 A Find and correct the mistakes in each conversation.

1 **A:** The world's fastest animal? Er, let me to think.
B: Well, I'm not much sure, but I think it's the cheetah.

2 **A:** The animal that lives the longest? Um, that's good question.
B: It's hard say, but it could be the tortoise.

B Work in pairs and practice the conversations.

SPEAKING

9 A Look at photos A–G below. Which animal/animal parts are shown? Why do you think the parts are special?

A: What do you think A is?
B: I don't know. It could be ...

B Compare your ideas with other students. Check your answers on page 164.

In most of the world, speed is measured in kilometers per hour, which can be written as km/hr, km/h, or kmph. In the United States, speed is measure in miles per hour, or mph.

9.4 THE NORTHERN LIGHTS

DVD PREVIEW

1 A Work in groups. Discuss the questions.

1 What part of the world do you think the picture shows?

2 Why do you think some people like going to places like this?

B Read the program information. Why do you think Joanna Lumley wants to visit the northern lights?

Joanna Lumley in the Land of the Northern Lights

Actress Joanna Lumley grew up in hot Malaysia. During her childhood, she dreamed of being somewhere cold and of seeing the amazing northern lights of Norway. Many years later she got the chance. This documentary follows her journey. She travels by plane, boat, train, sled and car to get to the far north, where she hopes her dream will come true. Will she see the lights?

DVD VIEW

2 A Watch the DVD. What do you learn about Joanna Lumley?

B Read sentences 1–5. Which word from the box completes each sentence?

lights books dogs people snow

1 As a child, Joanna never saw ______.

2 She feels as if she's in another world because there are no ______.

3 She brings essential things, for example, ______.

4 After the train journey, she meets a guide and his ______.

5 At night, she goes to see the ______.

3 A Read sentences a)–f). Match the words in bold to words in the box below with a similar meaning.

amazing difficult to find necessary
not definitely good or bad ~~hot and wet climate~~
happy to wait (maybe for a long time)

a) "As a little girl, I lived in the steamy heat of **tropical** Malaysia." *hot and wet climate–1*

b) "The weather near Tromsø is **uncertain**."

c) "And if we're lucky, we might see the **elusive** northern lights."

d) "This is the most **astonishing** thing I have ever, ever seen."

e) "I pack up things that are going to be **essential** on every trip."

f) "You just have to be **patient**."

B Watch the DVD again and number the sentences in the order you hear them.

4 Work in pairs and discuss the questions.

1 Would you like to do what Joanna Lumley did?

2 Is there anywhere you have wanted to visit "all your life"? Where? Why?

American Speakout an amazing place

5 A Listen to a woman talking about a natural place she visited and answer the questions.

1 Where is the place?
2 What is special about it?

B Listen again and check (✔) the key phrases you hear.

KEYPHRASES

What did you think of it?
It was (amazing / frightening / wonderful) ...!
The first thing you notice is (how big it is / how quiet the place is) ...
How did you get there?
The best thing about it was ... (the silence / how beautiful the place was) ...
How long did the journey take?
The journey took (two hours / two weeks) ...
Would you like to go back?

6 Answer the questions.

1 What's the highest place you've ever been to?
2 What's the wildest place you've ever been to?
3 What's the most beautiful place you've ever been to?
4 What's the longest walk you've ever done?
5 What's the coldest place you've visited?
6 What's the hottest place you've visited?

7 A Work in pairs. Choose two or three of the questions to discuss and compare your answers. Use the key phrases to talk about your experiences.

B Work with other students and tell them about your experiences. Decide which places are the most interesting, the most exciting and the most relaxing.

C Tell the class about your partner's experiences.

writeback a travel blog

8 A Read the travel blog. Which country did Lia visit? Did she enjoy the experience? Why/Why not?

Posted by Lia on December 14th, 2015 Previous post >> Next post >>

Day 4

Today was our final day trekking along the Great Wall of China, and it was probably one of the hardest days we've had. Today we walked for more than 12 km over 8 hours in very hot and humid temperatures. We climbed thousands of steps, and some parts of the Wall had no sides, just a very long drop on either side. It was terrifying. However, the views were spectacular, and, when we finally reached the watch tower, where we stopped for lunch and took some photos, we all felt incredibly proud of what we had achieved. Sitting on top of the Wall, looking down on the fields and listening to the silence is a feeling I don't think I'll ever forget.

B Choose a place you have visited. Write about your experience. Use these questions to help you.

1 Where did you go?
2 When?
3 With whom?
4 Why was it an amazing experience?
5 Would you like to go again?

V NATURE

1 A Take the geography quiz.

THE GEOGRAPHY QUIZ

① Which mountains are higher?
a) the Andes b) the Rockies

② Which country has a longer coastline?
a) Russia b) Canada

③ Which lake is larger?
a) Lake Toba b) Lake Michigan

④ Which river is shorter?
a) the Amazon b) the Nile

⑤ Which is the deepest ocean?
a) the Pacific b) the Atlantic

⑥ Which is the highest waterfall?
a) Niagara Falls b) Angel Falls

B Work in pairs and compare your answers. Then check your answers on page 164.

G COMPARATIVES AND SUPERLATIVES

2 A What are the comparative/superlative forms of the adjectives in the box?

hot	good	nice	cheap
high	boring	healthy	long
exciting	fast	old	cold

B Work in pairs and take turns. Student A: say an adjective. Student B: say the comparative and superlative form.

A: big
B: bigger, the biggest
B: expensive
A: more expensive, the most expensive

3 A Complete the questions with the correct form of the adjective in parentheses.

1 Who is ______ student in the class? (organized)
2 Who studies ______? (hard)
3 Who has ______ hair? (long)
4 Who is ______? (young)
5 Who is ______? (tall)
6 Who has read ______ books this month? (most)
7 Who drives ______ car? (fast)
8 Who lives ______ from the school? (far)

B Work in groups and take turns. Ask and answer the questions.

G ARTICLES

4 Add *a/an/the* or – (zero article) to the sentences where necessary.

1 Excuse me, where's nearest bank?
2 This city is big, but it doesn't have airport.
3 Cigarettes are bad for you.
4 Hi. Would you like drink?
5 Where's money I lent you?
6 I love ice cream. It's my favorite food.
7 She goes to small school in downtown Cincinnati.
8 We missed the bus and waited an hour for next one.
9 My sister is working in United Kingdom at the moment.
10 Is there Internet café near here?

5 Underline the correct alternative to complete the sentences.

1 I want to be a vet because I like *the animals/an animals/animals*.
2 She looked up and saw an eagle in *the sky/a sky/sky*.
3 He graduated and became *the journalist/a journalist/journalist*.
4 A lion attacked us. Immediately, Jan, our guide, shot *the lion/a lion/lion*.
5 They spent some time in *the Argentina/an Argentina/Argentina*.
6 We went on vacation, but it rained on *the first day/a first day/first day*.

V ANIMALS

6 A Find the names of nine animals in the word puzzle.

C	R	O	C	O	D	I	L	E	E
H	O	A	O	B	O	C	D	T	F
I	T	G	W	H	L	L	J	U	K
M	B	L	M	N	P	I	G	R	O
P	I	P	Q	R	H	S	T	T	U
A	T	V	W	W	I	X	Y	L	Z
N	A	B	H	S	N	A	K	E	C
Z	D	E	A	F	F	H	I	J	A
E	A	G	L	E	D	I	O	E	N
E	E	Y	E	L	I	P	M	S	O

B Work in pairs and take turns. Student A: describe one of the animals in the word puzzle. Student B: guess which animal it is.

F MAKING GUESSES

7 A Work in pairs. Guess the countries. Use *could/might be* or *can't be*.

Picture A can't be …

B Check your answers on page 165.

wordsearch, word puzzle — word square

10 society

SPEAKING
- 10.1 Discuss qualities of different places
- 10.2 Decide on the punishments that fit the crimes
- 10.3 Talk about problems in a school
- 10.4 Talk about an important issue

LISTENING
- 10.1 Listen to conversations about different cities
- 10.3 Listen to people complaining
- 10.4 Watch an extract from a documentary about an Internet sensation

READING
- 10.1 Read about the best cities for young people
- 10.2 Read an article about crime and punishment

WRITING
- 10.1 Use formal expressions to write an email
- 10.4 Write about an issue

How do you feel about city life?

INTERVIEWS

10.1 TOP CITIES

G uses of *like*
P sentence stress
V describing a city

New York

Dubai

SPEAKING

1 A Work in pairs. Discuss. What do young people want in a city? What do you think are the world's best cities for young people to live in? Why?

B Read the text. Which cities do you think will be on the list? Look at page 165 to find out.

Best Cities for Young People

The world's biggest and most important cities are not necessarily the best cities to live in, especially for young people. Many of them are really expensive, have traffic problems, poor public transportation systems and high crime rates. Young people looking for somewhere to study or to live are carefree and want to explore new lifestyles. Have a look at our list of the top ten cities for young people to live in.

VOCABULARY
DESCRIBING A CITY

2 A Read sentences 1–12 below. Are they positive (+) or negative (–)?

1 It has clean, safe streets.
2 The public transportation system is terrible.
3 There's a lot of traffic.
4 It has beautiful buildings.
5 The people are friendly and polite.
6 There's a lot of crime.
7 It's very polluted.
8 There are nice parks and green spaces.
9 It has good shopping and nightlife.
10 There are lots of things to see and do.
11 It's expensive to live there.
12 It's very crowded.

Prague

S10.1

B SENTENCE STRESS Listen to the sentences. Underline the words or syllables that are stressed.

1 It has clean, safe streets.
2 The public transportation system is terrible.

C Listen and repeat the sentences paying attention to the stressed words or syllables.

D Discuss. Which three factors are the most/least important for you?

LISTENING

S10.2

3 A Listen to the conversations and look at the photos. Which city does each speaker talk about? What do they think about it?

B Listen again. Which city has these things?

1 free streetcar *Melbourne*
2 beautiful buildings and squares
3 lots of bars and clubs
4 cafés and street art
5 cheap taxis
6 a castle

4 Read audio script S10.2 on page 174–175. Underline the phrases from Exercise 2 that the speakers use to describe the cities.

streetcar tram

Melbourne

New Orleans

Chicago

GRAMMAR

USES OF *LIKE*

5 A Match questions 1–5 with answers a)–e).

1 What's Prague like?
2 What's the weather like?
3 Do you like living in Melbourne?
4 What's the public transportation like?
5 And what do you like best about living in Melbourne?

a) I love it! Melbourne is a really great city.
b) It's a very beautiful city.
c) It's very cold in the winter.
d) I think it's probably the atmosphere.
e) Public transportation is really good, actually.

B Match questions 1–5 above with the rules below.

RULES

1 Use *like* (verb) to talk about something you enjoy/think is nice. ______

2 Use *be like* to describe or give your opinion about something. e.g., *Question 1*

▶ page 146 LANGUAGEBANK

6 A Complete the conversations using questions with *like*.

1 A: I've never been to **Madrid**. What's ______?
B: It's a beautiful city. There's a great atmosphere, and the people are really friendly.

2 A: Do ______ living in **Moscow**?
B: I love it! It's one of the best cities in the world.

3 A: ______ your **new apartment** ______?
B: It's very small, but it's near the city center.

4 A: What ______ best about living in **Rome**?
B: The food. I love Italian food!

S10.3

B Listen to check. Then listen again and repeat the questions.

C Rewrite the questions by changing or removing the words in bold.

D Work in pairs and take turns. Ask and answer the questions.

A: I've never been to Torun. What's it like?
B: It's a small city, so there isn't a lot of traffic.

SPEAKING

7 A Choose two cities you know well. Write down three positive things and one negative thing for each city.

B Work in groups and take turns. Describe the cities and say why you like/don't like them. Which of the cities should be in the top ten places to live? Why?

WRITING

USING FORMAL EXPRESSIONS

8 A Read the email. Why is Kristina writing? What information does she want to know?

Dear Sir/Madam,

I am writing to ask for some more information about your bed and breakfast. I am planning to stay in Malta for one month to study English, and I am interested in reserving a room. However, before I do that, I would like to check some information. First, is it possible to travel easily into the center of town by public transportation? How much does it cost? Second, my course finishes in the evening, so I would need to walk home alone. Are the streets around the area where you are located safe at night? Finally, since I plan to stay for the whole month, I would like to know if it is possible to have a discount on the price. I look forward to hearing from you.

Yours faithfully,

Kristina Paoli

B Is the language in the email formal or informal? How can you tell?

C Find formal expressions in the email that have similar meanings to the informal expressions in the table below.

Informal	Formal
Hi …	*Dear*
This is just a quick note to say …	
I want to … I want to know if … Can I ….	
Talk to you soon	
Best wishes	

D Imagine you are going to spend a month in another city studying English. Where would you go? You need some information. Write a formal email to the school. Include these things:

- the reason for your letter
- a question about the language program
- a question about the housing/accommodation
- a request for information about the city

In more formal emails, if you know the name of the addressee, you close with "Sincerely," (American English) or "Yours sincerely," (British English); otherwise, "Yours faithfully" is used.

apartment / First / Talk to you soon

flat / Firstly / Speak to you soon

10.2 CRIME AND PUNISHMENT

G present/past passive
P weak forms: *was/were*
V crime and punishment

SPEAKING

1 A Match photos A–D with the crimes in the box.

graffiti	murder	drunk driving	speeding

B Discuss. Are any of these crimes a problem in your town/city?

READING

2 A Read the introduction to an article and answer the questions.

1 What did the man do wrong?
2 What was his punishment?
3 What is "alternative sentencing"?

B Work in pairs. Discuss. What alternative punishments can you think of for the crimes in Exercise 1?

For graffiti, you should spend a month painting the walls of hospitals and libraries, etc., with no pay. For speeding, you should …

C Read the rest of the article. Does it mention any of your ideas?

D Work in pairs. Discuss the advantages and disadvantages of the alternative sentencing program.

The acronym DUI (driving under the influence) is commonly used in the U.S. and Canada to refer to drunk driving or being charged with it.

Make the Punishment FIT THE CRIME

A man is caught stealing books from a bookstore. The judge asks why he did it, and the **thief** says he loves books. What is the man's punishment? A **prison sentence**? A big **fine**? No. The man is sent to read stories and books to hospital patients. He enjoys the job and continues to do it for many years!

Welcome to alternative sentencing programs. Instead of traditional punishments, criminals get the punishments that fit their crimes.

What other examples of alternative sentencing are there? Two boys were caught **writing graffiti** on a wall. The normal punishment for this is a fine, but in this case the boys were told to do **community service**. They cleaned seventy walls in three weeks.

A **shoplifter** was caught **shoplifting** three times in one year in a small town in the United States. What was her punishment? She was sent to speak to store owners. She gave advice on how to stop shoplifters. In one month, she spoke to the owners of forty stores and told them all about the techniques that shoplifters use. It was a great service to the community because, after that, shoplifting almost disappeared from the town.

What about more serious crimes? Is alternative sentencing possible for crimes like **theft** or credit card **fraud**? It depends on many things. Who are the criminals? Are they young? Is this their first crime? Can they change their way of life? One recent story suggests it is possible.

A thief stole seventeen cans of paint. Instead of going to prison, he was told to spend several weeks painting local schools, a library, and other public buildings. He enjoyed the work, and now it's his job.

drunk driving — drink driving

VOCABULARY
CRIME AND PUNISHMENT

3 A Match the words in bold from the text in Exercise 2 with definitions 1–9 below.

1 a person who steals things *thief*
2 time that is spent in prison
3 writing or drawing on public walls, doors, etc.
4 doing unpaid work to help your town/city
5 stealing things
6 a person who steals things from stores
7 cheating someone to make money from them
8 stealing things from a store
9 an amount of money that you have to pay

B Put the words in the correct place in the table.

Criminal	Crime	Punishment
thief		

American Speak out TIP Sometimes words have the same stem, e.g., *shoplifter/shoplifting*. It is a good idea to write these words together. Write them in your vocabulary notebook.

▶ page 159 PHOTOBANK

GRAMMAR
PASSIVE VOICE

4 A Complete the tables with the passive form.

Present	
Active	**Passive**
The police **catch** a man stealing books from a bookstore.	A man ______ **caught** stealing books from a bookstore.

Past	
Active	**Passive**
The judge **sent** the man to read stories.	The man ______ **sent** to read stories.

B Read the sentences in Exercise 4A again. Which sentences say who does the actions: the active or the passive? Complete the rule below.

RULES

Use the passive to talk about what happens to things/people when we don't know who/what caused the action (or it's not important).

Form the passive with: subject + verb ______ (in the present, past or other tense) + past participle.

C Find five more examples of the passive in the article.

5 A WEAK FORMS: *was/were* How are *was* and *were* pronounced in the passive? Listen to the sentences below.

1 He was sent home.
2 It was eaten.
3 They were caught.
4 They were stopped.

B Listen again and repeat the sentences. Make sure you use a short, unstressed pronunciation for *was* /wʌz/ and *were* /wɜr/.

▶ page 146 LANGUAGEBANK

6 A Make passive sentences with the prompts and the verbs in parentheses. Use the present simple or the past simple.

1 When I was a child I / many stories (tell)
When I was a child, I was told many stories.
2 My real name is James, but I / Jim by my friends (call)
3 On my tenth birthday, I / to Disneyland (take)
4 These days, people in my company / a bonus every December (pay)
5 When I was younger, I / by many teachers (help)
6 On the first day, all the new students / around the school (show)
7 Even now, I / that I look like my mother (tell)
8 When we were young, all the children in my family / to become doctors (expect)

B Change four of the sentences so they are true for you. Use passives. Then work in pairs and compare your sentences.

My real name is Nicholas, but I am called Nico by my friends.

SPEAKING

7 A Work in pairs. Read about some crimes and think of alternative punishments.

1 Two boys were caught writing large graffiti on the wall of a private house.
2 A couple went sailing illegally in dangerous waters. A search team had to spend hours looking for them.
3 A man was arrested for playing loud music late at night for several days, ignoring his neighbors' requests to turn it down.
4 A girl was caught stealing eggs from a farm close to her home.

B Compare your ideas with other students' ideas. Which alternative sentences do you think (a) would work the best? (b) are the most imaginative?

C Turn to page 161 to find out what alternative sentences were given.

10.3 THERE'S A PROBLEM

F complaining
P sentence stress
V problems

VOCABULARY
PROBLEMS

1 A Work in pairs. Look at phrases 1–8 below. What do the words in bold mean? Which things can you see in photos A–E?

1 public transportation **delays**
2 **litter** on the streets
3 bad **service** in a restaurant or store
4 **faulty** equipment
5 someone speaking **loudly** on their phone
6 computers **crashing**
7 getting **stuck in a traffic jam**
8 receiving **spam** in your inbox

B Discuss. Which of the things in Exercise 1A annoy you the most? What other things annoy you (at home/ at work/in stores, etc.)?

I can't stand people eating in the street.

FUNCTION
COMPLAINING

S10.5

2 A Listen to three people complaining and answer the questions.

1 Where are they?
2 What problems do they describe?

B Listen again and answer the questions.

Conversation 1
1 What does the receptionist offer to do?
2 Does she sound rude or polite?

Conversation 2
3 How long did the man wait for a table?
4 How long did he wait for his meal?
5 What reason did the manager give?

Conversation 3
6 How long has the woman waited?
7 Why is she surprised?

3 A Complete sentences 1–6 below with a suitable word from the box.

sorry	look	nothing	over	work	problem

1 There's a ______ with the air conditioning. *C*
2 It doesn't ______.
3 We'll ______ into it right away.
4 I'm really ______ about that.
5 I'm sorry, but there's ______ we can do at the moment.
6 I've been here for ______ an hour.

B Are the sentences complaints (C) or responses (R)?

C Read audio script S10.5 on page 175 to check your answers.

▶ page 146 LANGUAGEBANK

4 Match complaints 1–4 with responses a)–d).

1 I bought this camera here last week, but there's a problem with it.
2 I had an appointment with Doctor Clarke at 3:00 p.m., but I've been here for over two hours.
3 Excuse me, the lights in my room don't work.
4 We were told there's a flight delay of over six hours. Is that right?

a) I'm really sorry about that. He's very busy at the moment.
b) I'm sorry, but there's nothing we can do at the moment. There's a problem with the electricity.
c) I'm afraid that's right. The plane has a faulty engine.
d) OK, can you leave it here? I'll look into it right away.

6 **There are words missing from conversations 1–3. Complete the conversations with the words in the box.**

could	into	doesn't	speak	ago	afraid	problem

Conversation 1

A: Excuse me, could I to the manager?

B: Yes, one moment, please.

A: There's a with the TV in my room. It work.

C: OK, I'll send someone up to have a look at it.

Conversation 2

A: Excuse me, I ordered room service over an hour. Can you look it, please?

B: Yes, of course.

A: Thank you.

Conversation 3

A: You help me? I'm I have a complaint.

B: What's the problem?

A: This soup is cold.

B: I'm sorry, sir. I'll take it back to the kitchen.

7 **Work in pairs. Student A: turn to page 165. Student B: turn to page 166. Role-play the situations.**

LEARN TO

SOUND FIRM, BUT POLITE

5 **A** **Read 1–3 below. In what situations could you use these expressions?**

1 Could you help me?

2 I'm afraid I have a complaint.

3 Excuse me, could I speak to the manager?

American Speak out TIP
When we want to criticize or complain, we usually use a phrase to introduce the complaint. This helps the listener to prepare for what we are going to say. Is this the same in your language? How do you say the phrases in Exercise 5A in your language?

10.6

B **SENTENCE STRESS** **Listen to the pronunciation of the sentences. Underline the stressed words. Then listen and repeat.**

Could you help me?

SPEAKING

8 **A** **Read sentences 1–6 about the Noparlo School of English. Which problems are the most annoying?**

1 Classes are delayed because the teacher is always late.

2 The equipment in the Self-Access Center is faulty.

3 The classrooms are full of litter.

4 Students use their phones in class.

5 The heating doesn't work, and it is winter.

6 The school food is terrible.

B **Work in pairs. Student A: you are a student at the Noparlo School of English. Turn to page 166. Student B: you are the director at the Noparlo School of English. Turn to page 161.**

criticize | criticise

10.4 MARY'S MEALS

DVD PREVIEW

1 **Work in pairs. Discuss. Do children in your country get free school meals? What do you think of the food that they eat? How could it be improved?**

2 **A** **Read the program information and answer the questions.**

1 Why did Martha start her blog? What was the problem?
2 Why did she decide to raise money?

Mary's Meals

Martha Payne, from Argyll in Scotland, became **an Internet sensation** when she started posting photos of her school meals on her blog NeverSeconds. Sometimes she wasn't happy with the meals that she was given and would give them a **score** out of ten. The local council **banned** her from taking photographs and posting them on the website, but Martha received support from around the world and soon was allowed to continue her blog. However, when she heard about how children in some parts of the world went to school hungry, she decided to use the blog to **raise money** for hungry children. She managed to raise over £100,000 to help feed school children in Malawi through a project called Mary's Meals. In this program, she visits the **charity** to see what they have done with the money.

B **Match the words/phrases in bold in Exercise 2A with meanings 1–5.**

1 collect money
2 an organization that gives money or help to people who need it
3 not allowed to do something
4 someone who becomes famous quickly on the Internet
5 a number of points

DVD VIEW

3 **A** **Watch the DVD. What did the charity Mary's Meals do with the money that Martha Payne raised?**

B **In the story, what is the significance of the words and numbers in the box?**

grow vegetables/raise sheep   school dinners/lunches
£100,000   100,000 people   2,000 children
kitchen   Hollywood

C **Watch the DVD again to check your answers.**

4 **Work in pairs. Discuss the questions.**

1 Do you think it was a good idea for Martha Payne to start a blog about her school meals? Why/Why not?
2 What do you think of the project Mary's Meals?
3 The host says, "What an achievement for nine-year-old Martha Payne." Do you agree/disagree? Why?

American Speakout an issue

5 A Listen to two people talking about issues that concern them. Check (✔) the issues that they talk about.

smoking drugs/alcohol crime green issues technology activities for teenagers traffic buildings in your town/city litter imported food cost of living fast food public transportation

B What is the problem? Listen again and complete the summaries.

1 He doesn't think that countries should import [1]______ from from around the world when they can [2]______ it in their own country. He thinks that people should buy their food locally.

2 She thinks that there are not enough things for [3]______ to do and this causes problems. She would like to see more [4]______ and youth clubs.

C Read audio script S10.7 on page 175 to check. Underline the key phrases in the audio script.

KEYPHRASES

One thing that really annoys me …

I don't understand why [we need to/there's] …

I get really fed up with [the fact that/the way that] …

I just think [it's really difficult/it's unfair] …

And another thing is …

I think … should … / it should be …

6 A Work in pairs. Choose an issue you feel strongly about from the box in Exercise 5A (or choose another one). Answer the questions.

1 What is the problem?
2 Why is it a problem? What has caused it?
3 Why do you feel strongly about it?
4 What do you think you or other people could do to change the situation?

B Work in groups and take turns talking about the problem. Do you agree/disagree with other people's ideas?

writeback a web comment

7 A Read the website comment below and answer the questions.

1 What is the problem?
2 How does the writer feel about the problem?
3 How do you feel about it?

COMMENT

One thing that makes me really angry is when people leave garbage on the streets and on the beaches. The problem is that nobody comes to clean it up. I go out every morning and collect litter that has been left on the beach. Nobody pays me for this. I do it because I love the beaches here. Every year there is more and more litter, and the beaches get dirtier and dirtier. I just don't understand it. I think people who litter should pay a fine, and the police should make them come with me in the mornings and clean up all the litter.

Sabrina, Newport Beach

B Write about an issue you feel strongly about. Use the prompts below.

One thing that makes me really angry is ______.

The problem is ______ .

I don't understand ______.

I think ______ should ______.

garbage / clean up rubbish / clear away

V DESCRIBING A CITY

1 A Complete the phrases.

1 a lot of tr_ _ _ _ _
2 beautiful bu_ _ _ _ _ _ _
3 friendly, po_ _ _ _ people
4 a good public tr_ _ _ _ _ _ _ _ _ _ _ _ _ system
5 a lot of cr_ _ _
6 clean, safe st_ _ _ _ _
7 good ni_ _ _ _ _ _ _
8 it's ex_ _ _ _ _ _ _ to live there

B Work in pairs and take turns describing a place you know. Use the phrases above to describe it.

G USES OF *LIKE*

2 A There is one extra word in each question below. Find the word and cross it out.

1 What's do the weather like today?
2 What food do you to like most?
3 What's your capital city it like?
4 What do you like about where do you live?
5 What's about the food in your country like?
6 What like are the people like where you live?

B Work in pairs. Ask and answer the questions.

V CRIME AND PUNISHMENT

3 Reorder the letters in the underlined words to complete the sentences.

1 He was given a <u>ironps teennecs</u> for committing the crime.
2 The graffiti artist had to do <u>icymountm viceers</u>.
3 The <u>filterposh</u> was caught in a store.
4 Unfortunately, <u>fehtt</u> is very common in my city.
5 Credit card <u>dufar</u> is a modern crime.
6 He received a <u>nife</u> for parking his car in the wrong place.
7 How did they catch the <u>hefit</u>?
8 She was caught <u>wingrit raigffti</u> on a wall.

G PASSIVE VOICE

4 A Match 1–6 with a)–f) to make sentences.

1 The television was
2 The American Constitution
3 Penicillin was discovered
4 The first airplanes
5 Surfing was first
6 The Statue of Liberty and the Eiffel Tower were

a) built by French architects.
b) invented by John Logie Baird.
c) practiced by Australian athletes.
d) was written in 1787.
e) were built by the Wright brothers and Alberto Santos Dumont.
f) by Ian Fleming.

B Work in pairs. Discuss. Do you think the sentences are true (T) or false (F)?

A: I don't think that penicillin was discovered by Ian Fleming.
B: No, he wrote …

F COMPLAINING

5 A Underline the correct alternative to complete the conversations.

Conversation 1

A: Hello. Could I speak to Mike Jones?
B: Yes, I'll get him.
A: Hi, Mike. I'm [1]*afraid/frightened* there's a problem with the computer. It has crashed.
B: OK, just bring it over, and we'll look [2]*up to/into it* right away.

Conversation 2

A: Excuse me. I'm afraid I [3]*have/make* a complaint.
B: Oh, really? What's the matter?
A: It's this remote control I bought from you. It [4]*doesn't/isn't* work.
B: Oh, yes, this part's faulty. Would you like another one?

B Work in pairs. Practice the conversations.

6 Work in pairs and role-play the situations. Student A: you are a customer. Read the situation and make complaints. Student B: you are the manager. Try to help the customer.

Situation 1
You are in Yumi Yumi, Europe's most expensive noodle bar. You have just found a hair in your noodles.

Situation 2
You are at the reception desk of the five-star La Plaza Mayor Hotel. An hour ago, you saw a mouse in your room. You called reception, but nobody came.

Situation 3
You are in a first class seat on a flight from New York to Paris. Your personal TV doesn't work; there's a strange smell in the cabin; and you are cold.

11 technology

SPEAKING
11.1 Talk about things you've done/would like to do
11.2 Talk about future consequences
11.3 Give your opinion
11.4 Talk about technology you couldn't live without

LISTENING
11.1 Listen to people talking about how they keep in touch
11.3 Listen to a discussion about the Internet
11.4 Watch an extract from a documentary about giving up television

READING
11.2 Read an article about social media
11.3 Read about wasting time

WRITING
11.1 Improve your use of pronouns
11.4 Write a comment about technology

How do you feel about technology?

INTERVIEWS

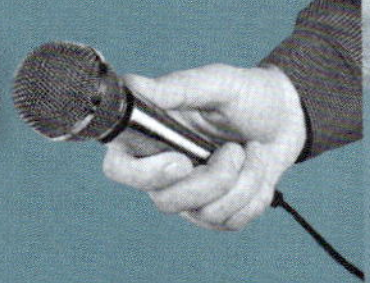

11.1)) KEEPING IN TOUCH

G present perfect
P sentence stress
V communication

VOCABULARY
COMMUNICATION

1 Work in pairs. Ask and answer the questions in the quiz.

How often do you and your partner do these things?

Write often (O), sometimes (S) or never (N) next to each thing.	You	Your Partner
use your cell (phone)		
write a blog		
use a video sharing site		
check your email		
send an SMS (text message)		
chat online		
update your webpage		
Skype someone		
follow a blog		
share links		
post messages		
use social networking sites		

LISTENING

11.1

2 A Listen to four people talking about how they keep in touch. Match each speaker to the type of communication in Exercise 1.

Speaker 1 _____ Speaker 3 _____

Speaker 2 _____ Speaker 4 _____

B What benefits of these communication technologies do the speakers mention? What negative points? Listen again to check.

C Read the sentences from the recording. Do you agree? Discuss with other students.

1 I get really annoyed when you're talking to someone … and they're texting someone else. I think that's really rude.
2 Generally, I think technology is wonderful.
3 The only problem (with a social networking site like Facebook) is that I keep checking it when I should be working.

GRAMMAR
PRESENT PERFECT

3 A Read sentences 1–3 and match them with sentences a)–c) below.

1 I haven't learned how to do it myself **yet**.
2 I've **just** started to use networking sites.
3 We've been to so many places **already**.

a) I started a few days ago.
b) We didn't think it was possible to travel so much.
c) But I hope to learn soon.

B Complete the rules with *just*, *yet* and *already*.

RULES

1 Use _____ in negative sentences or questions, for something you expected to happen before now.

2 Use _____ for something that happened a short time ago.

3 Use _____ for something that happened before now or earlier than expected.

▶ page 148 LANGUAGEBANK

4 A Make sentences with the prompts. Use the present perfect.

1 just / buy / new / I / car
I've just bought a new car.
2 sports / not / do / yet / I / week / this / any
3 have a baby / just / my best friend
4 already / have a vacation / I / this year
5 I / my studies / finish / yet / not
6 new / James Bond / see / movie / already / I
7 move / I / here / just
8 I / English class / already / next / pay for / my

B Make the sentences true for you.
I've had the same car since 1998!

C Work in pairs and compare your answers.

sports sport

5 Look at the cartoon and the "To do" list. What things has the woman already done? What hasn't she done yet?

5.11.2

6 A Listen and write the sentences you hear.

B SENTENCE STRESS Listen again and repeat, paying attention to the rhythm of each sentence.

SPEAKING

7 A Work in pairs. Look at the things in the box below and answer the questions.

travel abroad start an exercise program
write a regular blog learn to play an instrument
learn to drive a car/motorcycle
create my own webpage

1 Which of these have you done already?
2 Which haven't you done yet, but would like to do?
3 Which have you just done?

B Write a list of five things you want/need to do this week.

C Look at your partner's list. Ask questions to find out what he/she has done already and what he/she hasn't done yet.

A: I need to organize my vacation.
B: OK. Have you already decided where to go?
A: Yes. But I haven't reserved the tickets yet.

American Speak Out TIP

Every month, write a list of five things you want to do to improve your English, e.g., *watch a movie in English, read an English newspaper, write an email*, etc. Check your list at the end of the month to see how many of the things you have done.

WRITING
PRONOUNS

8 A Read the travel blog. Match the words in bold to the things they refer to in the box.

Izmir the class my new friends (x2) Ahmed (x2)
my new friends' and my downtown

It's big, beautiful and busy, … It = Izmir

Neil's Blog

August, Izmir

I've just arrived in Izmir. **It**'s big, beautiful and busy, and the people are so friendly. I've only been here for one week, and I've made lots of new friends already. Most of **them** are students too, and **they**'re new to Izmir. **Our** class hasn't started yet, but I'm really looking forward to **it**.

I'm going to share an apartment with another student, Ahmed. I haven't met **him** yet, but **he** sounds nice on the phone. The apartment is near downtown, and there are lots of bars and restaurants near **there**, so it should be good for going out at night. More news in September.

Reply | Previous Message | Next Message

B Underline the correct alternative.

Use pronouns (*it, them, they*, etc.) *to avoid repetition of words/to write longer sentences*.

C Rewrite this travel blog. Replace the underlined words with *we, us, it, there, he, them,* here, our, etc.

64 Ting 12 e ✓ Enjoy

Alecia and I have finally arrived in Bucharest, and <u>Alecia and I</u> love <u>Bucharest</u>. We thought we should update you on <u>Alecia's and my</u> tour. Last month we were in Hungary. We had a really good time <u>in Hungary</u>. We met a man called George, who was very friendly. <u>George</u> took us to some wonderful lakes and castles, and we really enjoyed <u>the lakes and castles</u>. The other news is that we have decided to stay <u>in Bucharest</u> for at least two years. We think <u>living in Bucharest</u> will be a wonderful experience for <u>Alecia and me</u>.

< back to top more >

an apartment a flat

11.2)) MAKE A DIFFERENCE

G real conditionals + *when*
P weak forms: *will*
V feelings

VOCABULARY
FEELINGS

1 A **Work in pairs. Discuss. Do you use social media? What sites are popular in your country? Do you use them? Why/Why not?**

B **Do you agree with the opinions below?**

I tend to use social media sites when I'm **bored** and there's nothing better to do.

Social media sites make me feel **nervous**. I'm **uncomfortable** sharing information with people I don't know.

I'm always **amazed** by how much useful information you can find on social media.

I'm **confused** about why social media sites are so popular. I'm **worried** that they actually make people feel **lonely**. Instead of having a few really good friends they can talk to, young people now have hundreds of "friends" they know nothing about.

I'm really **excited** about social media because I think they can help people to change the world.

C **Work in pairs. Look at the words in bold in the opinions above. Match them with definitions 1–8 below.**

1 How you feel when you have nothing to do.
bored

2 How you feel when you don't understand how something works.

3 How you feel when you are alone and have no friends.

4 How you feel when something special is going to happen and you are happy.

5 How you feel when you're unable to relax because you are embarrassed or worried.

6 How you feel when you are very positively surprised.

7 How you feel when you keep thinking about a problem or something bad that might happen, e.g., you might lose your job.

8 How you feel when you worry about something and cannot relax, e.g., before an test.

D **Work in pairs and take turns. Student A: think about the last time you were amazed/confused/excited/worried, etc. Tell your partner why you felt like that. Student B: ask for more information.**

A: The last time I was really excited was before my birthday party.
B: Really? What did you do?
A: I had a barbecue in the backyard.

Social Media as a Force for Change

For some people, using social media might be a good way to keep in touch with friends, chat about the latest music download, or play games with each other. But young people also use social media to change the world. 43 percent of people are 25 years old or younger, and many of these young people use mobile technology. If this generation isn't happy about something, it won't wait for politicians to change it; it'll use social media to change things itself. These are some examples of how young people from around the world use technology and social media to really make a difference.

READING

2 A **Read the introduction to an article and answer the questions.**

1 What kind of situations do you think people can change by using social media?

2 How do you think they might do this?

B **Read the rest of the article. Does it mention your ideas?**

C **Work in pairs. Answer the questions.**

1 How can social media help young people to cause political change?

2 What did McKenna Pope want to do? Was she successful?

3 How did the Karen Klein foundation start?

D **Work in pairs. Discuss. Which examples in the article do you think are good uses of social media? Would you use social media for these kinds of things? Why/Why not?**

Social Change

Social media sites have been very important for political protests and social change around the world. Large groups of people can now quickly organize themselves to protest against governments and use media to show the rest of the world what's happening. Groups like OccupyWallStreet build online communities that try to fight against what they see as an unfair global economy.

Online Petitions

13-year-old McKenna Pope saw that her younger brother enjoyed cooking and wanted to buy him a toy oven as a present. She went online, but found that she could only buy toy ovens designed for girls. She decided to start an online petition to Hasbro toys asking them to make toy ovens with pictures of boys on the package. In less than a month, her petition received 45,000 signatures and Hasbro decided to change the packaging for their ovens.

Raising Money

When teenage bullies in New York filmed themselves making their school bus driver cry, they uploaded the video to YouTube, and it went viral. Max Sidorov, a 25-year-old Canadian man, saw the video and was shocked. He started a campaign using social media to raise money to give the bus driver, 68-year-old Karen Klein, a vacation.
He wanted to raise $5,000. However, within three weeks, the campaign raised more than $600,000. When Karen received the money, she used $100,000 to set up the Karen Klein foundation to try and stop bullying across America.

So, whatever your problem is, if you use social media, you'll find people who will help you change the world.

GRAMMAR

REAL CONDITIONALS + *IF/WHEN*

3 A Look at sentences a)–d) and answer questions 1 and 2.

a) **If** you use social media, you**'ll** find people who will help you.

b) **If** we raise enough money, the bus driver **won't** need to work any more.

c) **When** people see what's happening, they **will** be shocked.

d) The protests **will** continue **if** they don't change the government.

1 Are the sentences talking about the present or the future?

2 The sentences are divided into two clauses. What tense is used after the *if/when* clause? What tense is used in the main clause?

B Underline the correct alternatives to complete the rules.

RULES

1 Use real conditionals (*if/when* + present simple + *will*) to talk about the *present/future* consequence of a specific situation.

2 Use *if* for a situation that is *likely/certain*.

3 Use *when* for a situation that is *likely/certain*.

4 The *if/when* clause *can be at the beginning or the end of the sentence/must be at the beginning of the sentence.*

▶ page 148 LANGUAGEBANK

4 A Put the verbs in parentheses in the correct tense to complete the sentences.

1 If you ______ (give) me your details, I ______ (send) you the photo.

2 If people ______ (sign) the petition, the company ______ (have to) respond.

3 When your friends ______ (see) the video, they ______ (not be) surprised.

4 If the situation ______ (get) worse, ______ you ______ (leave) your job?

5 If there ______ (not be) elections soon, people ______ (start) protesting.

6 When you ______ (see) this picture, I ______ (be) in the Everglades!

7 If the product ______ (be) really good, then people ______ (not write) bad reviews.

8 If they ______ (change) the design, ______ you ______ (buy) one?

S 1.3

B WEAK FORMS: WILL Listen to check. How is *will* pronounced?

I'll send you the photo.

S 1.4

C Listen and repeat the sentences.

5 A Make sentences 1–8 true for you.

1 If someone sends me an online petition, …

2 If I'm angry about the government or a big company, …

3 When I go on my next vacation, …

4 When I get home this evening, …

5 If I'm hungry later, …

6 If someone invites me to a party, …

7 If I go out this weekend, …

8 If I lose my cell phone, …

B Work in pairs and compare your answers.

Speaking

6 A Work in groups. Think of a situation in your town/city/country that you are not very happy about (lifestyle/politics/business/environment) and discuss the questions. Then make your plan and prepare to present it to other students.

1 How could you use social media to try and change the situation? What would you do?

2 Could you organize an online petition or a protest or try to raise some money?

B Listen to the other groups' ideas for social media campaigns and tell the group about the possible consequences of their actions.

VOCABULARY

INTERNET TERMS

1 **Work in pairs. Look at the Internet terms in the box below and answer the questions.**

travel website	search engine	online news
social media site	music download site	
photo sharing site	message board	

1 Do you use/visit any of these?
2 Which ones do you visit most frequently?
3 Do you think they are useful/not very useful? Why?

READING

2 **A** **Look at the picture. Do you think that people waste a lot of time on the Internet when they should be working? Read the text to find out.**

Stop wasting time!

Many of us find it difficult to concentrate on Fridays, so it's no surprise that nearly half of us waste our time at work on Friday afternoons by looking up funny news articles on the Internet, watching silly cat videos or planning our next vacation. But, unfortunately, the problem isn't just a Friday problem. People are wasting more and more time being distracted by the Internet and social media when they should be working or studying. A report has shown how computer users waste up to eight days a month on the Internet. Most of the people who were questioned said they were distracted "all or most of the time" when they work or study online. The study showed that the Internet can be bad for relationships, too, since people argue with their partners who spend too much time in front of their computer or mobile device. Luckily, there is a simple answer to the problem: get off the Internet and get on with life.

B **Answer the questions.**

1 What is the problem with Friday afternoons?
2 What kinds of distractions does the article talk about?
3 How much time do people waste not working?
4 Why is the Internet bad for relationships?

3 **Work in pairs. Discuss. Do you think being on the Internet is a good way to spend your free time or do you think people spend too much time on the Internet?**

FUNCTION

GIVING OPINIONS

S11.5 **4** **Listen to three people discussing the Internet. Are the statements true (T) or false (F)?**

1 The men both use the Internet at work.
2 The woman thinks people shouldn't use the Internet when they are at work.
3 The men both think that the Internet is a waste of time.
4 The woman says some people prefer the Internet to sports.

5 **A** **Look at statements 1–6. Check (✔) the ideas that are mentioned in the recording.**

Surfing on the Internet is:

1 addictive. Some people can't stop using it.
2 bad for relationships.
3 dangerous. You can meet dangerous people on the Internet.
4 good when you want a break from work.
5 causing people to fail their college degrees because they spend too much time on social media sites when they should be studying.
6 a waste of time.

B **Listen again to check.**

S11.6 **6 A Listen and complete the phrases in the table.**

Agreeing	Disagreeing	Giving an Opinion
That's ______ ______ true	I totally ______ I'm not ______ about that	I ______ I ______ think

B Look at audio script S11.5 on page 175–176. Underline the phrases for agreeing, disagreeing and giving opinions. Find one more phrase to add to each column in the table above.

▶ page 148 LANGUAGEBANK

7 A Find and correct the mistakes in the conversations below. There is a mistake in each response.

1 A: Everyone should learn a second language.
B: I think too. It's very useful.

2 A: It's not polite to arrive late for an appointment.
B: That true. I always arrive on time.

3 A: It's good to ask as many questions as possible in class.
B: I'm not sure by that. Some students ask too many questions.

4 A: It's best to live in a hot sunny country.
B: So definitely. Everybody loves the sunshine.

5 A: Children should study for tests from the age of six.
B: I am totally disagree. No child under ten should have to study for a test.

6 A: Everyone loves classical music.
B: I don't think. Most people like pop music.

B Work in pairs. Student A: read out A's opinions. Student B: respond with your own opinion. Then change roles.

LEARN TO
DISAGREE POLITELY

8 A Look at the responses in 1–5 below. Which do you think is more polite? Check (✔) A or B.

1 A: I'm sorry, but I really don't see what the problem is.
B: I really don't see what the problem is.

2 A: I disagree.
B: I'm not sure about that.

3 A: I don't think it's a waste of time at all.
B: It's not a waste of time.

4 A: That's true, but I don't think the problem is the Internet.
B: The problem is not using the Internet.

5 A: I totally disagree.
B: I'm afraid I totally disagree.

S11.7 **B POLITE INTONATION Listen to check your answers. Notice the intonation. What does the speaker do to sound polite?**

C Work in pairs. Practice saying the phrases using polite intonation.

American Speakout TIP
Use language carefully when you disagree. Don't be too direct. Use phrases like *I'm sorry, but …* , *I'm afraid …* , *I'm not sure …* and *I don't think …*

SPEAKING

9 A Choose two or three statements below. Do you agree/disagree? Write your opinion in a few words.

B Work in groups and compare your ideas.

You shouldn't believe what you read on the Internet.

The Internet has made the world a better place.

A lot of the technology we use is not necessary.

It's better to talk to someone than to send them a text message.

Downloading songs for free is OK.

Online books will mean the end of bookstores.

Everybody in the world should have a computer.

11.4 IS TV BAD FOR KIDS?

DVD PREVIEW

1 **Work in pairs. Discuss. Which of the things in the box do you own? Which do you use every day? Which items are the most useful? Rank the items.**

smart phone   laptop   TV   DVD player
microwave   tablet   digital camera

2 **A** **Work in pairs. What numbers do you think complete 1–5 in the quiz below? Check the answers on page 166.**

Did YOU know... ?

1 In the U.S.A., a child watches TV for an average of __ hours a day.
2 In parts of the U.K., more than __ percent of elementary school children have a TV in their bedroom.
3 The average person spends __ years eating and __ years watching TV.
4 Children under three years old who watch more than __ hour(s) of TV a day may have problems concentrating at school when they are older.
5 In the U.S.A., some families spend only __ minutes a week having meaningful conversations with their children. Those children spend __ minutes a week watching TV.

B **Discuss. How many hours do you spend watching TV per week? Do you think this is OK/too much/not enough?**

3 **Read the program information and answer the questions.**

1 What do you think the children will do when their televisions and video games are taken away?
2 How do you think the parents will feel during the experiment?

Panorama: Is TV Bad for Kids?

Panorama is a documentary series that looks at important issues. In this program, Jeremy Vine does an experiment in the U.K.: for two weeks, several families have to live without televisions, computers and video games. Can they survive? What can we learn from the experiment? Watch to find out.

DVD VIEW

4 **Watch the DVD. Were your ideas in Exercise 3 correct?**

5 **Watch the DVD again. Are the sentences true (T) or false (F)?**

1 Children who watch too much TV get fat.
2 The program *Panorama* went to a secondary school in Manchester.
3 They took the microwaves out of the homes of half the children in the class.
4 They gave the children a camera to record what happened.
5 The parents had to work a lot harder when there were no TVs.
6 After the experiment, the families watched the same amount of TV as before.

6 **Work in pairs and answer the questions.**

1 What do you think of the experiment? Do you think it was a good idea?
2 How do parents keep their children entertained in your country?

elementary school / high school — primary school / secondary school

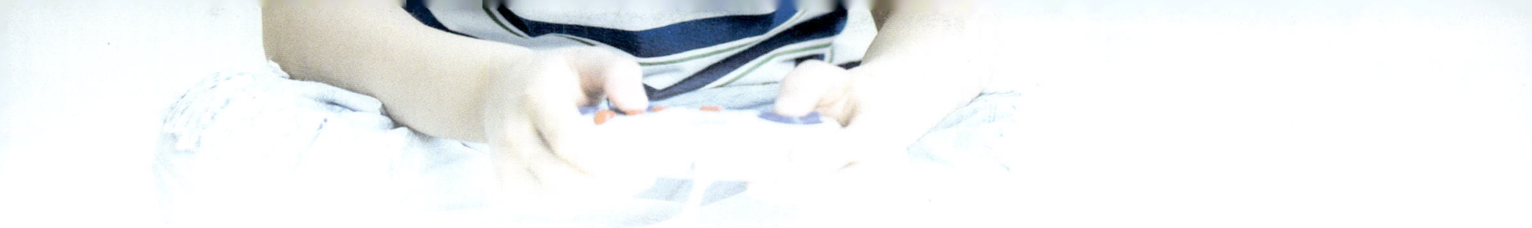

American Speakout technology

7 A Listen to people talking about essential gadgets. Write them in the correct column.

Speaker	Essential	Not Essential
1	*smartphone*	*television*
2		

B Listen again and Check (✔) the key phrases you hear.

KEYPHRASES

That's essential.

I love it.

I use it (all the time/every day) …

I couldn't live without …

It's good/important because …

I don't go anywhere without it./I take it everywhere.

I need it in case …

I suppose I don't need …

I can live without …

It's very useful.

C Decide which gadgets are essential/not essential for you. Think about why you need them. Make some notes. Use the key phrases to help you.

D Work in groups. Tell your group why you need the gadgets you chose. Which are the most popular?

writeback a web comment

8 A Read the comments. Do these people think technology is good or bad? Why?

PEOPLE FORUM TOPIC Archive

Is technology a good or a bad thing?

How have computers, the Internet, email and cell phones changed your life? Have they changed the way we do business? Are there good and bad things about technology? What do you think?

Shantanu, U.S.A./India
reply – Most people say technology has made our lives very fast and very convenient. But I don't think so. The fact is that it has also made us very lonely. We interact with machines for 8–10 hours a day and spend less than 2–3 hours interacting with other humans.

Jake, U.K.
reply – It seems to me that technology is a good thing. It allows me to find out what is **really** happening in the world, not just what the media want me to believe. The problem is that some governments want to control what is available on the Internet, too.

B Write your own comment using the structure below.

It seems to me that technology ______.

Most people say ______. But I'm not sure about that./I don't think so. In my opinion, ______.

For example, ______.

The fact is that/The problem is that ______.

Finally, ______. Technology ______ my life.

11.5 LOOKBACK

V COMMUNICATION

1 A Complete the words.

1 Can you remember life without a c_l_ ph_n_? Do you use one every day?
2 Do any of your friends have a w_b p_g_?
3 Do you prefer to speak to someone on the phone or send an S_S (t_xt m_ss_g_)?
4 What kind of l_ nks do you find interesting?
5 Are there any bl_gs that you read regularly? Why do you like them?
6 Do you like to ch_t online?

B Work in pairs and take turns. Ask and answer the questions.

G PRESENT PERFECT

2 A Write answers to 1–6 in the circle below.

1 The name of something you have just bought.
2 The name of something you would like, but you haven't bought yet.
3 Somewhere you have already spent a lot of time.
4 Somewhere you haven't been to yet, but you plan to visit.
5 Something you have just finished (a book/a class, etc.).
6 Something you have done already today.

B Work in pairs and take turns. Look at each of the words/phrases in your circles. Ask for more information.

A: A new car … Have you just bought one?
B: That's right.
A: What kind of car did you buy?
B: A Peugeot.

V FEELINGS

3 A Complete the sentence in different ways using the words in the box.

nervous	lonely	bored
uncomfortable	confused	
worried	amazed	excited

I feel ______ when …

I feel nervous when I have to take a test.

B Work in pairs. Discuss. What do you do in each situation to make yourself feel better?

G REAL CONDITIONALS + *WHEN*

4 A Match 1–6 with a)–f) to make sentences.

1 If you break a mirror,
2 If you walk under a ladder,
3 If you find a penny on the ground,
4 If you eat an apple a day,
5 If you give away a wedding present,
6 If a baby is born at 12 o'clock,

a) it will keep the doctor away.
b) he/she will be very lucky when he/she grows up.
c) paint might fall on your head.
d) your marriage will fail.
e) you will have seven years' bad luck.
f) you will have good luck all day.

B Work in pairs. Discuss. Do you have the same superstitions in your country? What other superstitions are there?

5 A Write down three things that might happen to you in the next six months.

I might find a job abroad.

B Work in pairs. Discuss the possible consequences.

A: I might find a job abroad.
B: What will happen if you do that?
A: I'll have to move.

F GIVING OPINIONS

6 A Put the words in the correct order to complete the conversations.

Conversation 1
A: I think video sharing sites are bad for children.
B: totally / disagree / afraid / I / I'm

Conversation 2
A: Nobody should eat meat.
B: not / that / I'm / about / sure

Conversation 3
A: all / drugs / my / be / opinion / should / in / legal
B: I'm sorry, but I don't think that's a good idea.

Conversation 4
A: I really think teachers should be paid more money.
B: right / that's / so / too / think / I

Conversation 5
A: government / do / the / better / next / think / be / you / will?
B: Definitely!

Conversation 6
A: Children under the age of ten shouldn't have a cell phone.
B: so / think / I / don't

Conversation 7
A: I can never find anything I want to watch on television. It's all garbage.
B: agree / true / that's / I

Conversation 8
A: Policemen should all carry guns.
B: totally / I / disagree

B Work in pairs and take turns. Practice the conversations. Give your own opinions and remember to use polite intonation.

A: I think video sharing sites can be dangerous.
B: Yes, I agree. Anyone can upload videos of illegal things.

12 fame

SPEAKING	12.1 Talk about your favorite movie 12.2 Talk about being famous 12.3 Make requests and offers 12.4 Talk about your ambitions
LISTENING	12.2 Listen to people talking about fame 12.3 Listen to people making requests 12.4 Watch an extract from a documentary about Lewis Hamilton
READING	12.1 Read a magazine article about writing a blockbuster 12.2 Read a magazine article about Internet fame 12.3 Read a text about personal assistants
WRITING	12.2 Write about a famous person 12.4 Write about your childhood ambitions

Would you like to be famous?

INTERVIEWS

12.1)) CAUGHT ON FILM

G reported speech
P contrastive stress
V movies

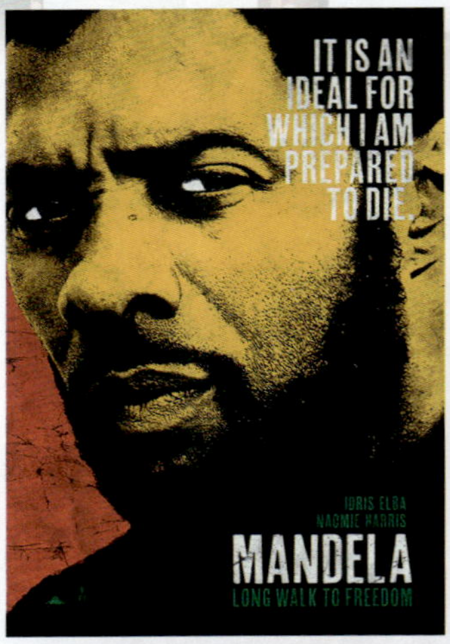

VOCABULARY
MOVIES

1 A Look at the movie posters and match them to the types of movie in the box. Which ones fit more than one category?

Mandela: Long Walk to Freedom *is a biopic and a drama.*

an action movie	a comedy	a science fiction movie
a (historical) drama	a horror movie	a thriller
a documentary	a biopic	a blockbuster	a cartoon

B Work in pairs. Discuss the questions.

1 Can you think of examples of the other types of movies in the box?
2 Have you seen any of the movies in the posters? What did you think of them?
3 What's your favorite type of movie?

In the U.S., a billion is a thousand times a million, while in countries like Colombia, a billion is usually a million times a million. Both definitions coexist in British English, where a billion originally meant a million times a million.

READING

2 A Discuss in pairs.

1 Can you name any movies that have been very popular recently? Why do you think they were so popular?
2 Do you think blockbusters have a "formula" (fixed rules for writing them)?

B Read the text to find an answer to question 2.

How to Write a HOLLYWOOD BLOCKBUSTER

Look at any list of Hollywood's biggest movies. What do you see? First, most use myths. The heroes' lives are world-shaking stories, part Bible, part fantasy. Myths are useful because they travel across cultures; and the biggest movies are seen everywhere, from Belgium to Bali to Brazil.

Related to myths is setting. Blockbusters are often set in amazing, alternative worlds. *Avatar* takes place in a natural paradise, but the movie involves blue people who can fly. Harry Potter goes to a British private school, but it's full of monsters and wizards.

Not all blockbusters need monsters, but the heroes and their opponents must be strong. The opponent might be an evil wizard (Voldemort in the Harry Potter movies), a cat-stroking genius (James Bond movies), or something inhuman and almost unstoppable (dinosaurs in *Jurassic Park*). If it's human, the bad guy needs good lines. Some phrases in movies are more memorable than the movie itself!

What about structure? Blockbusters come in three parts. The first act introduces the main character and the problem he/she faces. The second act sees the character trying to solve the problem, but failing. In the third act, the character finally defeats the opponent.

The third act is also where the biggest set piece happens. Set pieces are action scenes—a huge battle (*The Lord of the Rings*) or a car chase (Jason Bourne movies)—and they are big, expensive and memorable.

Include all of the above, find a studio and a director, and see your movie light up the world!

THE BIGGEST-SELLING MOVIES

1 *Avatar* (2009) - $2.8 billion
Famous line: *"Out there is the true world, and in here is the dream."*

2 *Titanic* (1997) - $2.2 BILLION
Famous line: *"I am the king of the world!"*

3 *The Avengers* (2012) - $1.5 billion
Famous line: Steve Rogers: *"Doctor Banner, now might be a good time for you to get angry."* Bruce Banner: *"That's my secret, Captain: I'm always angry."*

4 *Harry Potter and the Deathly Hallows—Part 2* (2011) - $1.4 BILLION
Famous line: Harry: *"We have to go there now!"*
Hermione: *"We can't do that! We have to plan!"*
Harry: *"Hermione! When have any of our plans ever actually worked?"*

3 Find words in the text that match the definitions below.

1 a very old story about gods, magical creatures, etc. (paragraph 1)
2 the place or time in which the events of a movie or book happen (paragraph 2)
3 someone who is competing against you (paragraph 3)
4 the way in which the parts of something are organized (paragraph 4)
5 a short part of a movie, where the events happen in one place (paragraph 5)
6 a movie company or the place where movies are made (paragraph 6)

4 Discuss with other students.

1 Do you think it's easy to write a blockbuster if you follow the "rules" in the text? What might be difficult?
2 Have you seen any of the top four biggest-selling movies? If so, do you think they follow the "rules"? Did you enjoy these movies? Why/Why not?

GRAMMAR

REPORTED SPEECH

5 Read the famous lines in the first column below. Compare the words spoken to the reported sentences in the second column. Answer questions 1–2 below.

1 How do the verb forms change?
2 Which verbs do we use to report speech?

Direct Speech	Reported Speech
"Out there is the true world, and in here is the dream."	He said out there was the true world, and in here was the dream.
"I am the king of the world!"	He said he was the king of the world.
"I'm always angry."	He told Steve he was always angry.
"We have to go there!"	He told Hermione they had to go there.

▶ page 150 LANGUAGEBANK

6 A Put the paragraph below into reported speech. Begin each sentence with *He told me* or *He said*.

"I'm an actor. I love my job, but I don't like playing criminals. I live in Hollywood, where I work as a waiter."

He told me he was an actor. He said he …

S12.1

B CONTRASTIVE STRESS Listen to different ways of saying *He told me he was an actor*. How does the stress affect the message?

S12.2

C Listen to the sentences and read audio script S12.2 on page 176. Which words are stressed? Why?

7 A Complete the favorite movie quotes quiz questions with *said* or *told*. Then circle the correct answer.

B Check your answers on page 166.

C Work in pairs. Read the quotes again and change them to reported speech.

1 She said she had a feeling they weren't in Kansas anymore.

Favorite Movie Quotes

1 Who ______ a dog, *"I have a feeling we aren't in Kansas anymore"*?
a) the dog owner in *Amores Perros*
b) Dorothy in *The Wizard of Oz*

2 Who ______, *"Greed is good"*?
a) Morgan Spurlock in *Super Size Me*
b) Michael Douglas in *Wall Street*

3 Who ______, *"It's alive!"*?
a) Sigourney Weaver in *Alien*
b) The crazy doctor in *Frankenstein*

4 Who ______ engineers in Houston, *"We have a problem"*?
a) Tom Hanks in *Apollo 13*
b) Harrison Ford in *Star Wars*

5 Who ______, *"I want to be alone"*?
a) Greta Garbo in *Grand Hotel*
b) The computer Hal in *A Space Odyssey*

6 Who ______ a policeman, *"I think this is the beginning of a beautiful friendship"*?
a) Humphrey Bogart in *Casablanca*
b) Hugh Grant in *Notting Hill*

SPEAKING

8 A You are going to describe one of your favorite movies. Think about how you can complete the phrases below.

1 The movie is about …
2 It's set in …
3 It's directed by …
4 The star(s) of the movie is/are …
5 He/She played a/an …
6 One of the best scenes takes place …
7 It has a happy/surprise/sad ending: …
8 I like the movie because …

B Work in pairs and take turns. Describe the movie and take notes on your partner's answers. If you have time, ask follow-up questions.

Who's your favorite actor? Do you have a favorite director?

C Work with other students. Tell them what your first partner said.

He said Mamma Mia was his favorite movie.

She said she liked movies by Akira Kurosawa because they told great stories.

12.2 A LUCKY BREAK

G hypothetical conditionals present/future
P word stress
V suffixes

Internet Fame

The Internet has changed the meaning of "celebrity." In the past, you had to be a successful actor, musician or athlete to be famous. Now all you need is the Internet. In 1968, artist Andy Warhol said, "In the future, everyone will be famous for fifteen minutes." With the invention of the Internet and YouTube, maybe that time is now. Now, a kid with a webcam can become an instant movie star, and even a cat with a grumpy face can make their owner famous. When Tabatha Bundesen's brother posted a photo of their cat on the Internet, Grumpy Cat became an overnight Internet sensation and later a company worth more than $1 million. Tavi Gevinson was twelve years old when she started her own fashion blog, but she quickly found herself on the front pages of newspapers and magazines and interviewed on television. These are the new superstars, celebrities of the future.

VOCABULARY

SUFFIXES

1 **Work in pairs. Do you think it would be good to be famous? What are the positive/negative things about being famous?**

2 A **Discuss. What do you think a "web celebrity" is? Read the article to find out.**

B **Answer the questions.**

1 What is different about fame now?
2 How do people become famous on the Internet?
3 Can you think of examples of web celebrities?

3 A **Look at the article above and find one example of a word with each suffix. Write them in the table.**

Adjective Endings		Noun Endings		
-ful	*-ous*	*-ion*	*-ity*	*-er/-or/-ian* (jobs)
successful				

B **Complete words 1–8 below and put them in the correct column in the table.**

1 celebrat______
2 photograph______
3 politic______
4 popular______
5 adventur______ (adj)
6 help______ (adj)
7 danger______
8 wonder______

5.12.3

C WORD STRESS **Listen to check your answers. Underline the main stress.**

D **Can you think of any other words with these suffixes?**

LISTENING

4 A **Work in pairs. Discuss. If you could be famous, what would you like to be famous for?**

5.12.4

B **Listen to eight people answering the question. Put the number of the speaker next to the thing they mention.**

an artist *1* an actress a singer/dancer
a musician successful in business
a politician/president a model
a soccer player/athlete a writer
a scientist/inventor

5 A **Listen again and complete the sentences.**

1 If I had more ______, I would love to paint.
2 If I were a politician, I would try to ______ the world.
3 Imagine if you scored a goal for your country in the ______ Cup; that would be such a good feeling.
4 I'd love to ______. If I could be famous for anything, I think I'd be a singer.
5 I'd like to be remembered as a great ______.
6 If I were famous, I would be ______, live in a big house, and have all those clothes.
7 If I invented something that made people's ______ better, that would be good.
8 If I were famous, I wouldn't be ______.

B **Work in pairs. Discuss. Do you agree with any of the speakers?**

A: I think I'd like to be a model.
B: Really? I wouldn't ...

soccer player — footballer

GRAMMAR
HYPOTHETICAL CONDITIONALS

6 A Look at Exercise 5A and complete the table.

If clause: *If* + present subjunctive*	main clause: *would/wouldn't* (+ infinitive)
If I [1]______ more time, If I were famous, If I [3]______ a politician,	I would love to paint. I [2]______ be happy. I would try to change the world.

*The present subjunctive is often the same as the simple past.

B Underline the correct alternatives to complete the rules.

RULES

1 Use hypothetical conditionals for *real/imaginary* situations in the present.

If I were famous (but I'm not …), I would …

2 Use hypothetical conditionals for *likely* (probable)/*unlikely* (impossible) situations in the future.

If I didn't have to work tomorrow (but I do), I would …

▶ page 150 **LANGUAGEBANK**

7 Underline the correct alternative.

1 If I *were/would be* a famous soccer player, I would live in a big house.
2 If she *worked/would work* harder, I'm sure she'd be more successful.
3 If I played more sports, I *would feel/felt better.*
4 If I *had/would have* the day off, I would stay in bed.
5 If I *didn't/wouldn't* work or study, I would be bored.
6 I would read more if I *didn't have/wouldn't have* a TV.
7 I *would use/used* my bicycle more if I didn't have a car.

8 A Use the prompts to make questions with hypothetical conditionals.

1 If / have / no money / what / do?
If you had no money, what would you do?
2 If / can / have dinner / with any two living people / whom / choose?
3 If / can / do any job / what / do?
4 If / have / more time / what / do?
5 If / can / change one thing about yourself / what / change?

B Work in pairs. Ask and answer the questions.

The hypothetical conditional of the verb *be* can take two forms. American English uses *were* (*If I were famous, I'd …*), whereas British English uses *were* and *was*, the latter as the more informal, e.g., *If I was famous, I'd …*

WRITING
PARAGRAPHS

9 A Put sentences a)–d) in the correct paragraphs to complete the profile of Jack Monroe.

a) Jack grew up in Essex and left school at age sixteen.
b) Jack is now a successful journalist who campaigns against poverty.
c) Jack Monroe was a 24-year-old mother of one who started writing an online blog ("A Girl Called Jack") when she was unemployed and looking for work.
d) She sold almost everything she owned (car, watch, TV, phone) in order to buy enough food for her and her two-year-old son to eat, but she found they were still hungry.

A Girl Called Jack

[1]______ She became an overnight celebrity when she wrote a blog post called "Hunger Hurts" talking about how difficult life is when you're living on very little money.

[2]______ She had a well-paid job with the fire department until she had a baby, and it became difficult to find childcare to allow her to work nights. After 18 months of being unemployed, she found herself living in poverty.

[3]______ She started the blog to talk about her experiences and give people recipes for eating healthily using very little money. The blog was a huge success, and soon Jack Monroe was asked to write articles in newspapers, appear on television and talk to the government about poverty.

[4]______ She has won awards for her blog and has published a book of her recipes.

B Choose the correct heading for each paragraph.

Achievements
Rise to Fame
Childhood and Education
Introduction

American Speak out TIP
Each paragraph should have a different topic. The first sentence of each paragraph (the topic sentence) should introduce that paragraph. Plan the topic of the paragraph before you start writing.

C Research the life of a famous person you admire or read the profile on page 167. Write the profile of this person using paragraphs.

play sports / fire department   do sport / Fire Service

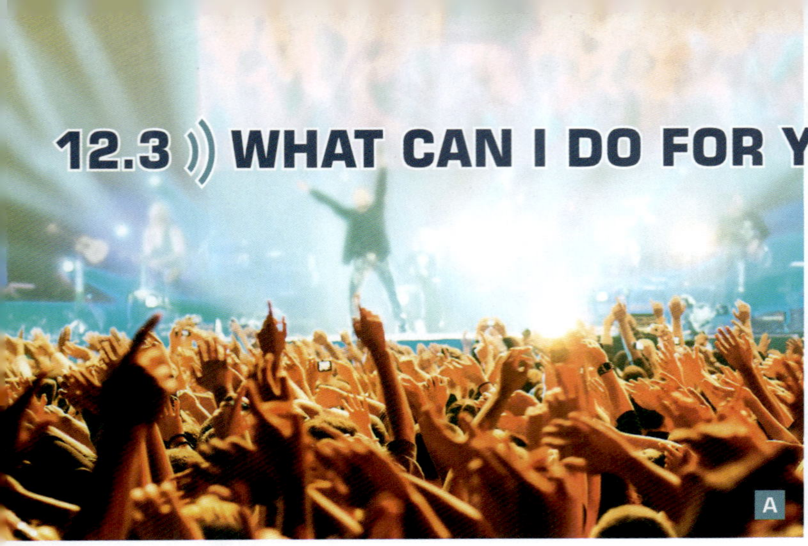
A

12.3 WHAT CAN I DO FOR YOU?

B

F requests and offers
P polite intonation: requests
V collocations

VOCABULARY
COLLOCATIONS

1 A Work in pairs. Complete phrases 1–6 by adding the correct letters.

1 *get* tickets for a concert/a good seat
2 r_ _t a car for the day/a vacation home
3 r_ s _ _ v _ a table for two/tickets for a show
4 _n_ _t_ someone to dinner/someone to a party
5 _ _c_ _m_ _d somewhere good to visit/a restaurant
6 _ _ g_n_z_ a private tour/a meeting

B Look at photos A–C. Which of the things in Exercise 1A can you see?

C Work in pairs. Discuss. How often do you do the things in Exercise 1A?

I sometimes get tickets for a concert. The last concert I saw was …

READING

2 A Read the definition. Discuss. What other things do you think a personal assistant does to help rich and famous clients?

P **personal assistant** *noun* someone who organizes things for (usually rich) clients, e.g., reserves tables in restaurants, buys tickets for concerts, etc.

B Read the text to find out.

Personal Assistant

He can reserve you a table at the world's top restaurants, get you the best seats for *The Lion King*, find you a private plane for the next day or organize a red carpet for you at the Oscars. He's a personal assistant, and he can get you anything you want … if you have enough money!

The personal assistants we spoke to have done some amazing things for their clients: one got twenty tickets for a Rolling Stones concert an hour before it started; he also flew some of Madonna's favorite tea to London and found some rare birds for Jennifer Lopez. Another asked former U.S. President, Bill Clinton, to have dinner with his client. Clinton said "yes"!

C

FUNCTION
REQUESTS AND OFFERS

12.5

3 A Listen to four conversations with a hotel concierge. What does each person want?

B Listen again. Complete the sentences with one word.

1 I'd ______ to go to a local restaurant.
2 ______ you recommend somewhere?
3 ______ you like me to call a taxi?
4 Would it be ______ to borrow one from the hotel?
5 Do you ______ me to send one up to your room?
6 Would you be ______ to reserve two tickets for us?
7 ______ I reserve the tickets for you?

C Look at sentences 1–7 again and answer the questions.

a) Which phrases are requests (R) and which are offers (O)?
b) Which request says what we want to do?
c) Which two requests ask if something is possible?
d) Which request asks for someone's opinion?

▶ page 150 LANGUAGEBANK

personal assistant / reserve — personal concierge / book

4 A **Put the words in the correct order to make questions or sentences.**

1 food / to / like / I'd / local / try / some
2 recommend / nightclub / a / could / good / you ?
3 reserve / be / tickets / would / to / three / you / able ?
4 car / rent / would / be / it / to / a / possible ?
5 I / ticket / buy / should / your ?
6 table / reserve / want / you / to / do / a / me ?
7 to / the / like / manager / me / you / call / would ?

B **Match questions 1–7 above with responses a)–g).**

a) Yes, I'll print out some information for you about the daily rates.
b) There are some excellent restaurants in this area.
c) There's a famous one that opens at midnight.
d) Certainly. I'll just call the box office.
e) Yes, for six people, please.
f) No, don't worry—I'll speak to him myself.
g) Yes, please. I'll pay you back later.

5 A **Complete the sentences in any way you choose.**

1 Could you recommend a ______?
2 Would you be able to ______ for me?
3 Would it be possible to ______?
4 Could you recommend somewhere to ______?

B **Work in pairs and take turns. Student A: read your sentence. Student B: respond.**

A: Could you recommend a good café?
B: Yes, go to The Café on the Bridge. It serves great coffee! Do you want me to take you there?

S12.6

C **POLITE INTONATION: requests** **Listen to the requests. Notice how the speaker's voice is high to start and then becomes lower. This sounds polite.**

D **Listen again and repeat. Pay attention to the intonation.**

LEARN TO
ASK FOR MORE TIME

6 A **Look at the extracts from audio script S12.5 on page 176. Underline four phrases to ask for more time.**

Extract 1
B: Could you recommend somewhere?
A: Yes, of course. Hang on. We have a list on a map.

Extract 2
A: Would you like me to call a taxi? It's about a five minute drive.
C: That would be wonderful.
A: OK, just a minute. I'll see if there's one waiting.

Extract 3
A: An adapter? Of course. Do you want me to send one up to your room?
D: Yes, please.
A: Can you give me a minute? I'll ask at the desk.

Extract 4
E: Would you be able to reserve two tickets for us?
A: Hold on. Let me just check where it's playing.

B **Are the phrases formal or informal? Which expression do you think is the most formal?**

7 **Complete B's responses with one word.**

Conversation 1
A: Can you get me a meeting with the CEO?
B: Hang. I'll call him.

Conversation 2
A: I'd like to rent the hall for a party on May tenth.
B: Can you give a minute? I need to see if it's free that day.

Conversation 3
A: Would it be possible to get tickets for the show?
B: A moment. I'll check online.

Conversation 4
A: Would I be able to get a flight this afternoon?
B: Hold. I'll call the airline.

SPEAKING

8 **Work in pairs. Student A: look at page 165. Student B: look at page 167. Read your roles.**

9 A **Write out one of your conversations. Try to use phrases for making requests and offers and asking for time.**

B **Act out your conversation in front of other students.**

should / adapter   shall / adaptor plug

12.4 BILLION DOLLAR MAN

DVD PREVIEW

1 Work in groups and discuss the questions.

1 Can you name any Formula 1 drivers?
2 What type of person do you think can become a Formula 1 driver?

2 Read the program information. Who is the program about, and what type of things might you learn by watching it?

Lewis Hamilton: Billion Dollar Man

Billion Dollar Man is a documentary about Formula One (F1) driver and celebrity, Lewis Hamilton. The program describes Hamilton's early life in the U.K. and how he used his talent to become one of the best and most famous drivers in the world.

DVD VIEW

3 Watch the DVD. What type of things do you learn about Lewis Hamilton and F1? Use the ideas in the box to help you.

who he is now	F1 facts	early days as a racer
teenage ambitions	route to F1	

4 A Read the notes about Lewis Hamilton's career. What words do you think complete the notes?

- Today, Hamilton is described as "Formula 1 driver, model, celebrity, [1]______."
- When he was six, he started racing electric [2]______.
- A few years later, he raced go-karts, but dreamed of joining [3]______.
- He won [4]______ British go-karting championships.
- He liked F1 because of the speed, being with "the big guys" and making [5]______.
- After go-carting, he joined [6]______.
- The best drivers are seen by F1 [7]______.
- Spent [8]______ years in Formula 3.

B Watch the DVD again to check your answers.

5 Discuss. Why do you think fans, journalists, etc. "love" Lewis Hamilton? What is unusual about this story?

American Speakout dreams and ambitions

6 A Listen to Marianna talking about her dreams and ambitions. Check (✔) the questions she answers.

1 Where did you grow up?
2 When you were younger, did you dream of doing a particular job?
3 What/Who inspired you to do this?
4 Did you have a teacher/someone to help you to learn a special skill?
5 Have you achieved any of your dreams? What did you do?

B Work in pairs. What are Marianna's answers to the questions?

C You are going to talk about the dreams and ambitions you had when you were younger. First, think about your answers to the questions in Exercise 6A. Then look at the key phrases. Underline any phrases you want to use.

KEYPHRASES

I always wanted to be a ...
As a child, I used to ...
It started with ...
I wanted to work ...
I spent a lot of time ...
As I grew up, I realized ...
One day, I had the chance to ...
Eventually, I ...

D Work in pairs and take turns talking about your childhood dreams/ambitions. Have they changed now that you are older? If so, how?

writeback a web comment

7 Read the website and answer the questions.

1 What did Damien want to be as a child?
2 What does he want to do now?

REFLECTIONS | CHILDHOOD AMBITIONS

How have your childhood ambitions changed? We asked people the following questions: What were your childhood ambitions? What do you do now? And what do you hope to become in the future?

Damien (31), Slovenia:
As a child, I always wanted to be a teacher. Both of my parents were teachers, and they inspired me with a love of learning. Now, I have achieved that dream. I teach geography, history, art and sociology to 12–15-year-old students at a secondary school here in Ljubljana. I love working with children. It's much better than an office job. But now I'm planning a career change. I want to open my own school. First, I'm going back to college to take some management classes. I hope to learn about the business side of owning a school. Next, I'll look for a building. I already have two teachers who want to work for me: my parents!

8 Write a comment for the website about your childhood ambitions using the model. Answer the questions below.

1 What were your childhood ambitions?
2 What do you do now?
3 What do you hope to become in the future?

realized | realised

V MOVIES

1 A Complete the text with the words in the box.

studio blockbuster scene opponent horror movies setting

Dream of Ice is a thriller by director Li Wang. Famous for several [1]______, here he leaves his usual monsters behind. The [2]______ is Shanghai, 2150. The main character, Chuan, competes with his [3]______, Oona, to find a box that contains a secret that can save the planet. In the best [4]______, Oona chases Chuan through a city on a mechanical eagle. *Dream of Ice* is certain to become a summer [5]______. In its opening week, it made $220 million for the [6]______.

B Work with other students. What recent movies can you recommend?

G REPORTED SPEECH

2 A Put the first lines (1–3) and the last lines (4–6) from these classic movies into reported speech.

1 "(Please, Sir,) I want some more." (*Oliver*)
He said he …

2 "I believe in America." (*The Godfather*)
He said he …

3 "The voice you hear is not my speaking voice, but my mind's voice." (*The Piano*)
She said the voice we …

4 "I'm too old for this." (*Lethal Weapon*)
He said he …

5 "It's a strange world … " (*Blue Velvet*)
He said it …

6 "The Grand Hotel. Always the same. People come. People go … nothing ever happens." (*Grand Hotel*)
He said The Grand Hotel was always the same. People …

B Work with other students. Do you know anything about the six movies in Exercise 2A? Which have you heard of?

V SUFFIXES

3 A Complete the questions with the correct suffix.

1 What is the most danger____ thing you have ever done?
2 Have you been anywhere wonder____ recently? Where did you go?
3 When was the last time you had a family celebrat____? What was the reason?
4 Have you ever met someone fam____ ? Who?
5 Which would you prefer to be: a politic____ or a music____ ? Why?
6 Are you success____ in your work/studies? Why/Why not?

B Work in pairs and take turns. Ask and answer the questions.

G HYPOTHETICAL CONDITIONALS PRESENT/FUTURE

4 Complete the sentences with the correct form of the verb in parentheses.

1 If I ______ (not have to) work tonight, I ______ (take) you out.
2 She ______ (be) very upset if I ______ (lose) her scarf.
3 If you ______ (be able to) do any job in the world, what ______ you ______ (choose)?
4 They ______ (be) ideal partners if they ______ (not argue) so much.
5 You ______ (not say) that if you ______ (know) more about it.
6 If I ______ (live) on a desert island, I ______ (be) perfectly happy.

5 Work in pairs. Play the consequences game. Student A: read and complete the first phrase. Student B: add another sentence, starting with the last consequence.

A: If I lived in Italy, I would eat more pasta.
B: If I ate more pasta, I would get fat.

1 If I lived to be 200 years old, …
2 If I met a good-looking man/woman this evening, …
3 If I lived in a bigger house, …
4 If I had more time, …
5 If I had to get a new job, …
6 If I were a famous movie star, …

F REQUESTS AND OFFERS

6 A Underline the correct alternative to complete the requests and offers.

1 Would it be possible *to see/see/seeing* the exhibition?
2 Would you like *buy/me buy/me to buy* a ticket for you?
3 Would you be *able for/able to/able* arrange dinner?
4 Could you *recommend/to recommend/recommending* a bar?
5 Should *to call/I calling/I call you* a taxi?
6 I'd *like to visit/like visit/like for visit* the museum.

B You have $50 million and a personal assistant. What would you like? Think of three things or choose from the box.

go shopping alone at midnight
buy a private island
hold a peace conference
buy a painting fly into space
meet your hero
buy a famous building

C Work in pairs and take turns. Student A: act out the role of client. Student B: act out the role of personal assistant.

A: What can I do for you, sir?
B: I'd like to buy a private island.
A: Where exactly, sir?
B: In the Caribbean, I think.

IRREGULAR VERBS

Verb	Past simple	Past participle
be	was	been
beat	beat	beaten
become	became	become
begin	began	begun
bite	bit	bitten
blow	blew	blown
break	broke	broken
bring	brought	brought
build	built	built
buy	bought	bought
catch	caught	caught
choose	chose	chosen
come	came	come
cost	cost	cost
cut	cut	cut
deal	dealt	dealt
do	did	done
draw	drew	drawn
dream	dreamed/dreamt	dreamed/dreamt
drink	drank	drunk
drive	drove	driven
eat	ate	eaten
fall	fell	fallen
feel	felt	felt
fight	fought	fought
find	found	found
fly	flew	flown
forget	forgot	forgotten
forgive	forgave	forgiven
freeze	froze	frozen
get	got	got/gotten
give	gave	given
go	went	gone
grow	grew	grown
hang	hung	hung
have	had	had
hear	heard	heard
hide	hid	hidden
hit	hit	hit
hold	held	held
hurt	hurt	hurt
keep	kept	kept
know	knew	known

Verb	Past simple	Past participle
leave	left	left
lend	lent	lent
let	let	let
lie	lay	lain
lose	lost	lost
make	made	made
mean	meant	meant
meet	met	met
pay	paid	paid
put	put	put
read	read	read
ride	rode	ridden
ring	rang	rung
run	ran	run
say	said	said
see	saw	seen
sell	sold	sold
send	sent	sent
set	set	set
shake	shook	shaken
shine	shone	shone
show	showed	shown
shut	shut	shut
sing	sang	sung
sit	sat	sat
sleep	slept	slept
speak	spoke	spoken
spend	spent	spent
stand	stood	stood
steal	stole	stolen
swim	swam	swum
take	took	taken
teach	taught	taught
tear	tore	torn
tell	told	told
think	thought	thought
throw	threw	thrown
understand	understood	understood
wake	woke	woken
wear	wore	worn
win	won	won
write	wrote	written

GRAMMAR

1.1 Question Forms

Yes/No questions are questions that only require a *Yes* or *No* answer.
For questions in the present and past simple, put the auxiliary *do/does/did* before the subject.

A: Does he live here? B: Yes, he does.

For questions with *be*, put *be* before the subject.

A: Is he married? B: No, he isn't.

Wh- questions are questions that ask for more than a *Yes/No* answer. Use the same word order as *Yes/No* questions.

Question Word	Auxiliary *do/does/did*	Subject	Infinitive
Where	does	he	live?
When	do	you	see your parents?
Why	did	they	phone me?
Whom	do	you	live with?

Question Word	*be*	Subject	adj/noun/verb + *-ing*, etc.
Why	are	you	sad?
What	is	he	doing?

Use *who/whom* for people. ***Who** is your boss?*
***Whom** do you live with?*

Use *where* for places. ***Where** is the bathroom?*

Use *what* or *which* for things.

***What** music do you like?*
***Which** do you prefer, football or hockey?*

Use *when* for time. ***When** do you want to meet?*

Use *how often* for frequency.

***How often** do you go to English classes?*

Use *how long* for length of time/distance.

***How long** does the class last?*

Use *how much/many* for quantity.

***How much** does this cost?*
***How many** brothers do you have?*

Use *why* for reasons. ***Why** are you studying English?*

Use *what time* for a time. ***What time** do you start work?*

Note:
Which has a limited number of possible answers.

***Which** do you want, the red or the blue sweater?*

What has a large number of possible answers.

***What** music do you like?*

1.2 Past Simple

Past Simple Regular Verbs				
+		I/you/he/she/it/we/they	worked	in a restaurant.
–			didn't work	
?	Did		work	in a restaurant?

Past Simple Irregular Verbs				
+		I/you/he/she/it/we/they	went	out.
–			didn't go	
?	Did		go	out?

Use the past simple to talk about finished actions in the past.
In negatives and questions, use the auxiliary *did* + infinitive.
Do not use *did* in negatives and questions with the verb *be*.

I wasn't very happy. NOT *I ~~didn't be~~ happy.*

Spellings: Regular Past Simple Verbs		
Verbs Ending in:	**Rule**	**Example**
	+ *-ed*	start—started
-e	+ *-d*	live—lived
-y	*-y* + *-i* + *-ed*	marry—married
consonant-vowel-consonant	double the consonant + *-ed*	stop—stopped

Form the past simple with regular verbs by adding *-ed*.
Many common verbs have an irregular past simple form.
Look at the list on page 67.
Use the past simple to talk about finished actions in the past.

1.3 Making Conversation

Making Conversation	Response
This is my friend (name).	Hi (name). Pleased to meet you.
Would you like a drink?	I'd love a coffee, thank you.
Nice day, isn't it?	Yes, it's beautiful.
Where exactly do you come from?	I come from …, near …
So, do you work here?	No, I'm a student.
Did you have a good weekend?	Yes, it was OK. I didn't do much.
Did you watch the game last night?	Yes, it was terrible.
We lost 48–0.	Oh, no! I'm sorry to hear that.
I'll see you later.	See you soon.

PRACTICE

1.1

A Complete the questions. How many can you answer?

1 _____ states are there in the U.S.A.?
2 _____ was the first person to walk on the moon?
3 _____ is the largest island in the Mediterranean Sea?
4 _____ is H_2O?
5 _____ did the Berlin Wall come down?
6 _____ is Lake Wanaka?
7 _____ country is famous for samba?
8 _____ long is the River Nile?

B Match questions 1–8 in Exercise 1.1A with answers a)–h).

a) Brazil	e) 50
b) Neil Armstrong	f) water
c) November 9, 1989	g) 6,695 km
d) in New Zealand	h) Sicily

C Find and correct the mistakes. There is a mistake in each sentence.

1 How much this cost?
2 You have any brothers or sisters?
3 What time starts the movie?
4 How often do you playing football?
5 Who your new teacher is?
6 Do want you to come and have a pizza?
7 Why don't you liking grammar?
8 Where you go on vacation last year?

1.2

A Complete the story with the correct form of the verbs in the box. Use the past simple.

~~ask~~ (x2) email say get (x2) arrive see know fall decide

A single father-of-two [1] *asked* his American girlfriend to marry him only four minutes after he [2] _____ her for the first time.

Carl Dockings, 36, from Wales, met Danielle on the Internet.

"We [3] _____ along so well. We always [4] _____ what the other was thinking." He said they [5] _____ and talked in chat rooms. They [6] _____ in love even before exchanging pictures.

After ten months, Carl [7] _____ to fly 4,000 miles to meet Danielle in person. He [8] _____ the important question at Chicago's O'Hare Airport soon after he [9] _____.

The 26-year-old [10] _____ "yes," and the couple [11] _____ married four months later.

They now live in his home city with their daughter Isabel.

B Put the verbs in parentheses into the correct form of the past simple.

1 My grandfather _____ (teach) me how to paint.
2 Where _____ you _____ (grow up)?
3 We _____ (meet) in Ireland last year.
4 At first, we _____ (not get along) very well.
5 I _____ (leave) college and _____ (get) a job in an office.
6 I _____ (live) in the U.S.A., so we _____ (not see) each other for six months.
7 _____ you _____ (enjoy) the concert last night?
8 They _____ (not have) children.
9 My sister _____ (finish) her degree last year.
10 She _____ (study) Russian.

1.3

A Find and correct the mistakes. There is a mistake or missing word in each sentence.

1 This is ~~the~~ *my* friend, Sara.
2 Hi. Pleased to know you.
3 Do you like a drink?
4 Where exact do you come from?
5 Did you have good weekend?
6 I see you later.

B Put the words in the correct order to make sentences.

1 meet / to / you / pleased
2 coffee / would / I / a / love
3 do / what / so / you / do?
4 I / you / see / 'll / later
5 come / where / do / from / exactly / you?
6 soon / see / you

GRAMMAR

2.1 Present Simple and Continuous

	Present Simple	Present Continuous
+	I work at home. He watches TV.	I'm working at home. He's watching TV.
–	She doesn't study now. We don't text in class.	She isn't studying now. We're not texting in class.
?	Does he live with you? Where do the workers have lunch?	Is he living with you? Where are the workers having lunch?

Use the present simple to describe something that is always or generally true.
It is common to use these words with the present simple: *sometimes, usually, every day, often.*

I usually get up at 7 a.m.

Use the present continuous to talk about:

- an activity happening right now, at the time of speaking.
- a temporary activity happening around now (maybe at the moment, but maybe not).

Spelling with *-ing* Forms		
Verbs Ending in:	**Rule**	**Example**
-e	~~-e~~ + -ing	take—taking
vowel + consonant	double the consonant + -ing	run—running
-ie	~~-ie~~ + -y + -ing	die—dying
-y	+ -ing	study—studying

Form the present continuous with the verb *be* + the *-ing* form of the verb.
It is common to use these words with the present continuous: *now, at the moment, currently, this month.*

I'm living with my parents at the moment.

Some verbs are not usually used with continuous tenses: *be, know, like, love, understand, want,* etc. These are called "state verbs."

I want to go to bed now. NOT
I ~~am wanting~~ to go to bed now.

2.2 Adverbs of Frequency

Use adverbs of frequency to say how frequently you do something. Some of the most common are: *never, rarely, occasionally, sometimes, often, usually, always.*
There are several adverbial phrases of frequency, e.g., *hardly ever, once in a while, every day/month/year.*
With *be*, put the adverb **after** the verb.

*I **am always** here.*
*They **were usually** early.*

We usually put the adverb **before** other verbs.

*I **sometimes spoke** to him.*
*We **hardly ever ate** there.*

With auxiliary or modal verbs, we usually put the adverb **after** the auxiliary or modal.

She doesn't stay here. → *She doesn't **usually** stay here.*
We haven't visited them. → *We have **never** visited them.*
I can help. → *I can **always** help.*

Adverbs of frequency can also go at the beginning, middle or end of a sentence.

***Occasionally**, I go dancing.*
*I **occasionally** go dancing.*
*I go dancing **occasionally**.*

Always and *never* do not normally go at the beginning or end of sentences.
Once in a while and *every day/month/year* usually go at the beginning or end of sentences.
There are other phrases to show how frequently something happens:

every day = one time per day
I have a shower every day.
once a week = one time per week
She writes to me once a week.
twice a week = two times per week
They go shopping twice a week.

2.3 Expressing Likes/Dislikes

There are a number of verbs and other phrases to show likes and dislikes. After these verbs and phrases, we usually use the *-ing* form.

Positive
I **like** sing**ing**/meat.
I **absolutely love** swimm**ing**/tennis.
I'**m interested in** runn**ing**/beach vacations.

Note: We can also use *like* + infinitive.
Like + infinitive means "do as a habit" or "choose to do."

*I **like** to go to bed early.*

Negative
I **can't stand** smok**ing**/computers.
I **don't like** work**ing**/rock music.
I **hate** watch**ing** TV/films.
I **don't really like** work**ing**/fruit.

Note: *I don't mind* means "It's OK for me. I don't like it or dislike it."

*I **don't mind** sleeping on the floor.*

PRACTICE

2.1

A Complete the conversations with the correct form of the verbs in the box. Use the present simple or present continuous.

eat	be	wait	know	work	wear	play

1 **A:** It takes him ten minutes to get to work.
B: I know. His house ___________ far from the office.

2 **A:** Isn't your son an actor?
B: Yes, but at the moment he ___________ in a restaurant.

3 **A:** What is all that noise? I'm trying to work!
B: I ___________ with the children.

4 **A:** What ______ you ______ about the new software program?
B: The new software program? Absolutely nothing.

5 **A:** Why ______ you ______ that jacket in the office? It's really warm!
B: Because I'm cold!

6 **A:** Would you like some beef?
B: No, thanks. I ___________ meat. I'm a vegetarian.

7 **A:** Why are you standing there?
B: I ___________ for a taxi.

B Find and correct the mistakes. There is a mistake in five of the sentences.

1 John works in sales, and he is going to the office every day at 8 a.m.
2 The new employee says she's eighteen, but I'm not believing it.
3 At the moment, I'm doing a task for my boss.
4 Don't buy a bottle of wine for her. She isn't drinking alcohol.
5 I can't speak Chinese, but my friend teaches me.
6 Excuse me, is anybody sitting here?
7 I'm taking art classes this term.
8 Hey! What do you do with that knife?

2.2

A Put the words in the correct order to make sentences.

1 I / dinner / on / weekend / cook / sometimes / the
I sometimes cook dinner on the weekend.
2 once / I / while / go / in / swimming / a
3 I / money / waste / never / my
4 Najim / often / tennis / play / doesn't
5 Akiko and Toshi / evening / stay / usually / the / home / in
6 why / late / are / always / you?
7 I / work / Fridays / rarely / late / on
8 Mary / ever / hardly / deals / with / customers
9 occasionally / a / team / work / I / on

B Underline the correct alternative.

1 *Always/Usually/Hardly ever* our IT consultant deals with these problems; it's his job.
2 I get up early *never/rarely/every day* and go to work at 6 a.m.
3 You *sometimes/every week/once in a while* need to risk your life in this job.
4 We *often/never/rarely* see each other—maybe once a year.
5 We *occasionally/always/rarely* work under pressure; we never have a chance to relax.
6 *Often/Hardly ever/Once in a while* I speak to my boss—maybe once a month.
7 We have a summer party *every year/always/never*.
8 I deal with customers *rarely/often/occasionally*, but only if my boss is out.

2.3

A Complete the sentences with one word.

1 I like ______ to music while I study. It helps me concentrate.
2 I ______ mind getting up early for my job. It's no problem for me.
3 Stefania is interested ______ traveling, so she's studying tourism.
4 Mick ______ like talking to customers. He says it's boring.
5 Lorenzo absolutely ______ dancing. He's really good at samba.
6 I can't ______ working on the weekend.

GRAMMAR

3.1 Present Continuous/*be going to* for Future

Present Continuous					
+		I	'm	spending	the day with my grandmother on Saturday.
–		We	're not	playing	football this evening.
?	What	are	you	doing	on the weekend?

It is common to use the present continuous to talk about things happening now or temporary situations. It is also possible to use the present continuous to talk about definite future plans and arrangements.
It is common to use an expression of future time with the present continuous, e.g., *this weekend, tomorrow morning, later.*

be going to					
+		I	'm going to	take	some time off work.
–		They	're not going to	win.	
?	Is	it	going to	rain?	

Use *be going to* + infinitive to talk about future plans and predictions.
Usually, we can use both the present continuous and *be going to* to talk about plans.

*I'm **meeting** my girlfriend later.*
*I'm **going to meet** my girlfriend later.*

But there is a small difference:
For plans that involve other people and have a fixed time and place, the present continuous is more common.
*We're **having** a barbecue on Saturday.* (We have invited people, bought food and drinks, etc.)
For plans that do not involve other people, *be going to* is more common.

*I'm **going to stay in** and read a book.*

When *be going to* is followed by the verb *go*, it is possible to omit *go to*.

*I'm **going to** (go to) the movies.*

3.2 Questions without Auxiliaries

Subject	Verb		Answer
Who	sent	the present?	David.
What	causes	this problem?	The water pipes.
Whose guitar	cost	$300?	Mine.
Which soccer players	played	for that team?	Beckham and Cole.

When *who*, *what*, *which* or *whose* is the **subject** of the sentence, do not use an auxiliary verb (*do*, *did*, etc.). The verb is in the third person.

***Who** ate all the pies? **Joe** ate all the pies.*
***Which** students forgot their homework? **Ben and Meg** forgot their homework.*

When *who, what, which* or *whose* is the object of the sentence, use an auxiliary verb as usual.

*What **do** you do? **I** work in a bank.*
*Whose book **did** you use? **I** used Tom's book.*

3.3 Making a Phone Call

Caller	
Start the Call	Hello, this is Andy. Hello, it's Wendy. (NOT ~~I am Wendy.~~)
Ask to Speak to Someone	Can I speak to …?
When the Person You Want Isn't There	Can I leave a message?
Finish the Call	See you soon. Goodbye.

Receiver	
Start the Call	Hello. Paul speaking.*
Find Out Who Is Speaking	Who's calling (please)?
When the Person the Caller Wants Isn't There	I'm afraid she's not here at the moment. Can I take a message? I'll ask her to call you back.
Finish the Call	Thanks for calling.

*We say this when we answer the phone at work.

PRACTICE

3.1

A Match prompts 1–4 with pictures A–D.

1 play / football
2 stay home / watch TV
3 go / to the movies
4 have / meeting

B Look at the pictures and make sentences with the prompts. Use the present continuous.

Next Week

This Evening

Saturday

Next Weekend

C Put the verbs in parentheses into the correct form of the present continuous or *be going to*.

A: What [1]______ you ______ (do) tonight?
B: I [2]____________ (go) John's house party.
A: Really? We [3]____________ (be) there, too.
B: Great! [4]______ you ______ (take) any food or drinks?
A: Yes, we [5]____________ (make) some food, but we [6]____________ (not take) drinks.
B: What type of music [7]______ he ______ (have)?
A: He's got a DJ, and he [8]____________ (play) dance music.
B: It sounds great. How [9]______ you ______ (get) there?
A: We [10]____________ (drive). Do you want a ride?

3.2

A Find and correct the mistakes. There is a mistake in five of the questions.

1 Do you like reading?
2 Who does read the most in your family?
3 Who be your favorite writer?
4 Which books have become famous recently?
5 What did be your favorite book when you were a child?
6 Who did write it?
7 How often you read on the Internet?
8 Where and when do you like to read?

B Make questions with the prompts. Use the past simple. One question needs an auxiliary verb.

1 What color / be / the Beatles' / submarine?
2 Who / write / "Stairway to Heaven"
3 Whose / home / be / Graceland?
4 Which country / Diego Rivera / come from?
5 Who / paint / the *Mona Lisa*?
6 Which painter / invent / Cubism?

3.3

A Put the words in the correct order to make a phone conversation.

A: speaking / David
B: it's / Johnson / hello / Mark
A: can / Mr. / help / how / I / you / Johnson?
B: to / like / Sara / please / I'd / to / speak / Torres
A: the / afraid / here / I'm / she's / moment / not / at
B: a / leave / I / can / message?
A: course / of / yes
B: you / me / her / can / ask / call / to / back?
A: problem / no
B: number / 276-7635 / is / my
A: repeat / you / that / can / please?
B: 276-7635
A: calling / thanks / OK / for
B: Bye

GRAMMAR

4.1 Present Perfect + *ever/never*

Present Perfect: Positive and Negative				
+	I/You/We/They	have ('ve)	finished	the project.
	He/She/It	has ('s)		
–	I/You/We/They	haven't/(have never)	visited	Mexico.
	He/She/It	hasn't/(has never)		

Present Perfect: Questions				Short Answers		
Have	I/you/ we/they	(ever) played	chess?	Yes,	I/you/ we/they	have.
				No,		haven't.
Has	he/she/it			Yes,	he/she/it	has.
				No,		hasn't.

***Note:** The present perfect is not that common in American English, which tends to use the simple past.

The past participle is verb + *-ed* for regular verbs. For a list of irregular verbs, see page 67.

Use the present perfect to talk about past experiences without saying an exact time.

I've been to Warsaw.

When we want to say an exact time, we use the past simple.

*I **went** to Warsaw in 2007.*

Use *ever* with the present perfect to mean "during your life until now." *Never* is the negative of *ever.*

*Have you **ever** visited Madrid?*
*She's **never** been to a nightclub.*

Spoken grammar 1: When we are asked a *Have you ever ...?* question, we often reply: *No, never* instead of *No, I haven't.*

A: Have you ever been to the Maldives?
B: No, never.

Spoken grammar 2: When we want to repeat the same *Have you ever ...?* question, we usually say *Have you?*

A: Have you ever been to Zurich?
B: No, have you?

4.2 *Can, Have to, Must*

Use modal verbs *can/can't, have to/don't have to, must/mustn't* to talk about present obligation.
Use *can* to talk about something that is possible/allowed.

*You **can** use dictionaries during the exam.*

Use *can't* to talk about something that is not possible/allowed.

*You **can't** park here.*

Use *must/must not/have to* to talk about rules or things that are necessary.

*We **have to** study for our exam.*
*You **must** return the books to the library before Friday.*
*You **must not** chew gum in the classroom.*

Use *don't have to* to talk about something that is not necessary (but it is possible/allowed).

We don't have to be there until eight o'clock. (But we can get there earlier if we want to.)

Use *he/she has to* in the positive and *he/she doesn't have to* in the negative.

*She **has to** pay for the exam.*
*He **doesn't have to** do any extra work.*

***Note:** In American English, *must* is not used that often to express obligation or necessity. It is more often used to express a logical conclusion, e.g., *He's never late; something must have happened., The computer won't turn on; the power must be out.* The contraction mustn't is rarely used.

4.3 Giving/Responding to Advice

Phrases for Giving Advice	Example
I think you should ...	I think you should study more.
You should ...	You should hear her play the trumpet.
You shouldn't ...	You shouldn't be late all the time.
Why don't you ...?	Why don't you finish your homework later?
I (don't) think it's a good idea to ...	I think it's a good idea to take some lessons.
Find/Write ...	Find a cheap hotel on the internet.

Phrases for Responding to Advice
That's a good idea.
I suppose so.
You're right.
I'm not sure that's a good idea.

PRACTICE

4.1

A Find and correct the mistakes. There is one mistake in each sentence.

1 Have you ever saw the movie *Titanic*?
2 Two days ago, she's been to a museum.
3 Unfortunately, we have ever won the lottery.
4 Has ever she visited you?
5 I haven't meet your brother.
6 In 2011, they've traveled to Geneva.
7 Have you seen that TV program last Wednesday?
8 He never has played a musical instrument.

B Complete the conversations with the correct form of the verbs in the box. Use the past simple or present perfect.

make	eat	visit	hear	do	work

Conversation 1
A: ___________ (ever) business in China?
B: Yes, I have. I did business there in 2014.

Conversation 2
A: Peter Duvall is a diplomat, isn't he?
B: Yes, he ___________ all over the world.

Conversation 3
A: She loves traveling doesn't she?
B: Yes, she ___________ fifteen countries last year.

Conversation 4
A: ___________ many speeches?
B: No, he hasn't. That's why I'm worried.

Conversation 5
A: Is Coldplay's new CD good?
B: I don't know. I ___________ it.

Conversation 6
A: Have you ever tried sushi?
B: Yes, we ___________ some yesterday!

4.2

A Underline the correct alternative.

1 We *have to/has to* get up early to catch the train.
2 Children *can't/can* stay with their parents if they are very quiet.
3 I'm afraid I *can't/must* leave work early. It's not allowed.
4 They *have to/don't have to* put a notice on the door so you know which room to go to.
5 You *can/don't have to* park your car here. It's free on Saturdays.
6 You *must not/have to* smoke in the office. It's against the law.
7 You *can't/have to* leave your coat on the floor. Hang it up!
8 We *must/don't have to* worry about transportation. A taxi will take us to the airport.

B Complete the sentences with *can/can't, have to/ don't have to* or *must/mustn't.*

1 You ___________ leave the room when you have finished the test. (it's allowed)
2 We ___________ reserve a table. That restaurant is never busy on Mondays. (it's not necessary)
3 You ___________ log in using your PIN number. (it's necessary)
4 You ___________ eat as much as you like. (it's allowed)
5 Sadie ___________ bring extra clothes. I have lots here. (it's not necessary)
6 You ___________ wear jeans in the nightclub. (it's not allowed)
7 Harry ___________ work on his pronunciation. (it's necessary)
8 You ___________ do that. It's illegal! (it's not allowed)

4.3

A Put the words in the correct order to make sentences.

a) a / idea / that's / good
b) think / I / out / after / lesson / go / should / the / we
c) not / I'm / sure / I / much money / don't have / because
d) for / we / a / out / meal / why / go / don't ?
e) OK / to / Butler's Café / let's / coffee / a / for / go

B Put sentences a)–e) in the correct order to make a conversation.

GRAMMAR

5.1 Past Simple and Past Continuous

	Past Simple	Past Continuous
+	I watched a movie yesterday.	I was watching a movie yesterday.
–	He didn't play here.	He wasn't playing here.
?	Did you talk to John?	Were you talking to John?

Use the past simple to talk about completed actions.

*I **ate** a salad last night.*

Use the past continuous to talk about actions in progress at a particular time.

*At 8 a.m. yesterday, I **was traveling** to work.*

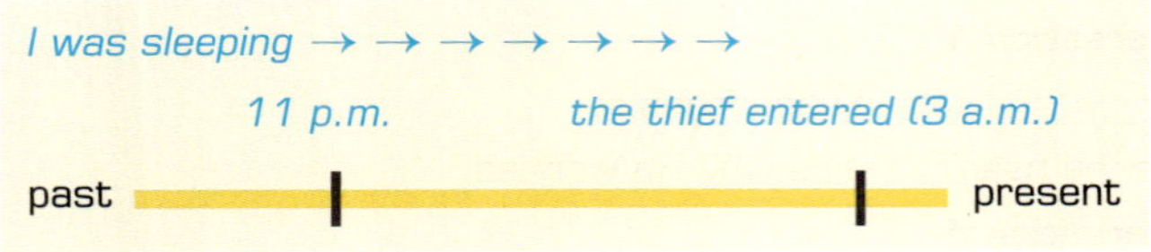

It is common to use the past simple and the past continuous together to tell stories. The past continuous describes an action that starts first, but is interrupted by a second action. Use the past simple for the second (usually short) action.

*What **were** you **doing** when the bus **crashed**?*
*I **was sleeping** when the thief **entered** the house.*

It is common to use *when* or *while* to link the two actions. Use *while* before the continuous action.

***While** I was sleeping, it started to rain.*

Use *when* before the continuous action or the short action.

***When** we **were talking**, the bus appeared.*
*We **were talking** when the bus **appeared**.*

Do NOT use *while* before the short action.

I was sleeping ~~while~~ it started to rain.

5.2 Verb Patterns

Sometimes we use two verbs together.

*I **love playing** football.*

After some verbs, put the second verb in the infinitive with *to*.

*She decided **to go** to Mexico.*
*We need **to make** a phone call.*

After some verbs, use the *-ing* form.

*I enjoy runn**ing**.*
*They avoided travel**ing** by bus.*

Some Common Verb Patterns	
Verb + *-ing*	**Verb + Infinitive with *to***
enjoy	choose
finish	hope
avoid	expect
imagine	would like
stop	decide
like	seem
don't mind	want
spend (time)	need
	help
	promise

Many verbs that show preference (things that we like or don't like) are followed by *-ing*, e.g., *like, enjoy, don't mind.*

After some verbs, it is possible to use the *-ing* form OR the infinitive with *to*, e.g., *love, hate.*

*I love **dancing**. I love **to dance**.*
*I hate **getting up** early. I hate **to get up** early.*

There is little change in meaning.

5.3 Asking for/Giving Directions

go left

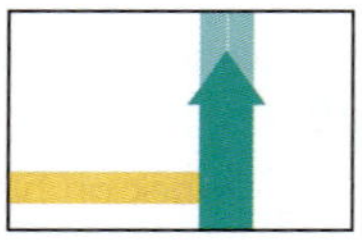
go past the turn

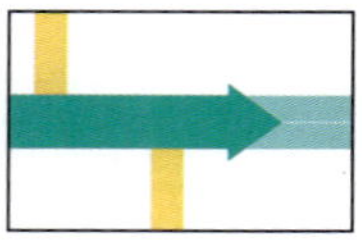
go along the main road

take the first right

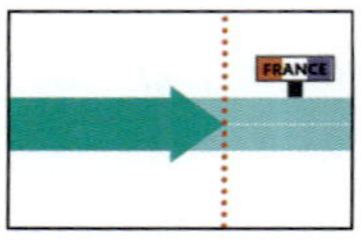
keep going until you reach ...

at the corner

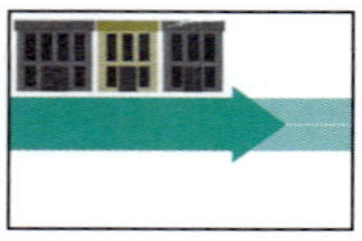
go through downtown

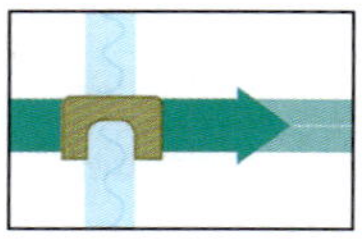
cross a bridge

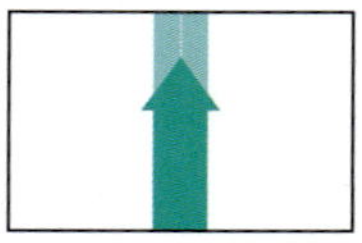
go straight ahead

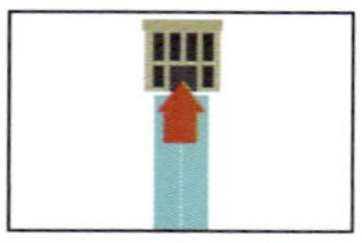
in front of you

Useful Questions	Directions	Saying You Understand
Can we walk? Excuse me, can you help me? Is this the right way? Can you show me on the map? Is it far?	It takes about twenty minutes. Keep going ... You'll see ... You can't miss it.	OK, so I need to ... Right.

PRACTICE

5.1

A Complete the story with the correct form of the verbs in parentheses. Use the past simple or past continuous.

Alvin Straight, a 73-year-old, [1]__________ (live) quietly on his farm in Iowa, when he heard the news that his brother, Lyle, was seriously ill. After ten years with no contact between the brothers, Alvin [2]__________ (decide) to visit Lyle. Alvin couldn't drive, so he [3]__________ (buy) a lawnmower, which moved at five miles per hour, and [4]__________ (begin) the 250-mile journey.

While he [5]__________ (travel), he met many people, including a priest and a teenage girl who was running away from her family. He helped them all simply by talking about life. Some of them also [6]__________ (help) him. For example, one day when he [7]__________ (drive) the lawnmower, it broke down. While two mechanics [8]__________ (fix) it, he met a friendly couple and [9]__________ (stay) with them.

The journey took him six weeks. And [10]______ the story ______ (end) happily? See the 1999 movie, *The Straight Story*, to find out!

B Make sentences with the prompts and the correct form of the verbs in the box. Use the past simple or past continuous.

pass	know	like	play	dance	swim	travel	have

1 He / tennis when he hurt his leg.
2 Sarah / the job because it was boring.
3 While they / they met lots of other tourists.
4 How / you / my name?
5 Whom / you / with in that nightclub when I saw you?
6 I / in the ocean when I saw the shark.
7 I / my exam?
8 The thief broke in while Jack / breakfast.

5.2

A Complete the sentences with the correct form of the verbs in the box.

live	read	drink	swim	visit	have	play	finish

1 They want ______ the monuments tomorrow morning.
2 I can't imagine ______ in that apartment—it's so small!
3 I don't like ______ water from a bottle.
4 They decided ______ football this morning.
5 Would you like ______ dinner in this restaurant?
6 Do you enjoy ______ in the ocean?
7 I hope ______ my degree next year.
8 I love ______ books about adventures.

B Find and correct the mistakes. There are eight mistakes in the advertisement.

MAD DOG TOURS

*** Are modern vacations too boring for you?**

*** Would you like doing something more exciting?**

Mad Dog Tours is perfect for people who hate spend time asleep on a beach. If you enjoy to travel to strange places, if you don't mind to stay in cheap hotels and want knowing how the local people really live, we promise helping you. Cheap vacations are our specialty. If you choose reserving your vacation with *Mad Dog Tours*, you can expect living your dreams!

5.3

A Match 1–10 with a)–j) to make sentences or questions.

1 Excuse me, can	a) about an hour.
2 Is this the	b) need to go left here.
3 Is	c) restaurant on your right.
4 Can you show	d) it far?
5 It takes	e) right way?
6 You can't	f) going.
7 Can we	g) me on the map?
8 So I	h) you help me?
9 You'll see the	i) walk?
10 Keep	j) miss it.

B Underline the correct alternative to complete the conversations.

Conversation 1

A: Excuse me, how do I get to the swimming pool?

B: You need to go [1]*along/at/with* the main road. Keep going until you [2]*go/have/reach* the town hall. Then [3]*go/make/be* left, and it's [4]*the/in/to* front of you.

Conversation 2

A: Excuse me, is this the right way to the Bach Concert Hall?

B: No, you need to turn around, then [5]*do/cross/go* the bridge. After that, you [6]*have/are/take* the first right and go [7]*at/with/through* downtown. The concert hall is at the [8]*first/corner/cross* of Ducane Road and Bright Street.

GRAMMAR

6.1 Present Perfect + *For/Since*

Use the present perfect to talk about things that started in the past and are still true now.

*We've **been married** for fourteen years.*
(We got married fourteen years ago, and we are still married now.)
Use *since* to talk about the specific time something started, e.g., *1992, last week, Monday, I was a child.*

*We've **known** each other **since** we were children.*

(We are friends now.)

*He **has played** football **since** 2002.*

Use *for* to talk about a period (length) of time, e.g., *ten years, two months, a long time, an hour, a few weeks.*

*I **haven't seen** him **for** a few weeks.*
*I've **lived** in Barcelona **for** twenty-five years.*

To ask about the length of time, use *How long have you …?*

***How long have you worked** for Dell?*

Use the past simple, not the present perfect, for things that happened at a specific time in the past.

*I **moved** to Spain in 2001.* NOT
I ~~have~~ moved to Spain in 2001.

6.2 *May, Might, Will*

Use *may/might* + infinitive to talk about probable situations.
We also use *may/might* + infinitive to talk about future possibilities.

*I **might go** to the party.*
*They **might** not **arrive** today.*
*We **may have** some problems.*
*She **may** not **like** the dress.*

Do not use contractions with *might not* and *may not*.
The question form with *might* is rare.
The question form with *may* is used for asking permission. It is a very polite form.

***May** I **sit** here?*
***May** I **open** the window?*

Use *will* + infinitive to talk about a future prediction. The negative of *will* is *won't* (or *will not*).

*I **will be** home at 9 p.m. tonight.*
*She **won't come** here tomorrow.*
***Will** they **win** the game?*

In spoken English, use the contracted form of *will ('ll)* in positive sentences. Do not use it in questions.

I'll be home at 9 p.m. tonight.

It is common to use *think/don't think* + *will*.

*I **think** she'll get the job.*
*I **don't think** I'll go to college next year.*

6.3 Seeing the Doctor

Doctor
What's the matter/problem?
How long have you had this problem?
Where does it hurt?
Can I have a look (at …)?
It's nothing to worry about.
I'll give you some pills/antibiotics/medicine.

Patient
I feel sick/terrible.
I can't sleep.
I'm worried about …
It hurts when I walk/talk.
It's very painful.

PRACTICE

6.1

A Underline the correct alternative.

1 I *didn't do/haven't done* much work *for/since* my boss left.
2 I *didn't go/haven't been* to China *for/since* 2010.
3 She *has been/was* a doctor *for/since* more than forty years. She retired in 2012.
4 Hi, Angela. How are you? I *haven't seen/didn't see* you *for/since* ages.
5 I *left/have left* college in 2000. I've worked in this company *for/since* about fifteen years.
6 I *didn't see/haven't seen* Sam yesterday. In fact, I *didn't see/haven't seen* him *for/since* Monday.
7 He's really tired. He hasn't stopped working *for/since* 5:30 a.m.
8 She *hasn't driven/didn't drive* a car *for/since* she had the accident.

B Complete the sentences with *for* or *since*. Put the verbs in parentheses into the correct form of the present perfect or past simple.

1 I've lived in this city ______ 2011. I ______ (come) here with my family.
2 I ______ (buy) this house in 2005, so I ______ (live) here ______ more than ten years.
3 I ______ (know) Marissa ______ a long time. We ______(meet) in 1998.
4 They ______ (move) to Australia last December, so they ______ (be) there ______ nearly a year.
5 We ______ (not be) back to Russia ______ 1990.
6 He ______ (not see) his father ______ he left home.
7 I've been learning English ______ I ______ (start) school.
8 She ______ (have) that car ______ ages!

6.2

A Match statements 1–6 with sentences a)–f).

1 I'm hungry because I missed breakfast.
2 You eat too much junk food.
3 I'm just going out to get a snack.
4 The movie was really good.
5 She looks a bit stressed.
6 We want to visit the museum this afternoon.

a) I won't be long.
b) I think she'll need a vacation soon.
c) We may not have time.
d) You might get fat.
e) I may have an early lunch.
f) I think my father might enjoy it.

B Find and correct the mistakes. There is a mistake in each sentence.

1 I don't will know my exam results until August.
2 Will you to go to college next year?
3 Anna is very busy, so she may not comes tonight.
4 The traffic is heavy, so they may to be late.
5 Edson mights be the best player we have ever seen.
6 I might go not to the exercise class today.
7 We'll to be back at 6 p.m.

6.3

A Complete the conversation with phrases from the boxes on page 138.

Doctor: Good morning. I'm Dr Gordon. [1]______ ______ ______?
Patient: [2]______ ______ ______. I have a sore throat and a cough.
Doctor: [3]______ ______ ______ ______ ______ ______ ______?
Patient: About a week.
Doctor: Do you have a fever?
Patient: Yes, I think so.
Doctor: [4]______ ______ ______ ______ ______ at your throat?
Patient: Yes. It's [5]______ ______. [6]______ ______ when I talk.
Doctor: Right. [7]______ ______ ______ some medicine. Take this for one week, and, if you don't feel better, come back to see me again.
Patient: Thank you.

GRAMMAR

7.1 *Used To*

		Subject	*Used To*	Infinitive	
+		I, you, he/she/it, we, they	used to	go	to the movies every Saturday.
–			didn't use to never used to	go	on vacation.
?	Did	you	use to	work	hard?

Note: Notice the spelling of *use to* in the negative and question form.

*We **didn't use to** live in a big house.* NOT
We didn't ~~used to~~ live …
***Did** you **use to** play a lot of football?* NOT
Did you ~~used to~~ play …?

Use *used to* to talk about a past habit or situation that is not the same now.

*We **used to** live in Rhode Island. (But now we live in Warsaw.)*
*I **used to** play a lot of tennis. (But I don't play any more.)*

It is possible to use the past simple instead of *used to.*

*I **used to go** out a lot. = I **went** out a lot.*

It is not possible to use *used to* to talk about something that happened just once or at a specific time. For this, use the past simple.

We moved in 2002. NOT *We ~~used to~~ move in 2002.*

It is not possible to use *used to* to talk about the present.

I usually eat at home. NOT *I ~~used to~~ eat at home.*

The negative of *used to* is *didn't use to*. In spoken English, *never used to* is more common.

*They **never used to** worry about money.*
*We **never used to** eat chocolate.*

7.2 Purpose, Cause and Result

Use the infinitive with *to* to talk about the reason or purpose for an action.

*I went to the store **to buy** some milk.*

Note: It is not possible to say *~~for to buy~~* some milk.
It is also possible to use *in order (not)* + infinitive with *to*.

*He came to class **in order** to learn English.*
*They came back early **in order not** to miss the party.*

It is also possible to use *so that* + subject + verb.

*I'll cook **so that** you can relax.*

Use *because* + subject + verb to talk about a cause.

*I left work **because** I hated the job.*
***Because** we don't eat meat, we buy a lot of fish.*

Use *so* + subject + verb to talk about the result of an action.

*It rained, **so** we went inside.*
*I forgot my wallet, **so** I didn't have any money.*

7.3 Finding Out Information

Getting Attention	Asking for Information	Thanking Someone
Excuse me, … Could you help me? Can you tell me …?	Where can I get/find/buy …? When can I use/start …? What time is the library open? What time do the classes start? Can I …? Do I have to …? Is it free/open/near? I need to find out about/speak to …	Thank you so much. That's very kind.

PRACTICE

7.1

A Complete the sentences with *used to/didn't use to* and the words in parentheses.

1 I ___________ (study) hard when I was at school, so I always passed my exams.
2 He ___________ (smoke) before he got ill, but he had to give up.
3 We ___________ (never/argue), but now we argue all the time.
4 They ___________ (live) in the city, but now they have moved to the ocean.
5 I ___________ (not/like) eating mushrooms, but now I love them!
6 ___________ you ___________ (enjoy) working in an office?
7 She ___________ (go out) with Steve, but now she has met someone else.
8 I ___________ (do) a lot of cooking, but now I don't have time.

B Look at the pictures. How have things changed? Complete the sentences.

1 He ___________ have long hair. Now it's short.
2 He ___________ drive a car. He rode a motorcycle when he was younger.
3 He ___________ wear a leather jacket. Now he wears a suit.

4 He ___________ play a lot of sports.
5 He ___________ win competitions.
6 He ___________ be fat.

7 He ___________ work as an actor. Now he's a politician.
8 He ___________ not ___________ be interested in politics.

7.2

A Complete the sentences with *so*, *to* or *because*.

1 She took the job ______ make some money.
2 The company became successful ______ it had amazing sales reps.
3 I became a doctor ______ cure people of their illnesses.
4 They treated her badly, ______ she left the company.
5 Put the key in your pocket, ______ you don't lose it.
6 You need to work hard ______ pass your final exams.
7 He spent twenty years in prison ______ he killed a man.
8 I have been at this school for ten years, ______ I know all the teachers.

B There are eight words missing from the text. Complete the text with *so*, *to* or *because*.

I usually get a newspaper I want to know what's on TV, but today I read a strange story. An Englishman was feeling terrible he was under pressure at work, he decided to disappear. He went to a beach go swimming (he said). Then he left his clothes there that someone could find them. He also left his wallet with a photo and ID the police knew who it was. The police went to his home speak to him, but he wasn't there. He was in Australia and had a different name! Three years later, he was caught when his cousin, who was in Australia attend a conference, recognized him. Where were they? On a beach!

7.3

A Find and correct the mistakes. There is an extra word in each line.

Conversation 1

A: Excuse me. Can you tell me where to can find a post office?

B: Yes, there's one just behind of you!

Conversation 2

A: I need to be find out about my housing.

B: There's a student services office on downstairs.

Conversation 3

A: Breakfast is in the restaurant from on 7 o'clock.

B: Sorry? Did you to say 7 o'clock?

Conversation 4

A: Do you is know where the main office is?

B: Yes, I'll show it you.

A: That's you very kind.

Conversation 5

A: Is it a free to park my car here?

B: No, it's you have to pay.

GRAMMAR

8.1 Relative Clauses

Use relative clauses to talk about what a person, place, or thing is (or does).

*This is the machine **that we used to make the copies**.*
*He's the man **who helped us**.*

Also use relative clauses to explain which one we are talking about.

*She's the girl **who has green eyes**.*
*That's the town **where I was born**.*

Use *who* for a person.

*He's the doctor **who** looked after your grandmother.*

Use *where* for a place.

*This is the city **where** she grew up.*

We use *that* when we are defining a place or thing.

*Paris is the city **that** I'd like to visit the most.*
*This is the knife **that** the killer used.*

It is quite common to leave out *that*.
Paris is the city I'd like to visit the most.

Use *which* for a place or thing when you add non-defining information.

*Paris, **which** is on the Seine, is a beautiful city.*
*This knife, **which** my aunt gave me, is very sharp.*

Using *that* instead of *who* is becoming more common.

*She's the girl **that** lives next door.*

When we define something by using a relative clause, we use *the*, not *a/an*.

*It's **a** car. We used it on the weekend.*
*It's **the** car **that** we used on the weekend.*

8.2 *Too Much/Many, Enough, Very*

Word	Use It Before	Meaning	Example
too	adjectives/adverbs	more than is necessary/right	I'm **too tired** to study.
too much	uncountable nouns		There's **too much water**.
too many	countable nouns		There are **too many people** here.
enough	nouns	the correct amount	Is there **enough gas** for the trip?
not enough	nouns	less than is necessary/right	There **aren't enough chairs**.
very	adjectives/adverbs	emphasis (can be good or bad)	She's **very nice**. He's **very ugly**.

Too is always used to say that something is negative (more than is necessary/right).

*These trousers are **too** small.* (negative)

Much is used with uncountable nouns, e.g., *rice, water, money, news*. These are called uncountable nouns because we cannot say ~~*one rice*~~ or ~~*two rice*~~.
Many is used with countable nouns, e.g., *days, people, dollars, computers*. These are called countable nouns because it is possible to say *one day, two days*, etc.
It is possible to use adjective + *enough* to say something is OK.

*The room is **big enough**.*
It is possible to use *enough* before a noun.

*Do we have **enough chairs**?*

Use *very* + adjective with positive or negative ideas.

*She's **very nice**.* (positive)
*This hat is **very expensive**.* (negative)

Spoken grammar: We sometimes use *enough* as a noun.

*That's **enough**. You're talking too much, children.*

It is common to end a sentence with *enough* when the listener already knows what we are talking about.

***A:** What about drinks?*
***B:** We have **enough**.*

8.3 Buying Things

Customer	Assistant
Excuse me. I'm just looking. Do you sell ...? Do you have one of these in red/blue/a larger size? Can I try it/this on? Where's the fitting room? It fits./It doesn't fit.	Can I help (you)? Are you looking for anything in particular? Who's next, please? Are you paying in cash or by credit card? Can you just sign here, please? Can you enter your PIN, please?

PRACTICE

8.1

A Rewrite the two sentences as one sentence. Use the prompts and relative clauses.

1 Laguna is a town. I spent my vacations there.
Laguna is the town *where I spent my vacations*.

2 Did you get the present? I sent it to you last week.
Did you get the present ______________________?

3 Burnham Place is a restaurant. You can watch the chefs make your food there.
Burnham Place is the ______________________.

4 Geekstore is a store. It sells cheap iPods and phones.
Geekstore ______________________.

5 Nichola Leeson is an accountant. She helped me complete my tax form.
Nichola Leeson is the ______________________.

6 Corleone is a town. I learned how to do business there.
Corleone is the town ______________________.

7 A man invested the money. He was a criminal.
The man ______________________.

B Match the endings in the box to 1–6 and write relative clauses. You need to change/cut some words.

~~you study there~~
she lends me
it sells insurance
he borrows $1,000,000 to buy a horse
she was working as a chef
we went on our honeymoon

1 A school is a place *where you study*.
2 The movie is about a man
3 I work for a company
4 I always give back the money
5 What happened to that girl
6 The Bahamas is the place

8.2

A Find and correct the mistakes. There is a mistake in five of the sentences.

1 The movie was great. It was too funny!
2 There aren't eggs enough to make a cake.
3 That child eats too much candy.
4 Do you earn money enough to pay the bills?
5 I spent too many time on the first question.
6 I can't help you because I'm too busy.
7 She's very generous—she always tips the waiters.
8 There isn't enough of time to do this exercise.

B Complete the sentences with *too, too much/many, (not) enough, or very*.

1 You spend ___________ time on your cell phone. It's bad for your work.
2 I didn't get ___________ money from the bank, so I need to go back.
3 He was ___________ lazy to study, so he failed his test.
4 I don't know how many coins I have in my collection. There are ___________ to count.
5 He did ___________ well to give up smoking after ten years.
6 I didn't take the dogs for a walk. It was ___________ cold.
7 The sofa takes up ___________ space. Let's buy a smaller one.
8 The company agreed to do more work, but this was a mistake. There were ___________ employees to do it.

8.3

A Complete the conversation with the words in the box.

help fitting enter on fit size one with

A: Hello, can I [1]______ you?
B: Do you sell jackets?
A: Yes, they're just over there.
B: Can I try this [2]______?
A: Yes, of course. How is it?
B: It doesn't [3]______. Do you have it in a larger [4]______?
A: I think so. Just a moment. Yes, here you are.
B: Thanks. And do you have [5]______ of these in black?
A: Yes, here it is. Would you like to try it on?
B: Yes, please. Where's the [6]______ room?
A: Just over there.
B: It fits. I'll take it.
A: OK. Are you paying [7]______ cash or by credit card?
B: Credit card.
A: OK, can you [8]______ your PIN, please?
B: OK.

GRAMMAR

9.1 Comparatives/Superlatives

Type of Adjective	Example	Comparative		Superlative	
one-syllable	cheap	+ *-er*	cheap**er**	*the* + *-est*	**the** cheap**est**
some two-syllable	quiet	+ *-er*	quiet**er**	*the* + *-est*	**the** quiet**est**
adjectives: ending in *-e* ending in *-y* ending in CVC	safe friendly big	+ *-r* ~~*-y*~~ + *-ier* double the final consonant + *-er*	safe**r** friendl**ier** bi**gger**	*the* + *-st* *the* + ~~*-y*~~ + *-iest* *the* + double the final consonant + *-est*	**the** safe**st** **the** friendl**iest** **the** bi**ggest**
many two- or more syllable	interesting	*more/less* + adjective	**more/less** interesting	*the most/least* + adjective	**the most/least** interesting
irregular	good bad far		better worse farther/further		the best the worst the farthest/the furthest

There are different ways to compare one or more things.

Superiority: *much/a lot more* + adjective + *than* *A is **a lot more** expensive **than** B.*
Equality: *the same as, as* + adjective + *as* *A is **the same as** B.*
Inferiority: *not as/so* + adjective + *as* *A is not **as big as** B.*
It is possible to use comparatives with nouns.
more/less + noun *He has **more money than** we thought.*
It is common to use the superlative with the present perfect. *It's the **best** restaurant **I've** ever **been** to!*

9.2 Articles

A/An (Indefinite Article)	Example
the first time something is mentioned	I saw a lion yesterday.
before singular nouns	There's a library in the town.
before job titles (in general)	I'm an actor.

No Article (Zero Article)	Example
to talk about things or people in general	Dogs are friendly animals.
before plural nouns	I'm taking four classes this term.
before most cities, countries and continents	I live in Germany.
in some phrases with prepositions	on Tuesday, at sea, in February, at work

The (Definite Article)	Example
to talk about something that has already been mentioned or information that the speaker and the listener already know	I saw a lion. The lion was sleeping.
to talk about something when there is only one	I looked at the moon.
before some plural place names	the United States
before seas/oceans/rivers	the Atlantic
before the names of some areas	the northwest of England
in some phrases with prepositions	in the evening, at the beginning
with superlatives	She is the tallest.

9.3 Making Guesses

It Is Possible	Example
It could + infinitive	It could be late because of weather.
It might + infinitive	It might be John at the door.
Maybe …	Maybe it's an antelope.
Perhaps …	Perhaps she went to bed late last night.

It Is Not Possible	Example
It can't be …	It can't be Mary's coat because she didn't come to the party.
It's definitely not …	What's the answer? It's definitely not "A."

PRACTICE

9.1

A Put the adjectives in parentheses into the correct form.

1 Eating at home is *cheaper* *than* eating in restaurants. (cheap)

2 People in cities work _______ hours _______ in the past. (long)

3 There is more traffic now, so the streets are _______. (noisy)

4 History is much _______ _______ _______ physics. (interesting)

5 Houses are _______ _______ _______ they were ten years ago. (expensive)

6 Life in the city is _______ _______ _______ it was before. (dangerous)

7 Cairo is even _______ _______ I expected. (hot)

8 South America is _______ _______ _______ Europe. (exciting)

9 I wish it were _______ _______ in this country. I'm freezing! (cold)

B Make superlative sentences with the prompts.

1 This / exciting / vacation / I ever have
This is the most exciting vacation I've ever had.

2 You / good / friend / I ever have

3 That / boring / movie / I ever see

4 This / short / day / year

5 That / long / run / I ever do

6 This / old / building / I ever see

7 That / hard / job / I ever do

9.2

A Underline the correct alternative.

1 Many people are frightened of *a/an/the/–* spiders.

2 I had a pet cat that I loved, but *a/an/the/–* cat didn't like me!

3 *A/An/The/–* vegetarians are people who don't eat meat.

4 The blue whale is *a/an/the/–* heaviest animal in the world.

5 We heard that there is *a/an/the/–* new gorilla in the zoo.

6 *A/An/The/–* bats drink blood.

7 There is *a/an/the/–* elephant that lived to the age of seventy-eight.

8 The mammal that sleeps *a/an/the/–* longest is the barrow ground squirrel.

9 We saw *a/an/the/–* eagle when we were in Namibia.

10 She used to work at Animals4U before *a/an/the/–* store closed down.

B There is an article missing (*a*, *an* or *the*) in each sentence in the text. Complete the text with the missing articles.

I was feeling bored, so I went for walk. The trees were green, and sky was blue. It was beautiful day. Suddenly I heard a strange noise, like animal. But I knew it wasn't cat because cats don't sound like that. Sound continued for a minute or more. I went home and turned on TV to watch the local news. The newscaster said, "Some animals have escaped from city zoo."

9.3

A Match statements 1–8 with responses a)–h).

1 She didn't come to school today.
2 The bill is 28 dollars.
3 Who is that man?
4 What's that smell in the kitchen?
5 When is her birthday?
6 I can't find my keys.
7 He lost his homework.
8 How many people are called Smith?

a) It might be onions. My mother is cooking.
b) I don't know, but it's definitely not today.
c) Perhaps the dog ate it again.
d) There could be millions. It's the most common name in the U.K.
e) She could be sick.
f) Maybe you left them in the car.
g) That can't be right. We only had two cups of coffee!
h) It can't be David. He's out of the country until next week.

GRAMMAR

10.1 Uses Of *Like*

Like (Verb)				
+		I	like	living in the city.
–		She	doesn't like	
?	Do Where do	you	like	going out in the evening?

Use *like* (verb) to talk about things you enjoy:

*What do you **like doing** in the evening?*
*I **like going out** at night.*

Be Like (Preposition)				
?	What	is	he/she/it/Antigua/your new house	like?

Use *be like* (preposition) to ask for a description:

A: *What's it (the city) **like**?*
B: *It's a big city, with lots of traffic.*

Note: Be careful not to confuse the two forms.

Question: *What's it like?*
Answer: *It's a beautiful city.* NOT ~~*I like it very much.*~~

10.2 passive voice *present/past*

Use subject + *be* + past participle to form the passive.

Present					
		Subject	**Be**	**Past Participle**	
+		I/you/he/she/it/we/they	am/are/is	told	that he is the best player.
–		Rugby	isn't	played	here.
?	Is	this dish		made	with potatoes?

Past					
		Subject	**Be**	**Past Participle**	
+		I/you/he/she/it/we/they	was/were	stopped	by a policeman.
–		The photo	wasn't	taken	here.
?	Was	the dog		killed?	

Use the active voice to talk about the things people do:

*John **stole** the camera.*
*Liz **ate** the bread.*

Use the passive voice:

- to talk about what happens to things or people:
  *The camera **was stolen** by John.*
  *The bread **was eaten** by Liz.*
- when the cause of the action is unknown:
  *Thousands of people **are killed** on the roads every year.* (We don't know who kills them.)
- when the cause of the action is not important:
  *The cakes **are made** in France.* (It is not important who makes them.)

If we want to say who does/did the action, we use *by:*

*The criminal was caught **by** the police.*
*Penicillin was discovered **by** Sir Alexander Fleming.*

10.3 Complaining

Before Making a Complaint	Complaint	Response
Could you help me? I'm afraid I have a complaint.	There's a problem with … It doesn't work.	We'll look into it right away. I'm sorry, but there's nothing we can do at the moment.
Excuse me, could I speak to the manager?	I've been here for over an hour.	I'm really sorry about that.

PRACTICE

10.1

A Put the words in the correct order to make questions.

1 like / job / your / what's / new ?
2 new / do / my / dress / like / you ?
3 like / what / are / tapas ?
4 there / the / what's / like / weather ?
5 like / in / you / living / the / do / country ?

B Match questions 1–5 with answers a)–e).

a) I love it. It's so peaceful.
b) Yes. It really suits you.
c) They are delicious. They are small dishes of vegetables, fish and meat. You can eat them as a starter.
d) It's great. I really like the people I'm working with.
e) It's terrible. It's windy and wet.

C Find and correct the mistakes. There is a mistake in each line.

1 I like listen to music. My favorite band is Jamiroquai.
2 How is the apartment like? Is it modern?
3 Have you seen *Terminator 4*? Did you like?
4 So, you've got a new boss. What's like he?
5 What's like the weather? Is it raining?
6 Are you like speaking English?

10.2

A Underline the correct alternative.

1 Only fresh fish *is serve/is served/is to serve* in this restaurant.
2 Yesterday she *has given/was given/is given* a ten-year prison sentence.
3 Shoplifters *aren't caught/not caught/aren't catch* very often.
4 This book *was written/is written/was wrote* by a French author in 1886.
5 At the moment, movies *are show/were shown/are shown* only on Wednesday evenings.
6 Hundreds of people *arrested/were arrest/are arrested* for drunk driving every day.
7 I made the mistake because I *am not telling/wasn't told/haven't told* what to do.
8 The prisoners *are sent/were send/were sent* home last night.

B Rewrite the sentences in the passive. Add *by* where necessary.

1 The French eat snails.
Snails ______________________.
2 Dostoyevsky wrote *Crime and Punishment*.
Crime and Punishment ______________________.
3 A journalist asked me some questions.
I ______________________.
4 Alejandro Ledesma produces all of our programs.
All of our programs ______________________.
5 Alec Guinness played most of the roles in that movie.
Most of the roles in that movie ______________________.
6 Swiss companies make the best chocolate.
The best chocolate ______________________.

10.3

A Put the words in the correct order to make conversations.

Conversation 1

A: me / excuse / complaint / have / afraid / a / I'm / I
B: what's / problem / the ?
A: doesn't / shower / work / the
B: look / away / it / into / we'll / right

Conversation 2

A: me / excuse / you / me / help / could ?
B: Yes
A: a / the / with / problem / Internet / connection / there's
B: nothing / sorry / can / but / I'm / the / we / at / moment / there's / do

Conversation 3

A: excuse / to / speak / me / could / manager / I / the ?
B: Yes
A: an / I've / been / hour / here / over / for
B: sorry / really / I'm / that / about

GRAMMAR

11.1 Present Perfect + *Just/Yet/Already*

It is common to use the present perfect with *just*, *yet* and *already*.
Use *just* to talk about something that happened very recently.
Put *just* before the main verb.

*I've **just** passed my driving test!*
*We've **just** got back from vacation.*

Use *yet* in negative sentences and questions to talk about something that hasn't happened, but you expect it to. Put *yet* at the end of the sentence.

A: *Are you ready?*
B: *No, we haven't finished **yet**.*
A: *Have you reserved a table **yet**?*
B: *No, not **yet**. I'll call the restaurant in a minute.*

Use *already* to talk about something that happened, maybe before you expected. Put *already* before the main verb or at the end of the sentence.

*I've **already** had four cups of coffee this morning.*
*He's found a job **already**!*

Spoken grammar: It is common to use *not yet* as a short response to a question. It means we expect to do something soon, but we have not done it.

11.2 Real Conditionals + *If/When*

If/When	+ Present	+ *will/won't* + Infinitive
If When	you don't study, the movie finishes,	you won't pass the exam. I'll turn off the TV.

Use *If/When* + present + *will* + infinitive to form a real conditional.
There are two clauses: the *if/when* clause and the main clause. You can reverse the order of the clauses, but the *if/when* clause always uses the present tense.

(*if/when* clause) (main clause)
*If we see Ann, we'**ll ask** her to call you.*
NOT *~~If we will see~~ Ann, we'll ask her to call you.*

(main clause) (*if/when* clause)
*We'll ask Ann to call you **if** we see her.*

Use real conditionals to talk about situations in the future and their consequences.
Use *if* for a situation that is uncertain. Use *when* for a situation that is certain.

If I pass my driving test today, I'll be very surprised. (I'm not sure about this.)
When I pass my driving test, my father will buy me a car. (I'm sure about this.)

It is also possible to use *may/might/could/should* in the main clause instead of *will*.

***If** it's sunny, we **might** have a picnic later.*
***When** they arrive, they **should** call to tell us.*

11.3 Giving Opinions

Agreeing	Disagreeing	Giving Your Opinion
That's right. That's true. Definitely.	I totally disagree. I'm not sure about that. I don't think so.	I think … I don't think … In my opinion …

To sound polite, use *I'm afraid* and *I'm sorry, but …* when you disagree.

***I'm afraid** I totally disagree.*
***I'm sorry, but** it's just not possible.*

PRACTICE

11.1

A Underline the correct alternative.

1 We're traveling around the Greek Islands. We've been to fourteen islands *just/yet/already*.

2 I'm leaving this evening, but I haven't packed my bags *just/yet/already*.

3 **A:** Have you seen Martha?
B: She's *just/yet/already* left. You might catch her in the elevator if you hurry.

4 **A:** Can you wait a minute, please?
B: I've *just/yet/already* been here for more than half an hour.

5 **A:** Do you know if your sister is coming to the party?
B: I'm not sure. I haven't spoken to her *just/yet/already*.

6 I thought Alf was going away for three weeks, but he's *just/yet/already* come back.

7 Great! I've *just/yet/already* reserved the tickets on the Internet. Now, we wait for the confirmation.

8 **A:** Can you call Emily?
B: I've *just/yet/already* spoken to her. That was her on the phone a minute ago.

B Find and correct the mistakes. There is a mistake in the word order in each conversation.

1 **A:** Have you read this book?
B: Yes, I've finished it just.

2 **A:** Are you ready to go?
B: No, Imelda hasn't called yet us.

3 **A:** Let's go to the Museum of Modern Art.
B: We've been already there.

4 **A:** Becky looks tired.
B: Well, just she's run five miles.

5 **A:** Are you coming out later?
B: I'd love to come out, but I haven't finished yet my work.

6 **A:** There's a movie on tonight.
B: Yes, but already I've seen it three times!

11.2

A Put the verbs in parentheses into the correct form.

1 I ______ home when I ______ my studies. (leave/finish)

2 If you ______ the class, I ______ some notes for you. (miss/take)

3 When I ______ Sandra, I ______ her what she thinks. (see/ask)

4 We ______ time for lunch if the train ______ at 12 o'clock. (not have/leave)

5 If I ______ my boss for a raise, he ______ it to me. (ask/not give)

6 I ______ dinner if you ______ the shopping. (cook/do)

7 If the weather ______ nice, we ______ out for a walk. (be/go)

8 We ______ on vacation when Al ______ some time off work. (go/get)

B Find and correct the mistakes. There are mistakes in four of the sentences.

1 If you will be in the office tomorrow, we talk about it then.

2 When Brian comes back from vacation, we'll arrange to go out.

3 When I hear from the rest of the team, I'll let you know.

4 We'll ask the doctor when we will get to the hospital.

5 If Theo behaves badly in class, the teacher speak to his parents.

6 They move into the house as soon as Mark will finish building it.

11.3

A There is a word missing in each sentence. Complete the sentences with the missing word(s).

1 I'm, but I don't think there is enough money for that.

2 I don't we should spend too much time discussing this.

3 I have to say I think right.

4 I'm afraid totally disagree.

5 Make them pay fines? I'm not sure that.

6 In opinion, we should start from the beginning.

B Complete the conversations with the phrases in the box.

I'm afraid	I think	totally disagree	my opinion
Definitely	not sure about		

A: [1]____________ we should all go home early today.
B: I'm [2]____________ that.
A: It's OK to hunt animals for sport.
B: [3]____________ I [4]____________.
A: In [5]____________, these politicians should go to prison.
B: [6]____________! They're criminals.

elevator / raise — lift /pay rise

GRAMMAR

12.1 Reported Speech

Direct Speech	Reported Speech
present simple → "I **play** the guitar." →	past simple She **said** she **played** the guitar.
present continuous → "They **are** watching a movie." →	past continuous He **told** us they **were watching** a movie.
will → "I'**ll** call you later." →	would She **said** she **would** call me later.
can → "He **can** work until 9:00." →	could She **told** me he **could** work until 9:00.

When we report speech, the pronouns sometimes change.

*"**I** eat meat." → **He** said **he** ate meat.*
*"**We**'ll help you tomorrow." → **They** said **they** would help me tomorrow.*

Use reported speech to tell someone what another person said.
It is common to change the verb tense/form when we report speech.
It is common to use *say* and *tell* to report speech.
Tell is followed by an object.

*He **told me** (that) he was hungry.* NOT
He ~~told that~~ he was hungry.

Say is *not* followed by an object.

*She **said** she worked in France.* NOT
She ~~said me~~ she worked in France.

When the present simple is used to describe a habit, we don't need to change the verb tense in reported speech.

*"I **get** up at 6 a.m." → She said she **gets** up at 6 a.m.*
*"We **don't** eat meat." → They told us they **don't** eat meat.*

12.2 Hypothetical Conditionals for Present/Future

If + Present Subjunctive	+ *Would/Wouldn't* + Infinitive
If I had more money,	I would buy a car.
If I wanted a job,	I would look for one.
If I were famous,	I wouldn't be happy.

Use *If* + present subjunctive + *would/wouldn't* + infinitive to form a hypothetical conditional.
Use hypothetical conditionals to talk about an imaginary situation in the present or future and its consequence.

*If I **knew** the way to the museum, I **would tell** you.*
(I don't know the way to the museum.)

*If I **won** the lottery, I **would** never **work** again!*

(I'm very unlikely to win the lottery—it's an imaginary situation.)

Would is often contracted (*I'd, you'd, he'd, we'd, they'd*).
Would not is contracted to *wouldn't*.

*If we had more money, we'**d** buy a bigger house.*
*We **wouldn't** live in the city if we didn't need to.*

It is possible to change the order of the clauses. Notice that there is a comma after the *if* clause in the first example, but no comma in the second example.

***If** we had children, our lives would be very different.*
*Our lives would be very different **if** we had children.*

With the verb *be* it is becoming more common to use *was* (instead of *were*).

*If he **was/were** a lawyer, he would tell you what to do.*
Use *If I were you …* to give advice.

***If I were you**, I'd tell him your plans.* NOT ~~*If I was you.*~~
It is also possible to use *could*.

*If I **could** sing, I would start a band.*

12.3 Requests and Offers

Requests	Responses	Offers
I'd like to …	No problem.	Would you like me to …?
Would it be possible to …?	Certainly.	Do you want me to (get a) …?
Would you be able to …?	Yes, of course.	Shall I …?
Could you recommend …?		

PRACTICE

12.1

A Rewrite the sentences as reported speech.

1 "My favorite movie is about an invisible man."
She told me ______________________.
2 "I don't like westerns."
He said ______________________.
3 "They are actors."
She told us ______________________.
4 "The movie isn't really about fashion."
He said ______________________.
5 "I work for a movie studio."
He told me ______________________.
6 "That director is famous."
We told her ______________________.
7 "I write thrillers."
She said ______________________.
8 "The scene reminds me of another movie."
He said ______________________.

B Rewrite the reported sentences as direct speech.

1 Gianella said she loved chocolate.
"I love chocolate."
2 He told us he was home by 6:00 p.m. every day.
"______________________"
3 Marina said she didn't want to do her homework.
"______________________"
4 They told me they were busy.
"______________________"
5 Yannick said he didn't understand the lecture.
"______________________"
6 I told you I didn't like flying.
"______________________"
7 Xun Li said she went back to China every summer.
"______________________"

12.2

A Match 1–6 with a)–f) to make sentences.

1 If you went to bed earlier,
2 If she asked Tim to marry her,
3 If we came in the summer,
4 We would visit you tomorrow
5 I'd get there early
6 She would earn more money

a) would we go to the beach?
b) if I were you.
c) you wouldn't feel so tired.
d) if the trains were running.
e) if she worked longer hours.
f) I'm sure he would say "Yes."

B Put the verbs in parentheses into the correct form.

1 I __________ to the doctor if I __________ you. He can give you some medicine. (go/be)
2 If they __________ ice cream here, __________ you __________ some? (sell/buy)
3 I __________ you if I __________, but I'm too busy right now. (help/can)
4 If I __________ my phone with me, I __________ him. (have/call)
5 If we __________ more food, I __________ them to stay for dinner. (have/ask)
6 If you __________ nearer to us, we __________ you more often. (live/see)
7 __________ your brother __________ happier if he __________ so hard? (be/not work)
8 If you __________ always __________ such a mess, the kitchen __________ cleaner! (not make/be)

12.3

A There are words missing from the conversations. Complete the conversations with the words in the box.

want	it	me	should	no	of	to	able	could

Conversation 1

A: You recommend a good coffee shop?
B: Certainly. There's one on Elm Road called Hot Beans.
A: Great.
B: Would you like to show you where it is?
A: Oh, yes, please. That's very kind of you.

Conversation 2

A: I'd like eat out tonight.
B: OK. Do you me to choose the restaurant?
A: Yes, why not?
B: OK. And I reserve a table for two?
A: Er, no—three. I'm inviting Bobby.

Conversation 3

A: Would you be to get me a good plumber?
B: Problem.
A: Would be possible to do it today? I have to travel tomorrow.
B: Yes, course.

Lesson 2.2 JOBS

1 **Match photos A–P to the jobs.**

1 accountant
2 architect
3 businessman/woman
4 chef
5 electrician
6 real-estate agent
7 homemaker
8 lawyer
9 PA (personal assistant)
10 plumber
11 receptionist
12 sales assistant
13 scientist
14 soldier
15 TV host
16 veterinarian

2 **Work in pairs. Discuss. Which jobs do you think are dangerous/enjoyable/boring? Why?**

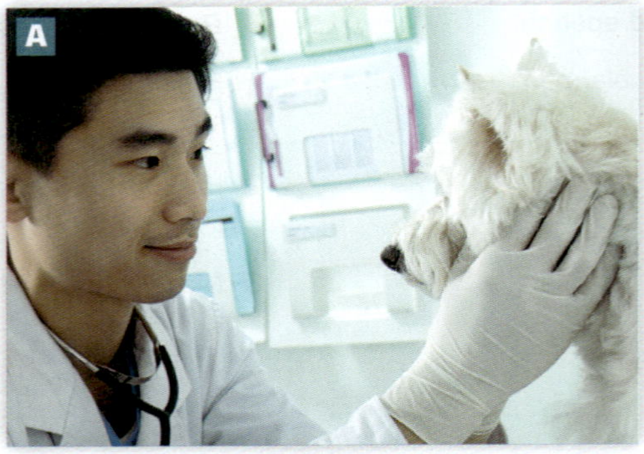

Lesson 3.1 TIME OUT

1 Match photos A–O to the activities 1–15.

collect:

1 stamps
2 coins

go to:

3 a concert
4 a nightclub
5 the gym

go to/see:

6 an exhibition
7 a show

play:

8 cards
9 chess
10 computer games
11 board games
12 hang out with friends
13 join a club
14 surf the net
15 walk/ride a bicycle/skate through a park

2 Work in pairs. Discuss. Which of these have you never done? Which would you like to do?

Lesson 4.2 EDUCATION

1 Answer the questions.

1 Where did you go to elementary school?
2 Which subjects did you enjoy in middle school?
3 Have you been to college? What did you/would you like to study?
4 Is the education system in your country similar to the one in the U.S.?

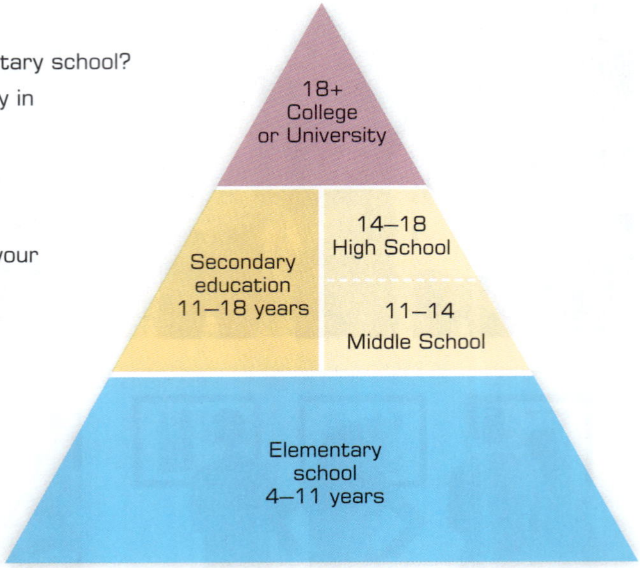

Public School in the U.S.A.

Math (Mathematics)

Physics

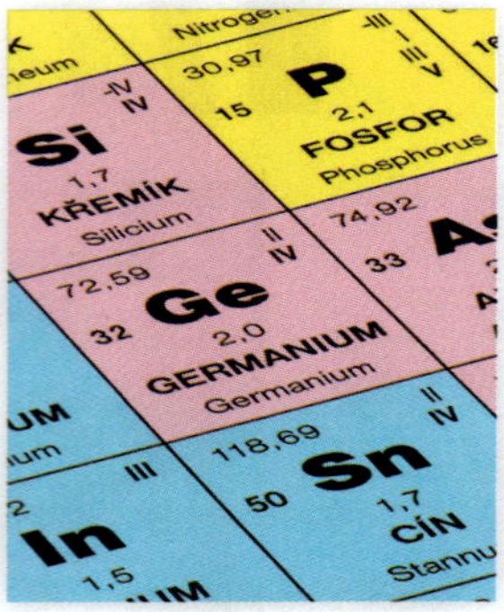

Chemistry

Biology

Geography

History

Languages

Art

Industrial Arts

PE (Physical Education)

Computer Science

Social Studies

Drama

Lesson 5.1 TRANSPORTATION

1 Match photos A–N to the transportation types.

1 airplane
2 tour bus
3 ferry
4 helicopter
5 hot air balloon
6 truck
7 city bus
8 scooter
9 motorcycle
10 ship
11 speedboat
12 taxi
13 streetcar
14 subway

2 Work in pairs. Discuss. Which transportation do you use regularly? Which do you think are the most enjoyable ways to travel?

Lesson 5.2 TRAVEL ITEMS

1 Match photos A–R to the travel items.

1 alarm clock
2 aspirin
3 binoculars
4 dictionary
5 digital camera
6 first aid kit
7 map
8 money belt
9 notebook
10 backpack
11 soap
12 souvenir
13 suitcase
14 sun hat
15 travel guide
16 umbrella
17 hiking boots
18 waterproof clothes

2 Work in pairs and take turns.
Student A: describe an item.
Student B: guess the item.

A: You wear these when it is raining.
B: Waterproof clothes.

Lesson 6.1 HEALTH

1 A Check the meaning of sports 1–30 below.

1 badminton
2 basketball
3 boxing
4 baseball
5 cycling
6 football
7 golf
8 hockey
9 horse racing
10 horseback riding
11 jogging
12 judo
13 karate
14 table tennis
15 rollerblading
16 rugby
17 running
18 sailing
19 scuba diving
20 skateboarding
21 skiing
22 squash
23 snorkeling
24 snowboarding
25 surfing
26 swimming
27 tennis
28 volleyball
29 windsurfing
30 yoga

B Which sports can you see in photos A–M?

2 Work in pairs. Discuss. Which sports are popular in your country? Which have you tried?

Lesson 6.2 FOOD

1 Which of these foods do you a) never eat b) eat a lot of?

2 Which types of food/drinks do you think are a) very good b) very bad for your health?

GRAINS

MEAT AND FISH/SEAFOOD

DAIRY

DESSERTS

DRINKS

VEGETABLES

FRUIT

Lesson 8.1 MONEY

1 Match photos A–H to the words.

1 bank statement
2 check
3 bills
4 ATM
5 credit cards
6 coins
7 bill
8 receipt

2 Work in pairs and take turns.
Student A: describe an item.
Student B: guess the item.

A: This is money made from metal.
B: Coins.

Lesson 9.1 NATURE

1 Which do you like to visit on vacation? Which of these do you have in your country? Work in pairs. Discuss.

ocean

lake

river

waterfall

mountain range

desert

glacier

rainforest

coastline

Lesson 9.3 ANIMALS

1 Write the names of the animals in the correct places.

1 bear
2 butterfly
3 camel
4 chimpanzee
5 cow
6 alligator
7 dolphin
8 eagle
9 elephant
10 fly
11 gorilla
12 leopard
13 lion
14 monkey
15 ostrich
16 penguin
17 pigeon
18 snake
19 spider
20 tiger
21 whale

2 Work in pairs. Discuss. Which do you think are dangerous/beautiful/intelligent?

WATER CREATURES

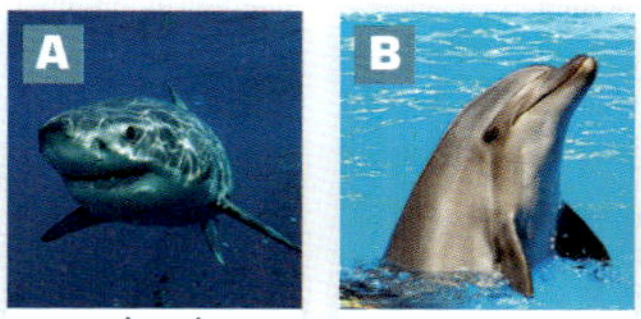

shark

BIG CATS

cheetah

REPTILES

turtle

BUGS

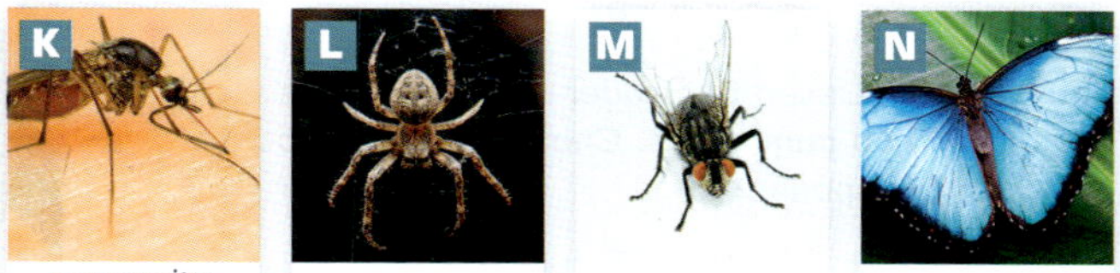

mosquito

BIRDS

PRIMATES

MAMMALS

sloth

Lesson 10.2 CRIME AND PUNISHMENT

1 Which words can you see in the pictures?

People:
1 criminal
2 police officer
3 judge
4 victim

Verbs:
5 steal
6 break in
7 shoot
8 arrest
9 investigate

2 Can you match any of the people to the verbs?

Criminals steal things.

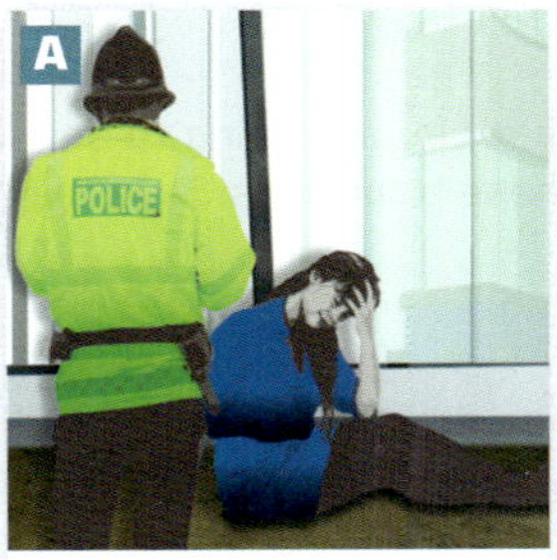

Lesson 1.3

4 A Student A: make questions or comments with the prompts for Student B. Listen to Student B's responses.

1 would / like / drink?
2 watch / game / last night?
3 nice / day?
4 work / here?

B Listen to Student B's questions and comments. Choose the correct response.

1 Hi, Pete. Pleased to meet you./ Dear Mr. Pete. How do you do?
2 Yes, thanks. I didn't do much./ Yes, thank you. I am enjoying it.
3 I'm coming from Toledo, near Madrid./ I'm from Toledo, near Madrid.
4 It's nice to meet you./ Yes, see you soon.

Lesson 3.5

4 C Answers to quiz

2 Reagan
3 *A Night at the Opera*
4 Raphael
5 Elton
6 "One Love"
7 Venice
8 Céline
9 Nelly Furtado

Lesson 4.3

9 A Student A: explain your problem. Then listen and respond to the advice.

Your son is eighteen years old and lives at home. He needs to study for his exams, but in the evening he goes out with friends until late. He often misses classes or falls asleep when he is studying. At home you do all the cooking and cleaning and give your son money every week.

B Listen to another student's problem. Give the student some advice.

Lesson 2.2

4 B Student B

Danger Rating 8/10

Motoboy Brazil

In Brazil, they are called motoboys, and, on average, one of them dies in traffic every day. Foreign correspondent Peter Lane met the motoboys of São Paulo. He learned that accidents are not the only problem—there are also robberies. It happened to Roberto Coelho.

"It was terrible, a really bad time for me. I lost everything. We don't have insurance, and the company doesn't help us." The motoboys usually earn just $450 a month.

Lane asks, "When you know the streets are dangerous, why do you still drive so fast?" Coelho says it's because they often work under time pressure. "We know it's dangerous, but we have no choice."

Lane also spoke to some car drivers. One said, "These motorcycle couriers are so dangerous. They drive too fast, and they don't care about the rules of the road." Another said, "Most of them are just kids. It's no surprise they have accidents."

Once in a while, they try to change the traffic laws—they want the motoboys to drive like everyone else. But the changes all failed, so the motoboys continue to risk their lives in one of the most dangerous jobs in the world.

Lesson 3.3

8 Student A: think about what you are going to say when you receive and make phone calls in these situations. Role-play the situations with Student B.

Answer the phone

1 You work for Nova Restaurant. Take a message.
2 You work for Amber Movie Theater. Answer the phone and tell a customer the times of the movie *The Magic Hat:* 2:30 p.m., 5:00 p.m., 7:30 p.m. and 10:00 p.m., with a special extra showing at 12:00 p.m. on the weekend.
3 Answer the phone normally. Listen and respond to the invitation.

Make a call

4 You are calling Ripping Yarns, a theater company. You would like six tickets for *Hamlet* for Friday.
5 You are calling Brandon's Restaurant. You want to change your reservation from 7:30 p.m. on Tuesday to 8:00 p.m. next Wednesday. There will now be ten people, not five, so you need a bigger table.
6 Ask your partner if he/she wants to go for a snack after class.

Lesson 5.1

3 Student B: read the text and make notes.

INTO THE WILD

When Chris McCandless graduated from Emory University, he knew he wanted more from life than a normal career. He gave away his savings—$24,000—to charity, abandoned his car, burned the money in his wallet, and gave himself a new name: Alexander Supertramp. He rejected the modern world and decided to experience life alone and in the wild.

With hardly any equipment or technology, McCandless went into the Alaskan wilderness.* While he was traveling, he met several people who helped him, giving him rides and food. One man even offered to adopt him as a grandson, but McCandless decided to keep going, into the wild.

Eventually he ended up in an abandoned bus, hunting and picking plants for food. While he was living wild, he wrote a journal. It described his day-to-day life and the difficulties and pleasures he had from living in nature. McCandless stayed in the bus for four months, and then his journal stopped. Eventually his body was found by a hunter.

Following a book describing his life, a film came out based on his adventures.

*__wilderness:__ a wild area where no one lives

Lesson 5.3

8 Student A: look at the map and ask Student B for directions to:

- a nightclub called Risky Business
- a restaurant called The Waterfall
- the Screen by the Pond movie theater
- a bar called The Courier's Rest
- the Museum of Fashion and Design

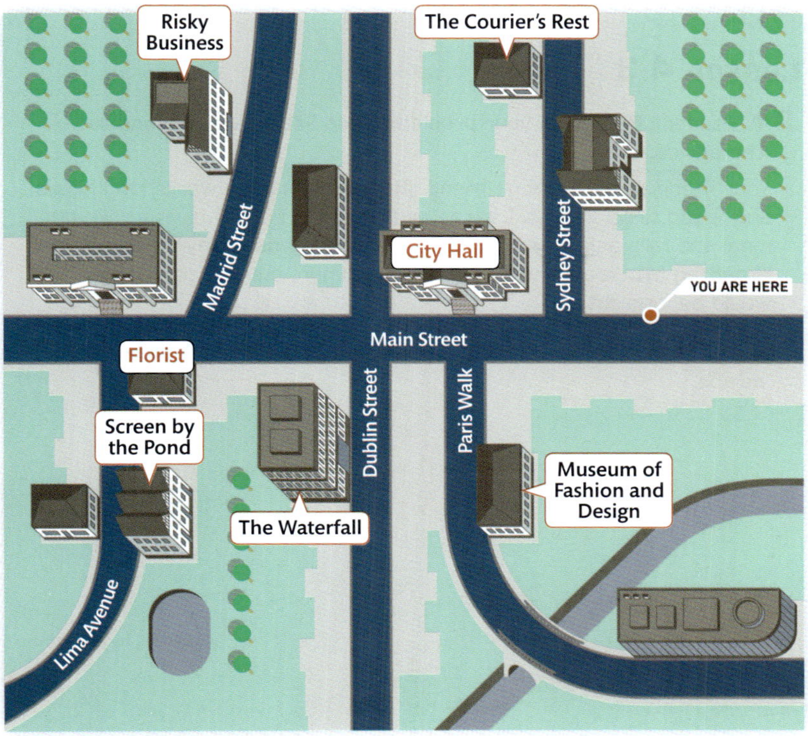

Lesson 6.3

6 A Student A: you are a doctor seeing a patient. Use the prompts to ask questions and make suggestions.

- how long?
- where / hurt?
- when / hurt?
- how / you / hurt?
- take painkillers
- get lots of rest
- don't play sports

Start like this:

Hello. How can I help you?

B Student A: now you are a patient seeing a doctor. Use the prompts to explain your problem.

- bad cough / few months
- tried antibiotics
- no fever / don't feel sick
- smoke / ten cigarettes a day

Lesson 10.2

7 C Here are the alternative sentences:

1 Over a period of two years, the boys had to clean the walls of every house in the street three times a year.

2 They had to spend a day at a festival standing in a small swimming pool and handing out water-safety leaflets.

3 He was made to listen to classical music for six hours a day.

4 She had to work on the farm for free for one month.

Lesson 10.3

8 B Student B: you are the director at the Noparlo School of English. A student is going to complain about some of the problems in Exercise 8A on page 103. Apologize to the student and think of reasons for the problems. Use these expressions:

I'm really sorry about that.
We had a problem with …
I'll look into it.

Lesson 1.3

4 A Student B: listen to Student A's questions and comments. Choose the correct response.

1 I'd love an orange juice, please./ I like orange juice, please.
2 Yes, it was awesome./Yes, it's beautiful.
3 Yes, nice to meet you./Yes, it's beautiful.
4 No, I'm a student./No, I'm working.

B Make questions or comments with the prompts for Student A. Listen to Student A's responses.

1 this / friend / Pete
2 have / good / weekend?
3 where / exactly / from?
4 see / later

Lesson 3.3

8 Student B: think about what you are going to say when you make and receive phone calls in these situations. Role-play the situations with Student A.

Make a call

1 You are calling Nova Restaurant. You reserved a table for Saturday, but you have to cancel it.
2 You are calling Amber Movie Theater. Ask what time the movie *The Magic Hat* is showing.
3 Invite your partner to a movie this evening. Say the name and time of the movie.

Answer the phone

4 You work for Ripping Yarns, a theater company. Answer the phone and confirm a ticket reservation.
5 You work for Brandon's Restaurant. A customer wants to change his/her reservation. Take the message and confirm whether it is possible.
6 Answer the phone normally. Listen and respond to the invitation.

Lesson 2.2

4 B Student C

Danger Rating 6/10

Jockey, France

"Bang!" goes the gun. The gates open, and the horses come running out. All eyes are on them. Money, fame and glory are the prizes.

Horseback riding looks so beautiful that it is sometimes easy to forget how dangerous it is. Life as a jockey is rarely safe, and it usually involves a few broken bones. Once in a while, jockeys even die during a race.

Jill Cleveland spoke to jockey Vincent Dax in France. As a young man, Dax was one of the best jockeys of his generation. He knows the sport is dangerous, but he never worries. "When the race starts, we forget about the danger. We know it's not like riding a bicycle or driving a car, but all we think about is winning."

During his career, Dax has broken many bones, including both arms and one leg, and he once fell off his horse and was knocked unconscious. So why do jockeys risk their lives? "We love racing. We love the speed, and we love the money. Jockeys know the risks involved, but we are good at what we do. If we get hurt, we just get back on the horse. That's life."

Lesson 4.3

9 A Student B: explain your problem. Then listen and respond to the advice.

Your friend would like a girlfriend. The problem is he works long hours and is too tired to go out in the evenings. He usually buys a take-out meal and falls asleep watching TV. He doesn't have any hobbies and is getting fat. You know lots of single women, but you don't think they would be interested.

B Listen to another student's problem. Give the student some advice.

Lesson 5.1

3 Student C: read the text and make notes.

RABBIT-PROOF FENCE

It is Australia in 1931. Three Aborigine girls, Molly, fourteen, her sister Daisy, eight, and their cousin Gracie, ten, were taken from their home by government officials because of their race. They were sent to live in a camp far from home. Life at the camp was terrible, and they hated it.

One night when it was raining, the girls decided to escape. They knew that the rain would hide their footprints in the mud, so they began the long journey home. In the desert, they had no food and nowhere to sleep.

They didn't have a map either, but while they were walking, they saw the "rabbit-proof fence," one of the longest fences in the world. It was there to stop rabbits from entering farmland. The girls recognized the fence and walked next to it for 1,200 miles. After nine weeks they got home.

Many years later, Molly's daughter, Doris Pilkington Garimara, wrote a book about the journey, and, in 2002, the story was made into a film, *Rabbit-Proof Fence*.

Lesson 5.3

8 Student B: look at the map and ask Student A for directions to:

- The Quick Snack Café
- The Ferry Theater
- the Concert Hall
- a bar called The Consultants' Rescue
- the Modern Art Gallery

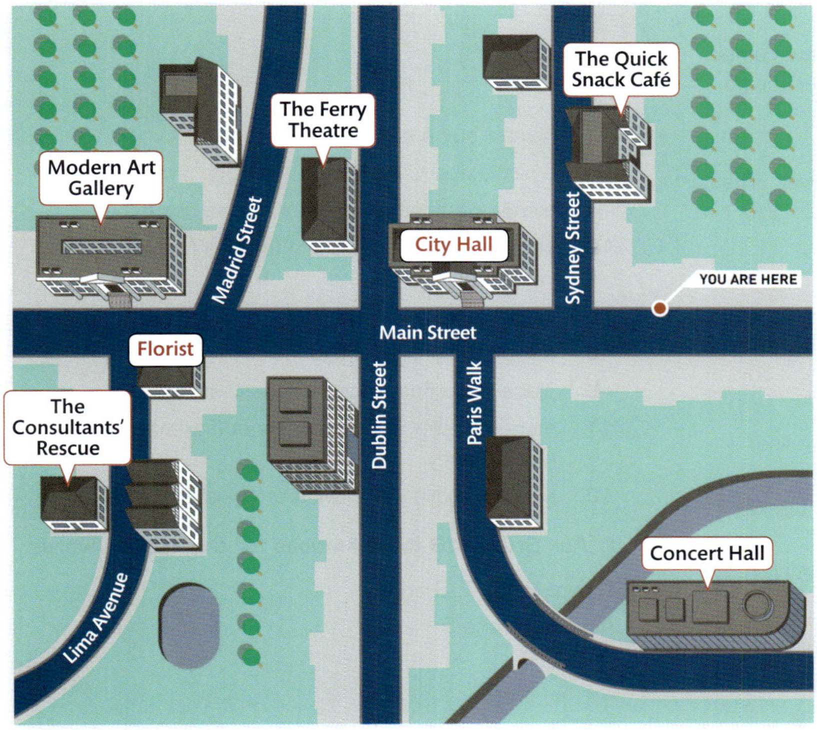

Lesson 6.3

6 **A** Student B: you are a patient seeing a doctor. Use the prompts to explain your problem.

- problem / two weeks
- pain / lower back
- hurts / walk
- accident / playing football

B Student B: now you are a doctor seeing a patient. Use the prompts to ask questions and make suggestions.

- how long?
- a fever?
- feel sick?
- smoke cigarettes?
- have an X-ray
- give up smoking

Start like this:

Hello. What's the problem?

Lesson 8.3

6 **A** Student A: you work in a clothing store. You start the conversation.

1 Offer to help.
2 Ask what color.
3 Give the customer the shirt and say, "Here you are. The fi tting room is over there."
4 Ask if it fi ts OK.
5 Ask how he/she wants to pay.
6 Ask him/her to enter his/her PIN.
7 Say thank you and goodbye.

B Student A: now you are in an electronics store. Student B starts the conversation.

1 Say you are looking for a camera.
2 Say you need a digital one.
3 Thank him/her.
4 Ask for a cheaper one.
5 Say "This one is fi ne."
6 Say you will pay in cash.
7 Say thank you and goodbye.

Lesson 9.3

6 B Answers

1 whale shark
2 spine-tailed swift
3 ostrich
4 python (a snake)
5 cheetah
6 mosquito (it kills people indirectly, by transmitting malaria)
7 whale
8 tortoise

Lesson 9.3

9 B Answers

A An elephant's skin:
Elephant skin is only thick in some places. It is very sensitive.

B An eagle's eye:
Eagles can see fish in the water from hundreds of feet away, and an eagle's sight is four times stronger than a human's.

C A dog's nose:
Dogs have an amazing sense of smell. Many dogs can recognize the smell of their old owners many years after they last saw them.

D A chameleon's skin:
A chameleon's skin can change color when the chameleon needs to hide.

E A shark's teeth:
Some types of shark have thousands of teeth. These teeth are extremely hard. A shark can bite through iron.

F A camel's hump:
Camels' humps are made of fat, and they allow camels to survive in the desert without food or water for up to two weeks.

G A fly's eyes:
Flies' eyes are very different from humans' eyes. The shape of flies' eyes allows them to see almost 360 degrees.

Lesson 9.5

1 B Answers

1 **a)** The Andes are higher than the Rockies.
2 **b)** Canada has a longer coastline (151,485 miles) than Russia (23,396 miles).
3 **b)** Lake Michigan in the U.S.A. is larger than Lake Toba in Sumatra.
4 **a)** The Amazon is shorter, but wider than the Nile.
5 **a)** The Pacific is the deepest ocean.
6 **b)** Angel Falls, in Venezuela, is the highest waterfall.

Lesson 4.3

9 A Student C: explain your problem. Then listen and respond to the advice.

Your roommate loves shopping. Every month she buys new clothes, shoes and designer bags using a credit card. Her room is full of clothes she never wears. She spends more money than she has and borrows money from you to pay her rent. She hasn't paid you back for two months.

B Listen to another student's problem. Give the student some advice.

Lesson 8.1

4 C Student A: write definitions for the completed words with the prompts.

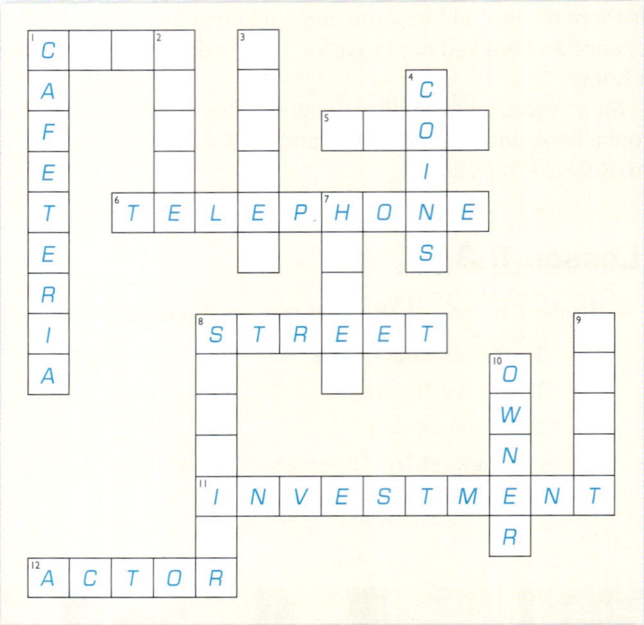

Down

1 place / buy a snack or a coffee
a place where you buy a snack or a coffee
4 pieces of money / made of metal, not paper
10 person / owns something (he/she bought it or was given it)

Across

6 thing / use / call someone
8 place / you find / cars, houses, stores, etc.
11 money / use / start a business and make more money
12 person / acts in / movies or theater

D Ask Student B for definitions for the missing words.

Down: 2, 3, 7, 8 and 9
Across: 1 and 5

Lesson 10.1

1 B Survey results

The World's Best Cities for Young People to Live in
1 Vienna
2 New York
3 Helsinki
4 Melbourne
5 Salvador
6 Dubai
7 Vancouver
8 Prague
9 Edinburgh
10 Paris

Lesson 10.3

7 A Student A: you are a hotel guest. You start the conversation.

1 Greet the hotel receptionist.

2 Say you have a problem: your fridge doesn't work.

3 Thank the receptionist.

B Student A: now you are a waiter. Listen to what Student B says, then:

1 Ask how you can help.

2 Apologize for the mistake. Say you will bring the right dish.

3 Apologize again.

Lesson 12.3

8 Student A: you are a concierge. Listen and respond to your client's requests. Ask for more time if necessary. Your client wants to:

- go to the best restaurant in town.
- get tickets to the theater.

Student A: now you are a client. Tell the concierge you want to:

- go shopping for clothes. Ask him/her to recommend
  a good area for shopping.
- visit a movie studio and meet some stars. Ask him/her if it's possible.

Lesson 7.3

8 A Student A: you are new to this town/city. Ask your partner questions to find out this information.

1 You want to know what time the stores open.

2 You want to know where the nearest train station is.

3 You need to exchange some money. Find out where to go.

Excuse me, …

B Student A: now answer Student B's questions using the information below.

The American Speakout School of English

Where are we?

We are open:
Mon–Sat: 8 a.m.–10 p.m.
Sun: 8 a.m.–1 p.m.

Join the American Speakout School of English and learn English fast!

Lesson 9.5

7 B Countries

A Chile

B France

C Japan

D Australia

Lesson 8.3

6 A Student B: you are in a clothing store. Student A starts the conversation.

1 Ask for a formal shirt.
2 Say you need a white one.
3 Thank him/her for the shirt.
4 Say it fits. Say "I'll take this one."
5 Say you want to pay by credit card.
6 Say yes (to enter your PIN).
7 Say thank you and goodbye.

B Student B: now you work in an electronics store. You start the conversation.

1 Offer to help.
2 Ask what type.
3 Say "They are over there."
4 Ask if it is what he/she is looking for.
5 Say "There are some cheaper ones over there."
6 Ask how he/she wants to pay.
7 Say thank you and goodbye.

Lesson 11.4

2 A Answers

1 In the U.S., a child watches TV for an average of **4** hours a day.
2 In parts of the U.K., more than 60 percent of elementary school children have a TV in their bedroom.
3 The average person spends **3.5** years eating and **12** years watching TV.
4 Children under three years old who watch more than **1** hour of TV a day may have problems concentrating at school when they are older.
5 In the U.S., some families spend only **3.5** minutes a week having meaningful conversations with their children. Those children spend **1,600** minutes a week watching TV.

Lesson 12.1

7 B Answers

1 b) 2 b) 3 b) 4 a) 5 a) 6 a)

Lesson 7.3

8 A Student B: answer Student A's questions using the information below.

B You are new to this school. Ask questions to find out this information.

1 You want to know where the nearest coffee shop to the school is.
2 You want to know where you can buy an English dictionary.
3 You want to know what time the school closes.

Excuse me, …

Lesson 10.3

7 A Student B: you are a hotel receptionist. Listen to what Student A says, then:

1 Greet the guest.
2 Apologize. Offer to send someone to the room to look into the problem.
3 Say "You're welcome" and apologize again.

B Student B: you are a customer in a restaurant. You start the conversation.

1 Get the waiter's attention.
2 Say you have a problem: you asked for pasta with chicken. You were given pasta with fish.
3 Thank the waiter.

Lesson 10.3

8 B Student A: you are a student at the Noparlo School of English. You are going to complain to the director of the school. Choose four of the problems in Exercise 8A on page 103. Think about what you are going to say. Use these expressions:

I'm afraid I have a complaint.
There's (also) a problem with …
Can you look into it?

Lesson 8.1

4 C Student B: write definitions for the completed words with the prompts.

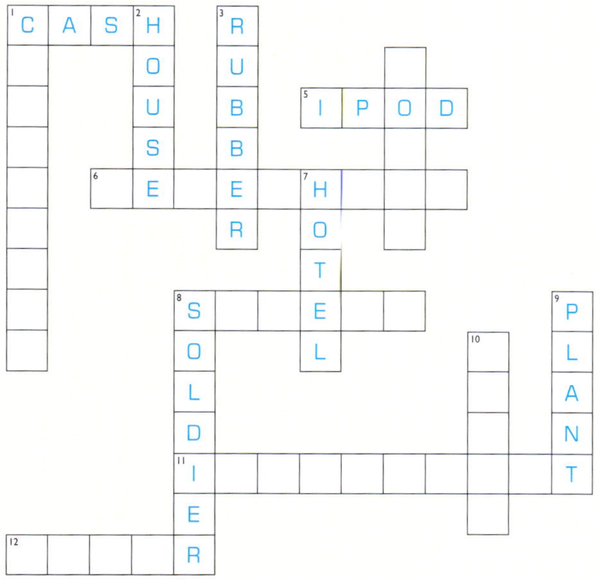

Down

2 place / people live

a place where people live

3 material / use / make car tires and chewing gum

7 place / stay when you are traveling

8 person / fight / for his country in wars

9 thing / grows in the ground and is usually green

Across

1 thing / use / pay for something (not a credit card)

5 thing / use / download and listen to music

D Ask Student A for definitions for the missing words.

Down: 1, 4, and 10

Across: 6, 8, 11 and 12

Lesson 12.3

8 Student B: you are a client. Tell the concierge:

- you want to go to the best restaurant in town. Ask him/her to recommend one.
- you want tickets to the theater. Ask if he/she can get six seats for tonight.

Student B: now you are a concierge. Listen and respond to your client's requests. Ask for more time if necessary. Your client wants to:

- go shopping for clothes.
- visit a movie studio and meet some stars.

Lesson 12.2

9 C Fact file.

Birth Name: Aung San Suu Kyi

Birth Place: Rangoon (now Yangon), Burma (Myanmar)

Date: June 19, 1945

Childhood/Education:
Father killed when she was young. Grew up with her mother and two brothers in Rangoon. Educated in a Methodist English school. Noted for having a talent with languages. Moved to India in 1960, graduated in Politics. Continued her studies at Oxford University, U.K.

Early Career:
Moved back to Burma in 1988 and entered politics calling for a democratic government. The military took power and Aung San was arrested. Offered freedom if she left the country, but she refused.

Rise to Fame:
Continued her non-violent action for democracy and refused to leave the country. In the 1990 election, her party received 59 percent of the votes, but Aung San was kept under house arrest causing an international outcry. Awarded the Nobel Peace Prize in 1991.

Later Life:
Spent more than 15 years under house arrest in Rangoon. Spent her time reading and playing the piano and sometimes meeting with diplomats. Wouldn't leave the country even when her husband was dying of cancer in 1999. Released from house arrest in 2010. Traveled the world as an ambassador for political freedom and peace.

Unit 1 Recording S1.1

1 How many people are in your family?
2 How often do you see your parents?
3 Do you enjoy spending time with your family?
4 When was your last family celebration?
5 Whom do you live with?
6 How often do you eat out with friends?
7 Where does your best friend live?

Unit 1 Recording S1.2

Story 1

My boyfriend and I were at a restaurant, and I don't know how he did it, but he put the engagement ring in my salad. I didn't see it, and I put it in my mouth. I think he panicked and tried to stop me. Anyway, luckily I felt something hard as I bit into my food, and I didn't swallow it. I took it out, saw what it was and accepted! So that was how we got engaged. It was almost a disaster. We got married one month later.

Story 2

We decided to go on vacation in Egypt, since we both liked diving. This was my girlfriend and I at the time. So we went on a dive, and I proposed to her underwater. I didn't say anything. I just gave her the ring while we were, I don't know, ten feet under. Luckily, she smiled. We got back on the boat, and she said yes.

Story 3

My husband and I are video artists. We met at art school, and honestly we fell in love immediately. And what he did was he made a funny two-minute video. He put it on YouTube and sent a link to me. And it was him proposing. And in the video there was music, and then all of our friends suddenly appeared, singing and dancing. It was amazing and such a surprise. I watched it, and then I surprised him. I accepted his proposal, but I didn't tell him. Instead I made a video of me saying yes.

Unit 1 Recording S1.5

Conversation 1

W = Woman D = David R = Rachel

W: Hi, David. This is my friend, Rachel.
D: Hi, Rachel. Nice to meet you. Would you like a drink?
R: Sorry. What did you say?
D: Would you like a drink, Rachel?
R: Oh. I'd love a coffee, thank you.
D: So, do you work here?
R: No, I'm a student.
D: Are you here on vacation then?
R: Um … yes.
D: Where exactly do you come from?
R: I'm from Huntington, near L.A.
D: OK, umm, I'll just go and get the coffee.

Conversation 2

W = Woman F = Felicia

W: Hi, Felicia. Nice day, isn't it?
F: Yes, it's beautiful.
W: Did you have a good weekend?
F: Yes, it was OK. I didn't do much.
W: Did you watch the game last night?
F: Yes, it was terrible. We lost 3-0.
W: Oh, no! I'm sorry to hear that.
F: That's OK. I'll see you later.
W: Yes, see you soon.

Unit 1 Recording S1.7

I've known Michelle for a long time. We met when we were at school together. We were about eleven years old, and I had to show her where to hang up her coat. And, we've been friends ever since. Er … we get along really well. She's one of those people who, if you haven't seen them for six months, six days, it's the same. It's like time hasn't passed. We have lots of things in common. We play tennis together. The only problem with Michelle is that she's a bit competitive, and we had a falling out over tennis. Sometimes, if she wins, I haven't spoken to her … erm … and she's just one of those people you can rely on. She's sort of like number one in my phone book. Umm … and, yes, she's a great person. We have lots of laughs together.

Unit 2 Recording S2.2

A: Today we're looking at how companies motivate their staff. Sarah, can you tell us more?
B: Absolutely. Internet companies are famous for this type of thing. At Yahoo, there's a free bus ride to work for employees. There's also a dentist and a hair stylist at the office.
A: Makes life easier for employees …
B: Exactly. And, wait for it, one day a month the employees watch movies together.
A: Great ideas.
B: Yep. Now at Google, lunch is free, and you can also get a cheap massage at the office.
A: Wow!
B: And other companies are bringing in new ideas, too. A company called Pontiflex in New York created a nap room where employees could sleep for 15 minutes.
A: Nice idea.
B: At several companies, we're hearing that the relationship between bosses and employees is changing. At one company, the boss writes thank you notes to employees. At another, the staff does a job swap two days a year. So a senior manager might clean floors for the day, and the cleaner can sit in an air-conditioned office.
A: Does that motivate everybody?
B: Well, it helps employees to see what everyone else is doing in the company, which I think is … very valuable and of course ….

Unit 2 Recording S2.3

Conversation 1

M = Man I = Interviewer

M: Hi. I work at Kinko's coffee store across the street. But, at the moment I'm taking a break here in the music store.
I: And what are you doing on your break?
M: I'm choosing my free CD for the week.
I: Free CD? Can you tell us a bit more? Why are you doing this?
M: Sure. Kinko's, the coffee shop, has an agreement with the music store. The employees at the music store get free coffee at Kinko's. They all come in during their break. And we get one free CD a week from the music store.
I: Great!
M: We all know each other, and it works really well.

Conversation 2

W = Woman I = Interviewer

W: So, this is the clothing store. And this is the study area.
I: Right. So you have a study area?
W: Yeah. As you can see, David, over there, is studying. And these two are taking an online course.
I: And this is during work hours? Does the boss know about this?
W: It's the boss's idea. The company pays for employees to take courses. So, during our breaks or after seven when the store closes, we can stay and study.
I: That's excellent. And are you studying at the moment?
W: Yeah, but I'm not studying anything related to fashion.
I: What are you studying?
W: I'm studying history.
I: And the company pays?
W: The company pays. It pays for about six of us. I think six of us are taking online courses.
I: Awesome!

Conversation 3

E = Employee I = Interviewer

E: Hi there. I work for a software company.
I: And what are you doing now?
E: Well, I'm checking my emails at the moment because I need to see what work I have to do today.
I: At one o'clock?
E: Well, the company has flexible hours. You can arrive when you want and go home at any time.
I: That sounds good.
E: It's great. We get a salary for good work, not for the time we spend in the office. So, really, the important thing is to do your job well. That's what the boss says, anyway!

Unit 2 Recording S2.5

I = Interviewer M = Man

I: Can you tell us a little about what you do and what you like about your job?
M: Yes. I'm a marine biologist. I work mainly in the ocean and also in the lab. One good thing about my job is that I like working outside.
I: I see.

M: In fact, I can't stand sitting at a desk all day. Um. What else?
I: Maybe you get to travel ...
M: I travel a lot, and I absolutely love traveling, particularly in South America and Australia.
I: And what about your colleagues, people you work with?
M: Actually, most of my time is spent alone, which kind of suits me. I don't like working on a team. I prefer working alone.
I: Really? And what about the type of work?
M: It's interesting—there's a lot of lab work, but it's a very practical job. You're working with animals and plant life the whole time. And, y'know, I don't mind getting my hands dirty. That's important. Also, I'm interested in learning new things—and you do learn all the time in this job. You're always discovering new things.
I: That's great. It sounds wonderful.
M: I couldn't do an office job because I hate working under pressure. And I'm not very interested in working for a company. I just want to be my own boss.
I: So, you found the right job for you.
M: I found the right job for me, yes.

Unit 2 Recording S2.8

A = Alistair   Z = Zeinab

A: Zeinab, can I ask you a few questions about your work/life balance?
Z: Of course.
A: OK. First question: how much time do you spend sleeping?
Z: Lots! Probably about eight or nine hours a night!
A: Really?!
Z: Yep.
A: OK. And what about studying?
Z: Well, I suppose usually about five or six hours a day, although it depends. I mean, if I have a test coming up or something, it's probably more.
A: And do you ever take a vacation?
Z: Oh, yeah. Probably twice a year. I try and go abroad and just completely relax.
A: OK. What about your weekends? Do you ever study on the weekend?
Z: Not usually, but once in a while I open a book!
A: Right. And do you think you have a good work/life balance?
Z: I think so, yeah. I'm not too stressed or anything.
A: Easy life being a student.
Z: Oh, yeah!

Unit 3 Recording S3.1

H = Host   R = Rafael   C = Carmen

H: You probably think there's nothing to do for free in New York, right? Well, New York may be one of the most expensive cities in the world, but, if you look carefully, there are still lots of fun things to do that will cost you next to nothing or may even be free. We sent two journalists, Rafael and Carmen, out onto the streets of New York with just $20 to spend. Their challenge was to organize a great day out, but not go over their budget. Let's listen to their plans. Rafael?
R: Yes.
H: Rafael, hi, can you tell us what you're planning to do with your $20?
R: Hi, yes, well, actually I'm going to start the day with a delicious bagel from a great bagel shop I've discovered on 3rd Avenue. They are really cheap and tasty. Then I'm going to spend the morning in Central Park. The park is filled with free events and street musicians, so I'm just going to listen to music and watch people. In the afternoon, I'm going to the Museum of American Finance. You have to pay to go in, but I'm really interested to find out about the history of American banking. After that, I'm taking the Staten Island Ferry. It's free, and it's a great way to see views of New York from the water. In the evening, I'm going to see some live music on 2nd Avenue. I'll need to buy one drink, but the music is free.
H: That sounds great, Rafael. Enjoy the day.
R: Thank you. I'm sure I will.
H: OK, so Rafael has chosen bagels, Central Park, the Finance Museum and live music in the evening. Let's hear about what Carmen is planning for her day. Carmen?
C: Hi.
H: Carmen, can you tell us what you've planned for your day in New York City?
C: Yes, of course. I'm really excited, because I'm going to the High Line to see some sculptures and just walk around and see what's happening.
H: The High Line? What's that?
C: It's an old railway track. Now, it's used as a park, and there's lots of different activities and artists there. It's a really peaceful and beautiful place, right in the middle of the city. Lots of people go jogging there. I'm not going running, though. I'm going to see a free art exhibition. After that, I'm going to Times Square. It's such a famous place, and there are a lot of tourists there. But, I really like the atmosphere, and there's an Italian restaurant that makes the best cheesecake just nearby. So, I'm going to have something to eat. Then, in the evening, I'm meeting with a friend and we're going to a free hip-hop class. I'm going to learn to dance like a real New Yorker.
H: Wow, that sounds good. So, first you're going to eat cheesecake, and then you're going dancing. Right?
C: Exactly!
H: That sounds like a great plan. So, two great plans there. Which would you choose?

Unit 3 Recording S3.4

Conversation 1

A: Como's Restaurant.
B: Hello, I'd like to reserve a table for four on Saturday night. Around eight thirty if possible.
A: Let me just take a look. This Saturday?
B: Yes.
A: Saturday the fifteenth. Sorry, we're completely full on Saturday. There's nothing at all.
B: Ah, what about Sunday?
A: Sunday, Sunday. Um ... the best I can do is a table at nine o'clock.
B: Nine o'clock? Don't you have anything earlier?
A: Nothing at all, I'm afraid.
B: OK, let's go ahead. Nine o'clock.
A: Can I take your name, please?
B: The table is for Jack Hopper.
A: Jack ... hang on ... can you repeat that, please? Did you say Jack Hopper?
B: Yes. H-o-double p-e-r.
A: OK, that's reserved. Table for four, nine o'clock, Sunday.
B: Great. Thank you.
A: Thank you.

Conversation 2

A: RSA Theater. Jenny speaking. How can I help you?
B: Hello, I was wondering if you could help me. I've reserved tickets for the show on the tenth of June, but I'd like to change the date.
A: OK, one moment. Can I just check? What's the name, please?
B: The tickets are in the name of James King.
A: Sorry, I didn't catch that. Did you say King?
B: James King.
A: OK. Two tickets for June the tenth. What date would you like to change to?
B: What dates do you still have seats for?
A: There's nothing on the twelfth or thirteenth. There are two seats for the eleventh, but they're separate. We have ...
B: Sorry, can you slow down, please? Two seats for?
A: Sorry, two seats for the eleventh, but they aren't together. We can give you two seats together on June the fourteenth.
B: June the fourteenth. That's fine.
A: OK. I'll just go ahead and reserve those.

Conversation 3

A: Hello?
B: Hello, it's Mary here. ... Hello? Can you hear me OK? It's Mary here.
A: Oh, hi, Mary. How are you?
B: Very well, thanks. And you?
A: Yeah, fine.
B: Are you doing anything on Saturday? Because a few of us are going out for dinner.
A: Sorry, Mary, can you speak up, please? I'm at the station and I can't hear a thing.

B: D'you want to go for dinner on Saturday?
A: Oh, that sounds nice.
B: There's going to be a few of us, Mohammed and Clare and Robin.
A: That sounds like fun.
B: Are you free?
A: I think so.
B: Good. Eight-thirty, Saturday. Pauly's.
A: OK. Pauly's on Saturday at eight-thirty.
B: That's right. Great. See you soon.
A: OK. Thanks for calling.

Conversation 4

A: Witherton's. Who's calling?
B: Hello, this is Kim. Kim Brower. Can I speak to Alexandra Sanders, please?
A: I'm afraid she's not here at the moment.
B: Ah, do you know when she'll be back? I've tried her phone three or four times and left messages, but she hasn't called back.
A: She's visiting a customer. She should be back this evening. Can I take a message?
B: It's about dinner tonight. I've had to cancel because of work.
A: OK. I'll ask her to call you back.
B: Thanks.
A: Does she have your number?
B: It's 182-2766.
A: Can you repeat that, please?
B: 182-2766.

Unit 3 Recording S3.8

OK. I'm going to tell you about how to go local in Pisa, Italy. I'm going to take you on a tour that only the locals would know about. First of all, we're starting the day with a coffee and a fresh pastry from a little bar near the Vettovaglie market. I love this place because it's where all the locals who sell in the market go to have their coffee. And the coffee is delicious. We're going to spend the morning walking through the market and the old part of the city near the university. Afterward, for lunch, we're going to one of the best restaurants I know. It's called Le Bandierine and they specialize in home-made spaghetti and seafood, and we're going to have a fantastic meal there. In the afternoon, we're planning to go a little outside Pisa to San Rossore park. It's a beautiful place to walk, but they also have horse races there, so we can have some fun watching the horses. In the evening, we're going back toward the Leaning Tower for an early evening drink to look at the Piazza dei Miracoli as the sun goes down, when all the tourists have gone home. We'll finish the evening with a wonderful pizza from a restaurant on the other side of the city. I'm sure you'll love it. It's going to be a day to remember.

Unit 4 Recording S4.3

I = Interviewer M = Mario

I: So, Mario, can you tell us how you used your talent in your job?
M: Um, well, I've always enjoyed cooking. I come from a big Italian family, and I learned to cook by watching my mother in the kitchen.
I: But, no one knew you could cook, right?
M: That's right. No one knew. I only cooked at home, but I did it well. Then, in my twenties, I started to make meals for my friends. And, well, I was working in an office. And I brought food to office parties, things like that.
I: Then you had an idea …
M: I had the idea to sell my food at work.
I: So your colleagues buy your food every day.
M: Yeah, I started selling it to friends and colleagues and then to other people at work. I prepared all kinds of things: bread, pasta, desserts.
I: And then you made a decision.
M: Yeah, office work was OK, but I wanted to do something more interesting. So, eventually, I asked the boss if I could open a café in the office.
I: And he was happy to …
M: He agreed. They gave me a room. Now I take food there every day. We have chairs and tables. And now that's my job.
I: Have you ever thought, "Oh, I prefer my old office job. This is too difficult"?
M: Never. I've never thought that because this is what I love doing: cooking and preparing different menus. Really, it's the best decision I've ever made.
I: And have you thought about expanding the business, maybe opening a restaurant one day?
M: I've thought about it, but it's a long way away!

Unit 4 Recording S4.6

G = Glynn M = Magda

G: Magda, many of my students are too shy to speak in front of the class. They worry about making mistakes.
M: Yes, this is a common problem. Teachers should give students time to prepare. Tell them the question, and give them a few minutes to think about what they'll say. They can take notes first.
G: That's a good idea.
M: Also, let them practice in groups before they speak in front of everyone. This well give them confidence.
G: Yes, you're right. I do usually give them a chance to practice first. Now, what about those students who have problems listening to English?
M: Problems listening. That's common, too.
G: Native speakers, for example, people from the U.K. or Australia or the States, speak really fast and it's difficult to understand them.
M: Yes. Students should practice listening to native speakers. Fortunately, if they have the Internet, there are lots of opportunities. They can listen to the news and to podcasts. But even better is to go on YouTube and watch film clips. When we can see the people speaking, it makes it easier. We can watch the mouth and the hands and the body language, and it helps us to understand.
G: And using subtitles? Some teachers say we shouldn't use them. Ever!
M: I'm not sure that's a good idea. Subtitles can be a real help. Students can see the differences between the spelling and the pronunciation of words. They can see which words are swallowed …
G: I suppose so.
M: For me, students should use subtitles … maybe the second time they watch.
G: OK, and what about … students' pronunciation. They have a lot of problems …

Unit 4 Recording S4.7

A: OK, well, I think the most important invention is probably the Internet. For me, it's number one.
B: Uh-huh.
A: It's opened up the world, and we can get lots of information for free now. And it joins people together from all different cultures and countries.
B: That's true, but I think there are more important inventions. Really simple things that are so common we forget about them.
A: Like what?
B: Well, things like aspirin. It's not really an invention, I suppose, but can you imagine life without aspirin?
A: Umm, not really.
B: And all the other medicines we use.
A: Antibiotics to cure illnesses. That's true actually. Painkillers.
B: And another invention that I see as really important is the car.
A: Oh, yeah, definitely.
B: Before the car, travel was so slow it took days to get anywhere.
A: That's true. People went everywhere by horse, didn't they?
B: Yeah, and so the car opened up possibilities …

Unit 5 Recording S5.3

1 These days, we always expect to hear English in tourist areas. Most people working in tourism speak it, but I always want to talk to local people and many of them don't speak English. So I try to learn a few words of the language, especially "please" and "thank you." And I always take a small dictionary.
2 I love walking when I go on vacation … 'cause I think … I think you see more, so I always take a really good pair of walking shoes.
3 I think a good digital camera is important when you travel. I always take a lot of pictures. And I also take binoculars.
4 When I'm not traveling for work, I usually spend my vacations in a warm place, so I always take a sun hat. But, when I go somewhere during the

winter or rainy season, I always take waterproof clothes.

5 I think it's a good idea to buy a really good suitcase. And when you pack, leave enough space for souvenirs. On the other hand, I enjoy traveling to wild places, so often I take a backpack not a suitcase. If you decide to go walking, a backpack is much easier to carry.

6 It's best to avoid carrying too much money because you don't want to look like a rich tourist! Because of this, I always take a money belt when I'm on vacation.

7 I need to write things down to remember them so I take a notebook and pen.

Unit 5 Recording S5.4

1 To get to Argentina, you wait at the corner for the bus. It takes you down Avenida das Cataratas and right into Avenida Mercosul. The bus goes straight ahead for about 25 minutes. Cross the bridge, and you're in Argentina.

2 To see the Iguaçu Falls on the Brazilian side, you turn right and go straight ahead down Avenida das Cataratas and Highway 469, and the Falls are in front of you. You can't miss them—they're the biggest in the world!

3 To get to Paraguay, you have to go left. You go along the main road through the park past the trees. Then you turn right and you're on Avenida Kubitschek. Let's see. From there you keep going until you reach Highway 277. Go left. The bridge is at the end of the highway. Cross the bridge and you're in Paraguay.

Unit 5 Recording S5.5

Conversation 1

A: Excuse me. We're trying to get to the carnival. Is this the right bus stop?
B: Yes, but you don't need the bus. It's very close.
A: Oh! Can we walk?
B: Yes, it takes about ten minutes from here. Just go straight ahead. You'll hear the music!
A: OK. Thank you very much.

Conversation 2

A: Excuse me, can you help me? I'm looking for the Plaza Hotel. Is this the right way?
B: Um … Plaza Hotel, Plaza Hotel. Yes, keep going, past the movie theater and take the first left.
A: OK.
B: Then keep going for about fifteen minutes until you reach the end of the road. And you'll see the sign for the hotel. You can't miss it.
A: OK. Can you show me on the map?
B: Sure.

Conversation 3

A: Excuse me, we want to get to the Grand Motel. Is it far?
B: Um … sorry, I have no idea. Jim, do you know?
C: What?
B: The Grand Motel?
C: The Grand Motel? Yeah, it's just over there. Just go to the end of this street. Go left and go past the … um … there's a restaurant. Go past the restaurant, and it's on the left.
A: On the left. So I need to go to the end of the street, turn left, go past the restaurant, and it's on the left.
C: Yeah, that's it.
A: Thanks a lot.

Unit 5 Recording S5.8

OK, well, we would like to go to Easter Island. It is very isolated, very far from other places, and the nearest country is Chile, over two thousand miles away. We are going to travel there by plane and stay with different families. The trip is going to take three months. We want to experience the local culture, the music, food and way of life. So our plan is to speak to the local people about these things and to film them. We hope to find out about their traditions and to see what they think of their history. Well, finally, my husband and I always wanted to go to Easter Island. I read about it when I was a child and I saw pictures of these amazing stone heads on the island. So for us, this is our dream trip.

Unit 6 Recording S6.1

1 Do you live in a town or by the ocean?
2 How long have you lived there?
3 How long have you lived in the house you live in now?
4 What is the name of your best friend?
5 How long have you known him or her?
6 Do you work or study?
7 How long have you worked or studied where you are now?
8 What hobby do you enjoy?
9 How long have you done it for?
10 Do you have a bicycle or a car?
11 How long have you had it?

Unit 6 Recording S6.3

I = Interviewer S = Sue

I: Sue, what are the latest food trends?
S: We have lots of interesting developments and even possible solutions for world problems related to food.
I: Great. So you can kind of …
S: Well, the key question is always what to eat, and here we may see some changes, things that you might not understand as food groups.
I: Can you give an example?
S: An example is insects.
I: As a food group?
S: Well, in Latin America, Asia and Africa, people have eaten insects for thousands of years, but it's only now that we in the West are seeing what a good food source they are. Insects are rich in protein, low in fat, and easy to farm.
I: So spiders and ants may be on the menu?
S: We might see them on menus in the West. Now, technology will also play a part in the future of food. Scientists have already found ways to create meat in the lab.
I: Right, but it tastes awful, doesn't it?
S: It tastes awful now, but maybe it won't in the future. And as well as making meat in a lab, we're also looking at ways to make proteins out of things like mud and wood and also seaweed.
I: It seems incredible that mud might be something we can eat.
S: Well, it's the same for seaweed, which again is easy to farm because it's everywhere. Um. Other developments on your kitchen table include an intelligent knife.
I: What's that?
S: An intelligent knife will tell you all about the food it's cutting. So, say you cut a slice of meat, the knife will tell you how much protein and fat is in the meat, where it's from, how old it is.
I: That's amazing.
S: Really giving people more information about their food.

Unit 6 Recording S6.6

Conversation 1

D = Doctor W = Woman

D: Hello. I'm Dr. Andrews. Now, what's the matter?
W: Well, doctor, I feel terrible. I get these headaches, and I feel sick.
D: Oh. How long have you had this problem?
W: A few weeks now. And I can't sleep at night because my head hurts.
D: You can't sleep?
W: That's right.
D: And are you very worried or under pressure at the moment?
W: No, I don't think so.
D: Do you have a healthy diet?
W: Hmm. Quite healthy.
D: Do you drink tea or coffee?
W: Yes, I do.
D: How much?
W: Tea? Probably about eight cups, or ten.
D: A day?
W: Yes.
D: I see. And has that changed in the last few weeks?
W: Not really.
D: OK. Well, the first thing is I think you should stop drinking so much tea and coffee. Try to drink just one small cup a day. I'll give you some painkillers for the headaches. Take two of these three times a day. I don't think it's anything to worry about, but if …

Conversation 2

D = Doctor M = Man

D: Good morning. How can I help?
M: Well, I'm worried about my foot.

D: Your foot?
M: Yes. It hurts when I walk.
D: I see. Did you do anything to it? Did you have an accident?
M: Um. Well, sort of.
D: What happened?
M: I kicked a wall.
D: I see. When did you do that?
M: About a week ago.
D: OK. Did you go to the hospital?
M: No.
D: Can I have a look?
M: Yes, of course.
D: Where does it hurt? Here?
M: Argh. Yes, there.
D: Can you move it?
M: Yes, a little, but it's very painful.
D: Hmm. I think it might be broken. It's nothing to worry about, but I think you should go to the hospital for an X-ray. I'll write you a note, and if …

Unit 6 Recording S6.8

To get healthy, you need a combination of things. You need the right diet. You need to exercise. You need to sleep seven or eight hours. Then there are other things related to lifestyle: how many friends you have, how happy your relationships are. These are really important, and they affect your general health. In this person's case, there are some changes he can make. For example, he needs to do some exercise. I understand that his back gives him problems, which is quite common in someone of his age. But he could really help himself by doing more activity. He could try going for walks or riding a bicycle. Also, six hours of TV every day is too much. He should spend some of that time exercising or seeing his friends. He must lose weight, so maybe he could eat less meat, perhaps once a day instead of twice. Now, some of these changes are related to the people around him. For example, if it's his wife who does the cooking, she'll need to …

Unit 7 Recording S7.1

Part 1

H = Host J = Jessica

H: Now, have you ever daydreamed about changing your life forever, about giving up your job and setting off for a distant country where you could find love and happiness? Well, Jessica Fox did just that, and she's on the line now to tell us about her journey. Jessica, welcome to the program.
J: Oh, thank you for having me. It's a pleasure to be here.
H: Now, you started your journey in Los Angeles. Tell me about your life there. What was your job? What sort of lifestyle did you have?
J: Ahh, I was consulting for Pixar. I was doing what I loved. I was living in a city that I adored, and I had a fantastic network of friends. There was, I can only describe it as like a … an abstract taste that I was missing. And so I really began … it was about a year … I began daydreaming about something quite different.
H: Did you have an actual vision of what the change might be?
J: I would often sit down in my studio and just dream of different things, and usually they turned into the screenplays I was writing, and this dream kept on coming back of working in a used bookstore by the ocean. And I …
H: Working in a used bookstore by the ocean?
J: In Scotland, yeah.
H: In Scotland, right. Had you ever had any connection with used bookstores or Scotland before?
J: None, absolutely none.

Part 2

H: And so did you set about doing something to realize … Or make your dream come true?
J: Yeah, it happened quite quickly, actually. I typed in "used bookstore, Scotland," into Google, and Wigtown came up, Scotland's national book town of … I think it was about sixteen bookstores. And, I thought "Oh, my gosh, one of them, hopefully, will take me in for a kind of live/work exchange while I was on vacation, and I could realize this dream of …"
H: So, did you just send an email to these bookstores and ask them to take you in?
J: I sent one email to the first bookstore on the list, which was The Bookshop, and it was the largest used bookstore in Scotland. And, within a couple of emails, this sort of amazing, generous bookstore owner said, "Yes, I host a lot of other artists. Come on over for the festival."
H: And so you came over and you stayed at The Bookshop. What sort of a bookstore was it? What sort of impression did it make on you when you first arrived?
J: I would describe it as, if Harry Potter had a bookstore, this would be it.
H: And what about the bookstore owner? Did you get along with him?
J: I did. You know I was … I was here for a specific reason. I really wanted to get away from things. I wanted to write. So, when I first met the bookstore owner I, it was just … it was a friendly, a kind of a friendly relationship I had with him. I didn't get to know him very much until toward the end of my stay …

Part 3

H: Your month ended, and you went back to L.A. Did you find yourself missing the bookstore and missing the owner?
J: Yeah, I loved the store, I loved the town itself and the people there. It took me a while to admit that it was actually most of all the bookstore owner I was missing.
H: And how did you find out that he was missing you, too?
J: We would correspond over email and Skype, and I'd get beautiful packages from him with things I missed about Wigtown.
H: Such as?
J: Such as, this is terrible, such as the cookies, digestives, the digestive cookies I absolutely adore, um, and a lot of the candy and movies. I fell in love with Scottish movies.
H: So your relationship deepened? Did you think, "Well, maybe I'm falling in love with this man"?
J: Yeah, and I think the reason it took so long for me to admit was that it meant a radical life shift. And, luckily, my job shifted at Pixar. So, suddenly I had this freedom of being able to be anywhere in the world that I wanted. And I just thought, "Well, why let all my characters in my movies have all the fun?" I really wanted to jump in and try this. This was a true challenge, an adventure.
H: So, tell me about your life now, living above the bookstore in Scotland.
J: Well, right now there's a heater underneath my legs—it is absolutely freezing—there is ice crawling up the windows. But, it's very cozy, and the snow has just hit here. It's beautiful outside, and Wigtown remains, four years after, remains as charming as when I first came.
H: … and how is it going with the bookstore owner?
J: Wonderful! You couldn't find a more beautiful place, and you couldn't find more excellent people, and you know … the love of my life is here so …
H: Jessica, it's been wonderful to speak to you.
J: Thank you so much for having me.

Unit 7 Recording S7.5

Conversation 1

A: Excuse me, where do I register for my course?
B: Do you know where the main office is?
A: Sorry?
B: The main office.
A: Oh, yes.
B: The registration desk is there.
A: Thank you so much.

Conversation 2

A: Excuse me, where's the reading room?
C: It's next to the cafeteria.
A: The cafeteria? Where's that?
C: Follow me. I'll take you there.
A: Thank you. That's very kind.

Conversation 3

A: Where can I use the Internet?
D: You can use the computers in the library or in the study center.
A: Do I have to pay?
D: No.
A: So, it's free for students.
D: Yes, that's right.

Conversation 4

A: Excuse me, what time is the library open?
E: It's open every day, from 9 a.m. until 6 p.m.

A: Did you say "every day"?
E: Yes, that's right. Every day, from nine in the morning until six in the evening.
A: Thank you.

Conversation 5

A: Could you help me? Where can I get a new student ID card? I've lost mine.
F: OK. If you go to the main office you can get a new one.
A: Thank you.

Conversation 6

A: Excuse me, can you help me find my classroom?
G: Sure. What number is it?
A: 301.
G: OK. You need to go up to the third floor. And it's on the right.

Conversation 7

A: Where can I buy a notebook?
H: There's a stationery store downstairs.
A: Sorry?
H: There's a stationery store downstairs.
A: Thank you so much.

Conversation 8

A: Can you help me?
I: Yes, maybe.
A: I need to find out about my housing. Can you tell me where to go?
I: Housing? I think you have to go to the student services office over there, next to the bookstore.
A: Thank you.

Unit 7 Recording S7.8

Well, when I first arrived in the U.S., it was a very interesting time for me. The biggest problem was that I couldn't really speak the language very well. I learned English at school and at college in Poland, but it's very different when you are living in the country and you need to speak it all the time. I felt very nervous when I had to speak to American people, like in stores or when you meet friends. And I couldn't understand what people were saying to me. It was terrible. I used to stay at home and watch lots of television to try and understand what people were saying. Luckily, I made friends very quickly with some American girls, so we used to go out together. That really helped me. After a few months, my English was much better. I felt more confident. And now I talk to people all the time, but it was hard at the beginning.

Unit 8 Recording S8.2

Speaker 1

I work as a nanny, looking after children, aged two, three, and five. I'm actually a live-in nanny. I live with the family. I came into the job with my eyes open. I knew it would be hard work because children can be difficult, though, of course, they're fun, too. Also, we work long hours, and too many of us do extra work like cleaning and cooking when we should only look after the children. Nannies, particularly live-in nannies, aren't paid enough. Some of us need two jobs. We should earn enough just from being a nanny because working with children is a really important job. It's like teaching. It affects the future.

Speaker 2

I'm a fireman. It's one of the most dangerous jobs that exists. Really, it's too dangerous to be paid so little. People see us relaxed and calm, and maybe we go and rescue a cat from a tree and people think, "Oh, they earn too much. Their job is easy." But, when there's a serious fire, we have to be ready, even if it's just once a year. We risk our lives to save people, sometimes stupid people who fell asleep with a cigarette in their mouth or forgot to switch off the oven. You know, we save people, we save buildings, we save businesses. Anything and everything can burn down, and that's why we're so important.

Speaker 3

I'm a research biologist. I work on finding solutions to some of the world's major problems, such as disease and hunger. The thing is, it's always difficult to get funding, to get enough money to actually do the research. Some of our projects are very expensive. They can cost millions of dollars, and it can take years before you see results. So, actually, I'm not asking for a bigger salary for myself, but I'd like more money for the lab. Too many scientists spend too much time applying for grants to get money rather than actually doing their job in the lab. When things go well for us, the whole world benefits, so I think this work should be better funded.

Unit 8 Recording S8.4

Conversation 1

S = Store Assistant W = Woman

S: Can I help you?
W: No, thanks. I'm just looking.
S: OK, just let me know if you need anything.
W: Thanks.

Conversation 2

S = Store Assistant M = Man

S: Hi there. Are you looking for anything in particular?
M: Yeah, do you sell those things that photographers wear? Er ... it's like a vest.
S: Um, a type of vest.
M: Yeah, a light green vest with lots of pockets.
S: Ah, you mean like a safari vest?
M: Yes.
S: They're just on your left.
M: Ah, yes. Thank you. Can I try this on?
S: Of course.
M: Where's the fitting room?
S: Just over there.
M: Thanks.

Conversation 3

M = Man S = Store Assistant

M: Excuse me. Do you have one of these in a larger size? It doesn't fit.
S: Is that the large? I'll just go and check for you. I'm sorry. This is all we have in stock at the moment. There are some other T-shirts over there on the other side. There might be some extra large sizes there.

Conversation 4

W = Woman S = Store Assistant

W: Hello. I was wondering if you have any of that stuff you use for cleaning swimming pools.
S: Um ... yeah, we usually sell a liquid cleaner. You pour it into the pool. There's one here.
W: Can I take a look?
S: Yup.
W: How much is it?
S: This one's twenty-eight dollars ninety-nine cents for a quart.

Conversation 5

S = Store Assistant M = Man
W = Woman

S: Hi. Are you paying in cash or with a credit card?
M: Credit card.
S: Can you enter your PIN, please? Thanks. Here's your card.
M: Thanks.
S: Thank you. Who's next, please?
W: Do you take Mastercard?
S: Yes, that's fine. Can you just sign here, please?

Unit 8 Recording S8.6

Our business is called Ragbags. Our idea is to make beautiful bags out of recycled material, so old jeans and clothes that you would normally throw away. We hope to make money by reusing old material and turning it into different types of bags—all types of bags: shopping bags, beach bags, handbags, whatever you need. So, you can either buy one of our ready-made bags, or, if you have some material that you really like, we can make one especially for you. To be successful, we need to make sure the bags are really good quality and look wonderful. We don't need a lot of money to start the business because we'll make the bags at home. We plan to sell Ragbags at markets, in local stores and also online. We'll have a website with lots of beautiful photos, where people can choose their design and colors and then order their wonderful bag. And the best thing about the company is that you will have an amazing bag, made from your own favorite recycled material. Each bag will be unique, one of a kind, and we'll have fun making them, too. It's a win-win.

Unit 9 Recording S9.1

Hi, and welcome to Green Ideas. Now, the problem with some of the traditional ways of saving the environment is that they can be really boring. So, today we're looking at ideas for protecting the environment that are a bit different, and we think they sound fun.
Our first project is called Hug it Forward. This great project started in Guatemala where communities decided to work together to build schools out of old plastic bottles. In the first project, over 1,800 kids from the region filled 10,000 plastic bottles with bits of plastic, food wrappers and other garbage or trash found in the streets. They then used the bottles as bricks to help build a school. By the time they had finished, they had a new school, and the area was a lot cleaner, too! Now the idea is spreading, and, around the world, more communities are using the bottle school technology to build their own schools. What a fantastic idea!
And here's an idea for those of you who enjoy going out clubbing. The Surya nightclub in London was one of the first eco-friendly nightclubs in the U.K. The club has a special dance floor that uses the movement people make when they dance to generate energy. The dancers manage to produce 60 percent of the energy that the club uses for light and music. The owner of the eco-club had another great idea. If you walk or cycle to the club, rather than using a car or public transportation, you get free entry. I love it.
And our final idea for today is the story of Seoul River Park. It's getting more and more difficult to find green spaces in cities, so when Dr. Kee Hwang had a "crazy" idea to take down the city's main highway and uncover the river that flowed below to make a green park, most people thought he was crazy. They told him that his idea would create traffic chaos and would be a disaster for the area. But Dr. Hwang went ahead with the project and created the 5.8 kilometer green river park. It's a place where the residents of Seoul can walk, relax and really enjoy the city. And do you know what? People are happier, and there's a lot less traffic chaos than before! It just shows that sometimes even the craziest ideas can work.

Unit 9 Recording S9.6

1 I met wonderful people in the Amazon.
2 The birds we saw were amazing.
3 I have a great idea.
4 We need to put up a tent.
5 We took photos of the beautiful scenery.

Unit 9 Recording S9.7

M = Man W = Woman

M: Why do we use rats after an earthquake? I'm not sure. It might be to help find people or other animals?
W: Yeah, they're used to rescue people. They can move in small spaces, and they have a good sense of smell, so they can find people.
M: Why do some prisons use abandoned dogs? Mmmm, let me think. It could be as prison guards. Maybe they use the dogs to guard the prisoners? Actually, no, it can't be that because they'd be trained dogs, not abandoned dogs. I don't know.
W: OK. It says: it was a program that started some years ago. Abandoned dogs are taken to prisons, and then the prison inmates take care of them until the dogs are adopted.
M: Why does the army use dolphins? It's definitely not to attack people because dolphins are kind of nice. Um, it's hard to say. I really don't know.
W: Dolphins are used to protect areas of water. They can detect swimmers who shouldn't be there. A light is attached to the dolphin's nose. The dolphin bumps into the swimmer, and the light falls off its nose. This tells the army where the swimmer is.
M: Why did airport security plan to use gerbils in the 1970s? Perhaps they can smell drugs or something like that?
W: Gerbils can smell people's adrenaline. When someone is excited, scared or angry, adrenaline is released by the body. The airport security bosses hoped the gerbils would smell terrorists or other criminals in airports. In the end, the idea was abandoned because gerbils didn't know the difference between terrorists and people who were just scared of flying.
M: Why do we use seals for research in the ocean? Um ... that's a good question. It might be because they can live in very cold temperatures.
W: They can dive deep down into freezing water. Scientists can attach research equipment to the seals' bodies, and this doesn't stop the seals from diving and swimming.

Unit 9 Recording S9.9

A: OK, the most beautiful place I've been to. Well, a few years ago I went to Fish River Canyon.
B: Where?
A: Fish River Canyon. It's the second biggest canyon in the world.
B: After the Grand Canyon?
A: After the Grand Canyon.
B: Where is it?
A: It's in Namibia, in Africa.
B: Wow. And what did you think of it?
A: It was amazing. The first thing you notice is how big it is, of course.
B: Of course.
A: It just goes on and on as far as your eye can see. But the best thing about it was the silence.
B: Really?
A: It was so amazingly quiet. We went there in August, and there weren't many tourists, and it was just so quiet.
B: Would you like to go back?
A: I would love to go back. One day!
B: One day.

Unit 10 Recording S10.2

Conversation 1

I = Interviewer D = Daniela

I: Daniela, so you live in Melbourne, right?
D: Yeah, that's right.
I: Well, Melbourne has been voted one of the best cities to live in for young people. So what do you think? Do you like living in Melbourne?
D: I love it! Melbourne is a really great city. It's very friendly and fun. Umm ... there are lots of things to see and do.
I: OK, so you can go out a lot?
D: Yeah, it's very artsy, there are lots of cafés and street art, music ... and the nightlife is really good. People like to enjoy themselves in Melbourne.
I: That's great. And what about getting around? What's the public transportation like?
D: Public transportation is really good, actually. It's quite cheap, and it's efficient. You can go everywhere by streetcar, and sometimes it's even free.
I: So, what do you like best about living in Melbourne?
D: I think it's probably the atmosphere. Also, it's a great location. It's really close to some fantastic beaches, so there's surfing. It has everything really. It's a great city.

Conversation 2

I = Interviewer R = Rick

I: Rick, you've lived in Dubai for ... what, four years, right?
R: Yeah, four years.
I: So what's it like, living in Dubai?
R: Well, I read that Dubai is one of the world's fastest growing cities, so there are a lot of people, and it's very crowded. It's a great city for shopping and going out. And it has a really good nightlife, with lots of bars and clubs.
I: Is it a safe city?
R: Yes, there isn't a lot of crime. The streets are very safe. But one of the biggest problems is the traffic. Everyone drives a car here—gas is still cheap, so the traffic's terrible. One good thing is the taxis though. There are lots of them, and they're cheap, so you don't have to drive.

Conversation 3

I = Interviewer M = Matt

I: What about Prague? What's Prague like, Matt?
M: I've always loved Prague. I think it's definitely one of the best cities in the world.
I: What do you like best about living in Prague?
M: I think it has to be the city itself. It's so beautiful. It's like the city of your dreams, with beautiful buildings and squares. The old streets are wonderful to walk along. It is full of culture, music, bars, restaurants ...
I: What about the weather? What's the weather like in Prague?

M: Yeah. OK, when I arrived in Prague, it was minus seven degrees Celsius. So, obviously, it gets very cold in the winter, and there is a lot of snow. But, in the summer, the sun shines, and you can sit outside in the cafés or walk up to the castle. It's a very special city, and the people are so friendly.

Unit 10 Recording S10.5

Conversation 1

G = Guest R = Receptionist

G: Oh, hello. Could you help me? There's a problem with the air conditioning.
R: Oh, yes?
G: I've just tried to switch it on, but it doesn't work.
R: Is it completely dead?
G: Completely. Absolutely nothing.
R: OK, we'll look into it right away. I'll send someone up. It'll take about five minutes, OK?
G: Thanks.
R: You're welcome. And sorry about that.

Conversation 2

D = Diner W = Waitress
M = Manager

D: I'm afraid I have a complaint. Could I speak to the manager, please?
W: Yes, of course.
M: Good evening, sir. I understand there's a problem.
D: Yes. I'm afraid I have a complaint.
M: Oh?
D: Well, we got here at eight. And then we waited about twenty minutes for a table.
M: Right.
D: This is for a table we'd reserved for eight, OK? Then we waited another hour for our meal.
M: Right.
D: One hour. Then when the check arrived, they put this extra charge on it.
M: An extra charge? That's probably the service charge.
D: Well, could you check this for me, please?
M: Yes, that's service.
D: Well, to be honest, I don't want to pay this.
M: Of course not. Well, sir, I'm really sorry about that. It's a very busy time of year.

Conversation 3

M = Man W = Woman

W: Excuse me. Do you work here?
M: Yes.
W: Do you know when the next train will be arriving? I mean, I've been here for over an hour.
M: I'm sorry, but there's nothing we can do at the moment. Everything is delayed.
W: And you don't know when the next train is coming?
M: No.
W: Or why there's a delay?
M: Snow.
W: What?
M: Snow on the track. It was the wrong type of snow.
W: What do you mean "the wrong type of snow"? You're kidding, right?

Unit 10 Recording S10.7

1 One thing that really annoys me is the fact that we import so much food from overseas, rather than growing our own food here in this country. So, you go to the supermarket, and you can buy strawberries in the middle of winter. I suppose that's OK. But, then you try to buy an apple, and the apples are from New Zealand, and you think, "Well, that's just crazy." I mean, I don't understand why we need to fly apples all over the world when we could just grow them here in this country. It really makes me angry. It would be so much better for the environment if people bought food locally. So, I'd like to start a campaign to encourage people to buy and eat local food. Perhaps I could start a website or publish articles in newspapers to try to get people to stop buying food that comes from all over the world.

2 I get really fed up with the fact that there's nothing for teenagers to do in this town. I just think it's really difficult because people complain that teenagers are just on the streets, causing problems. But actually, there isn't really anywhere else for them to go. There are no sports facilities or clubs where they can spend time together and have some fun. And another thing is we get a lot of crime because there are too many bored teenagers around. I'd like to raise money to build sports centers and youth clubs where teenagers can go to enjoy themselves or practice sports or learn something. I think there should be more things for teenagers to do, and they should be better and cheaper.

Unit 11 Recording S11.1

1 I use my phone for everything. I text most of the time because it's quick and cheap, so I text my friends and my boyfriend. I like texts because they're quiet; nobody knows what you're saying. My mom used to call me all the time to check that I'm OK, but now she can text me, which is much better. I get really annoyed when you're talking to someone though, and they're texting someone else. I think that's really rude.

2 I use the Internet a lot. I use Skype to keep in touch with my family because my daughter lives in France, so I don't see her very often. And the phone is expensive. With the Internet, I can see my grandchildren; it's wonderful. My son sets up the computer for me. I haven't learned how to do that yet. And sometimes it crashes during the phone call, which is annoying, or I can't see the picture properly. But usually it's fine. Generally, I think technology is wonderful. When I was younger, we only dreamed of having video phone calls, but now it's possible, and it's free.

3 We use a blog. It's a great way to tell people about your travel experiences. We've been to so many places already, and it's nice to tell people about them. And you can put photos there of the people you meet and the places you visit. The best thing is that, as soon as you write the blog, people all over the world can read it. The only problem we have is when we can't find an Internet café.

4 I've just started to use social media sites like Facebook. I found some friends I haven't seen for years, and it was great to get in touch again. The only problem is that I keep checking it when I should be working.

Unit 11 Recording S11.3

1 If you give me your details, I'll send you the photo.
2 If people sign the petition, the company will have to respond.
3 When your friends see the video, they won't be surprised.
4 If the situation gets worse, will you leave your job?
5 If there aren't elections soon, people will start protesting.
6 When you see this picture, I'll be in the Everglades!
7 If the product is really good, then people won't write bad reviews.
8 If they change the design, will you buy one?

Unit 11 Recording S11.5

M1 = Man 1 M2 = Man 2
W = Woman

M1: I use the Internet all day at work, and I still get my work done.
M2: Yeah, me, too.
M1: I'm sorry, but I really don't see what the problem is.
W: I think the problem is that lots of workers spend all day surfing the Internet and wasting their time instead of doing their work.
M1: Hmm.
W: And students at college are failing their courses because they spend all their time checking Facebook and watching videos that friends send them.
M2: Yes, that's true, but … um … I don't think that the problem is the Internet. You know, I think the problem is with the websites like Facebook.
M1: Yeah, definitely, like YouTube.
M2: Some companies and colleges stop you from using certain websites. And, in my opinion, that's OK.
W: But, it's so easy to waste time. I don't think you should use the Internet when you're trying to work, unless you need it for your work, for research or something.
M1: I'm not sure about that. Going on the Internet sometimes gives you a break. It's like having a cup of coffee or talking to someone in the office. People should use the Internet as much as they like.
W: I don't think so …

M2: Yes, that's right. I think it's good. I run a small business, and my staff uses the Internet as much as they want to. I don't check what they are doing. They do all their work, and they are happy. I don't think it's a waste of time at all. It's the same as going to a bookstore …
W: No, but …
M2: … or looking through a pile of magazines.
W: I'm afraid I totally disagree. The problem is that people are addicts. People aren't addicted to reading books, but the Internet is different. People spend too much time in front of their computer or their phone. They choose the Internet over sports and going out. They forget how to live in the real world, and I think it's a real problem.

Unit 11 Recording S11.8

1 OK—smartphone? That's essential. I love it. I use it all the time, for everything. I talk to people, chat, text, take photos. I couldn't live without my phone. Microwave? That's … essential. I don't have lots of time for cooking, so I use the microwave a lot. Television? Not essential. I don't watch much television. DVD player, no … not essential. Digital camera? Not essential. I use my phone. So, what else? Umm… laptop? That's essential really. I use my laptop for work, so, yes, I need that. Tablet? Hmm. I guess it's not essential.
2 Which are essential? All of them! Goodness. Right. Smartphone? Essential. I don't go anywhere without my phone. I need it in case there's an emergency and I have to call someone. Or if there's a problem with one of the children. Yes, I definitely need my phone. TV? That's essential really. I couldn't live without my television and DVD player. Umm … Laptop? Well, I need a computer really, so, yes, that's essential. Tablet. Well, no that's not essential. Digital camera? I suppose I don't need that. Someone else can take the photos! What else? Microwave. No. I can live without that.

Unit 12 Recording S12.2

He told me he was an <u>actor</u>, not a <u>dancer</u>!
He told <u>me</u> he was an <u>actor</u>, but he told <u>John</u> he was a <u>doctor</u>!
<u>He</u> told me he was an actor, but his <u>wife</u> said he was a <u>waiter</u>!

Unit 12 Recording S12.4

1
A: If I could be famous for anything, it would be art. I love painting. And, if I had more time, I would love to paint seriously. If I could have a painting in a museum, I'd be really happy.
2
B: I'd be a famous politician. If I were a politician, I would try to change the world, to stop all these wars and do something to help poor countries. You know, I think it's terrible how most politicians don't seem to worry about things like that.
3
C: If I could do anything, um … I think I'd be a famous soccer player or something like that. Imagine if you scored a goal for your country in the World Cup, that would be such a good feeling. You would remember something like that forever.
4
D: I'd love to sing. If I could be famous for anything, I think I'd be a singer. Or a dancer. I'd love to be a famous dancer. I'm terrible at both of those things. I can't sing or dance! I guess that's why we have dreams, isn't it?
5
E: I would love to be a famous writer, or poet, like Shakespeare. I think it's a wonderful thing to be able to write a book that people all around the world want to read, to be able to speak to people in that way. Yes, I'd like to be remembered as a great writer. But I don't think that'll happen.
6
F: If I could be famous for anything, well, let me see … for being beautiful! That would be good. One of those beautiful actresses who wins at the Oscars. If I were famous, I would be rich, live in a big house and have all those clothes. Oh, yes, that would be nice.
7
G: If I could be famous for anything, it would be for inventing something, like a medicine or a cure for cancer, not for being an actor or a musician. If I invented something that made people's lives better, that would be good.
8
H: What would I want to be famous for? Hmm. I wouldn't like to be famous. If I were famous, I wouldn't be happy. No, I prefer just being me, thank you.

Unit 12 Recording S12.5

Conversation 1

A: Hello.
B: Hello.
A: How can I help you?
B: I'd like to go to a local restaurant. Maybe something with traditional food. Could you recommend somewhere?
A: Yes, of course. Hang on. We have a list on a map.
B: Ah, OK.
A: OK? So here's the hotel. And if you want to walk, you can go to this one here.
B: OK.
A: This is a reasonably priced restaurant that serves mainly …

Conversation 2

A: Hello.
B: Hello. How are you?
A: Fine, thanks. What can I do for you?
B: I read that there's a local market in the area. Is it a food …
A: The food market. Yes, it's a bit of a walk. Maybe thirty minutes.
B: Oh, that far?
A: Would you like me to call a taxi? It's about a five-minute drive.
B: That would be wonderful.
A: OK, just a moment. I'll see if there's one waiting.
B: Thank you very much.

Conversation 3

A: Good morning.
B: Morning. I forgot my adapter for the laptop. It's from the United States. Would it be possible to borrow one from the hotel?
A: An adapter plug? Of course. Do you want me to send one up to your room?
B: Yes, please.
A: Can you give me a moment? I'll ask at the front desk. It's just for a laptop?
B: Yeah, that's right. A U.S. laptop. I just forgot the adapter.
A: OK, no problem. What's your room number?
B: Fourteen.
A: Room fourteen. OK.
B: Thanks a lot.

Conversation 4

A: Hello.
B: Hello.
A: How can I help you?
B: I want to see a show this evening. *Cats*.
A: Oh, yes. *Cats*.
B: Would you be able to reserve two tickets for us?
A: Hold on. Let me just check where it's playing. OK, here we are. Yes, should I reserve the tickets for you? Do you have any preference about the seats?
B: Any seats. Two together.
A: Two together, yes. OK, and it starts at 7 o'clock. So you should have plenty of time, and if you'll just wait here while I …

Unit 12 Recording S12.7

I grew up by the ocean. My father and my uncle are fishermen, and, as a child, I used to spend all my time on the beach. Every morning I watched the fishermen come in with their nets full of fish, and these men seemed so free and happy. So, I had this idea that I wanted to work on a boat. But the problem was: it was a very male profession. Only men did it, and fishermen didn't accept that women could go fishing. They thought we should stay at home and clean the house, do the cooking, have babies. I always asked my father to go on the boat with him, and he always said, "No, stay at home and help your mother." Anyway, it's a long story, but eventually I became a cleaner in a hotel. And then one day I had the chance to work as a cleaner on a ship, one of the big cruise ships. It's a great job, and I've done it for the past six years. It's a dream come true because … I spend a lot of time at sea. My next dream is to have a houseboat and actually live on the water. We'll see. I can make it happen!

Catalogue Publication Data

Authors: Antonia Clare, JJ Wilson

American Speakout Pre-Intermediate Student Book with DVD-ROM and MP3 Audio CD

First published

Pearson Educación de México, S.A. de C.V., 2017

ISBN: 978-607-32-4059-8

American Speakout Pre-Intermediate Student Book with DVD-ROM and MP3 Audio CD & MEL Access Code

ISBN MEL: 978-607-32-4039-0

Area: ELT

Format: 21 x 29.7 cm   Page count: 184

Managing Director: Sergio Fonseca ■ **Innovation & Learning Delivery Director:** Alan David Palau ■ **Regional Content Manager - English:** Andrew Starling ■ **Publisher:** A. Leticia Alvarez ■ **Content Support:** Erin Ferris ■ **Editorial Services Manager:** Asbel Ramírez ■ **Art and Design Coordinator:** Juan Manuel Santamaria ■ **Design Process Supervisor:** Aristeo Redondo ■ **Layout:** Lourdes Madrigal ■ **Cover Design:** Ana Elena García ■ **Photo Research:** Beatriz Monsiváis ■ **Photo Credits:** Pearson Asset Library (PAL)

Contact: soporte@pearson.com

This adaptation is published by arrangement with Pearson Education Limited

Pearson Education Limited
Edinburgh Gate
Harlow
Essex CM20 2JE
England
and Associated Companies throughout the world.

Used by permission and adapted from
Speakout 2ND EDITION Pre-Intermediate Students' Book
ISBN: 978-1-2921-1597-9
First published, 2015
All Rights Reserved.

Every effort has been made to trace the copyright holders and we apologize in advance for any unintentional omissions. We would be pleased to insert the appropriate acknowledgement in any subsequent edition of this publication.

First published, 2017

ISBN PRINT BOOK: 978-607-32-4059-8
ISBN PRINT BOOK MEL: 978-607-32-4039-0

Impreso en México. *Printed in Mexico.*

1 2 3 4 5 6 7 8 9 0 - 20 19 18 17

Avenida Antonio Dovalí Jaime #70
Torre B, Piso 6, Colonia Zedec Ed. Plaza Santa Fe
Delegación Álvaro Obregón, México, Ciudad de México, C. P. 01210

www.PearsonELT.com

Pearson

Pearson Hispanoamérica

Argentina ■ Belice ■ Bolivia ■ Chile ■ Colombia ■ Costa Rica ■ Cuba ■ República Dominicana ■ Ecuador ■ El Salvador ■ Guatemala ■ Honduras ■ México ■ Nicaragua ■ Panamá ■ Paraguay ■ Perú ■ Uruguay ■ Venezuela

Acknowledgements
The Publisher and authors would like to thank the following people and institutions for their feedback and comments during the development of the material: **Hungary:** Tom Boyle; **Japan:** Will Pearson; **Poland**: Lech wojciech Krzeminski, Piotr Swiecicki; **UK:** Ben Hodge, Joelle Finck, John Barron, Prakash Parmer .

Text acknowledgements
We are grateful to the following for permission to reproduce copyright material: Extract on page 172 from Outlook, Matthew Bannister interviewing Jessica Fox, 31/01/2013, http://jessicafox. info/wp-content/ uploads/2013/01/BBCWorld- Interview-Service-Interview-1_21_2013.mp3, copyright © BBC Worldwide Learning.

Illustration acknowledgements
Fred Blunt pgs 9, 11, 39, 43, 56, 66, 76, 86, 91, 106, 109, 126, 133, 138, 141, 145, 148; **Stephen Cheetham** (Handsome Frank) pgs 80; **Matt Herring** pgs 159; Infomen pgs 161, 163; **Joanna Kerr** pgs 60; **Andrew Lyons** pgs 90; Harry Malt pgs 165, 166; **Vicky Woodgate** pgs 18, 39, 80; **Jurgen Ziewe** pgs 103; **In house** pgs 16, 46, 52, 53, 56, 7 8, 136.

Photo acknowledgements
The Publisher would like to thank the following for their kind permission to reproduce their photographs:

(Key: b-bottom; c-centre; l-left; r-right; t-top)

123RF.com: Andrei Shumskiy 7b (icon), 17b (icon), 27b (icon), 37b (icon), 47b (icon), 57b (icon), 67b (icon), 77b (icon), 87b (icon), Seanjoh 93 (g), Andrei Shumskiy 97b (icon), 107b (icon), 117b (icon), Cathy Yeulet 152 (j), Hieng Ling Tie 157(soya); **4Corners Images:** Antonino Bartuccio/ Sime 27r, 34-35; **Alamy Images:** Purepix 7t, Cultura Creative 12l, Anna Stowe 12tr, Cultura Creative (RF) 17cr, XiXinXing 17l, imageBROKER 20(b) Alvey & Towers Picture Library 20c, Paul Springett 08 23c Alex Segre 28tl, Prisma Bildagentur AG 29t, New York City 30-31b, Dbimages / Allen Brown 32, Ammentorp Photography 37cr, Blend Images 37l, Hi Brow Arabia 38c, Juice Images 38cr, Adrian Sherratt 41tl, PhotoAlto / FredericCirou 42tr, Ammentorp Photography 43b, fStop / Andreas Stamm 43t, Mediacolor's 47r, Viktor Cap 50bl, Age Fotostock/Caroline Webber 52cr, Cro Magnon 52tr, Image Source Salsa 57cr, ZUMA Press Inc. 58c, EpicStockMedia 58tr, Freer Law 63l, Image Source Salsa 64-65, ICIMAGE 77t, Tetra Images 81(a), Image Source 83, Sabena Jane Blackbird 85r, Ian Dagnall 87cr, dbimages 88(c), Mikael Karlsson 92c, Eagle Visions Photography/Craig Lovell 93f, Kevin Foy 100(b), Mark Jordan 102(b), Paul Brown 102(c), Andrew Fox103t, Lucie Lang 110-111tc, imageBROKER 113, Eniz Umuler 122(c), Gregg Vignal 153(n), Tetra Images 153(e), BriggsMorris 153(o), Jonny White 154 (12), H. Mark Weidman Photography 154(13), Jose Pedro Fernandes 155 (travel guide), Manfred Grebler 156(m), Steven May 158(f), Cyrille Gibot 162; **BBC Photo Library:** Gary Moyes 7r, 14-15; **BBC Worldwide Ltd**: 14l, 24l, 34l, 44, 44cl, 64l, 64r, 67r, 74l, 94l, 114bl; **Camera Press Ltd:** Telegraph / Martin Pope 121; **Corbis:** Ocean 27cl, Tim Clayton 28bl, Flame / Simon Marcus 30, 31t, Image Source 38bl, Aflo /Naho Yoshizawa 41tr, Sopa / Antonino Bartuccio 52tl, Tetra Images 57cr, Redchopsticks 59t, Jabruson / Nature Picture Library 67t, Karen Kasmauski 79b, Move Art Management 102 (a), Tetra Images /Mike Kemp 107r, Silke Woweries 109t, Tetra Images / Mike Kemp 114-115, Arman Zhenikeyev 117l, Crave / Hbss 122(b), Image Source 156(f), Hello Lovely 160; **Datacraft Co Ltd:** 41(b), 154(5); **DK Images:** Rough Guides / Nelson Hancock 29b, Steve Baxter 60cr, Dave King 77l, Rough Guides / Nelson Hancock 83(d), Mockford and Bonetti 155(b), Rough Guides/Victor Borg 155(d), Dk Images 155(first aid kit), Lorenzo Vecchia 157 (grapefruit), William Shaw 157 (lamb); **Fotolia:** goodluz 10b, CandyBox Images 13rb, whitelook 17r, Franz Pfluegl 20(d), eurobanks 20(g), whitelook 24b, EpicStockMedia 48, Amax 51tr, M.studio 57cl, Maksud 60cl, Monart Design 61, fovito 67cr, Maksym Yemelyanov 70bl, Belman 70br, Spinetta 70cr, Vicgmyr 70tl, Kletr 70tr, Oleg_Zabielin 81(f), barneyboogles 82b, Sergey Nivens 87l, Thegoatman 93 (a), runique 93(b), Igor Norman 93 (c), Taboga 93(d), Nicola Vernizzi 93 (e), courtyardpix 97l, Zharastudio 98b, mangostock 152(n), drx 153(l), Syda Productions 153(j) Pressmaster 153(m), Marek 154(7), Calado 155(g), lowonconcept 155 (souvenir), Natika 157(carrots), natalyka 157(courgetti), Mates 157(cucumber), Swetlana Wall 157(duck), Mariusz Blach 157(garlic), stockphoto-graf 157(ice cream), margo555 157(peas), yvdavid 157(shrimps), Joe Gough 157(steak), Route66, 158(a), PhotoSG 158; **Getty Images:** Betsie Van Der Meer 7cr, Jean-Erick PASQUIER/ Contributor 17t, Andersen Ross 13bl, Javier Pierini 18, Digital Vision 20(f), AFP / Calle Toernstroem 21, Shaun Lombard / Vetta 27t, Hulton Archive 45b, China Span /Keren Su 47cl, Connie Coleman 51bl, www. ExtremeSportsPhoto.com /David Spurdens 51br, Mary Kate Denny 52b, iStock / Hadynyah 54b, Oil Scarff 58tl, Maskot 62, PhotoAlto/ James Hardy 77cr, AFP /Stringer 77r, 84l, (backround) Moment 84-85, Christopher Kimmel 96, iStock / Helena Lovincic 97cl, E+/ Mark Bowden 97cr, Robert Cianflone 97t, E+ /Ilbusca 100(a), The Image Bank 102(d), Travel Ink 104b, Dan Kitwood 107cl, The Image Gate 107t, Image Source 111c, Daniel Zuchnik 117cl, 120tr, WireImage /Amanda Edwards 120tl, Shaun Botterill 124l, Caiaimage/Chris Ryan 153(b), Blend Images/ Tom Grill 153(c), iStock / 360 /Jacob Wackerhausen 153(h), Altrendo Images 153(k), Cultura RM / Nancy Honey 154(10), iStock/Pixdeluxe 156c; **Hug it forward**: 88(a); **Imagemore Co. Ltd.:** 156(b); **John Foxx Images**: Imagestate 92l, 159t(g), 159t(r), **Masterfile UK Ltd:** Thomas Dannenberg 47cr, **Nature Picture Library:** Edwin Giesbers 87t, **Pearson Education Ltd:** Jules Selmes 23b, Gareth Boden 81c, 81d, 153a, Tudor Photography 155 (walking boots), Coleman Yuen 155(h); Pearson Education Ltd 155(dictionary); **Pearson Asset Library:** Pavel L. Photo and video 24(t), Studio 52 25(t), 702400 38(t), Roxana Bashyrova 45(tl), Pavel Isupov 45(tc), Monkey Business Images 45(tr), Pincasso 53(t), 123RF.com 61(t), Alexey Boldin 64(t), Pressmaster 73(t), Constantine Pankin 85(t),331177 88(t), Oksana Perkins 90(t),123RF.com 91(t), SF photo 91(t), Bryant Aardema 92(t), KellyNelson 93(t), Kentoh 102(t), 123RF.com114(t), corbis 154 (social studies), Peter Kim 156(E), Andrew Chambers 158(H), Constantine Pankin 158(C), **Alan Peebles:** alanpeebles.com 67l,68; **Plainpicture Ltd:** Kniel Synnatzschke 33; **Press Association Images:** AP /Denis Farrell 79tl, Zak Hussein 89(b), PA Archive /Andrew Milligan 97r, 104l; **Reuters:** Claudia Daut (CUBA) 57t, **Rex Features:** 31cr, Csu Archv / Everett 37r, 44-45, Image Broker 47t, Duncan Bryceland 54l, Associated Newspapers 67cl, 70c, Most Wanted 78b, Peter Brooker 79tr, Dan Tuffs 100(c), Robert Harding /David C Poole 104-105, Crispin Thruston 117r, Staley Lat 124, 125b, Crispin Thruston 125b; **Robert Harding World Imagery:** 28tr; **Shutterstock.com:** javarman 7cl, My Good Images 8, Monkey Business Images 8(t), gpointstudio 9(t), Gladius Stock 10(t), JonMilnes 10tr, michaeljung 10tl, Syda Productions 11(tl), Svitlana Sokolova 11(tr), William Perugini 12br, A and N photography 13(t), lightwavemedia 15(t), Todd S. Holder 17cl, lightwavemedia 18(t), baranq 19(t), wavebreakmedia 20 (e), Rawpixel.com 20(t), Alex Brylov 21(t), Wollertz 22(t), Ekkachai 22-23(a), wavebreakmedia 23(d), sgm 27cr, IM_photo 27l, Songquan Deng 29(t), goodluz 30(t), Pressmaster 31(t), bikeriderlondon 32(t), CREATISTA 33(t), Stanislaw Tokarski 34(t), stockcreations 35(t), Konstantin Chagin 37cl, Nata-Lia 37t, Monkey Business Images 38br, Lucky Business 38cl, Monkey Business Images 38t, Pavel L Photo and Video 39(tl), Catalin Petolea 39(tc), Jack.Q 39(tr), Denys Kurbatov 40(t), wavebreakmedia 41(t), spaxiax 42(t), Dmytro Zinkevych 43(t), Chones 44(t), Baimieng 49(t), Lavandaart 50(t), Siberian Art51(t), PhotoBarmaley 51tl, Manamana 54(t), javarman 55(t), Creativa Images 28(t), EpicStockMedia 59(t), Alaettin Yildirim 59c, EM Arts 59b, Viachaslau Kraskouski 59t (backround), Javier Impelluso 60(t), gkrphoto 60b, Igor Dutina 60t, s_bukley 62(t), Infocus 63b (background), Nomad_Soul 63t (background), Andrii Gorulko 63tr, Littleny 65(t), Milles Studio68(t), Giancarlo Liguori 69(tl), Li Hui Chen 69(tr), Ian Law 70(t), ra3rn 71(t), Jorge Salcedo 72, dramaj 74(t), Gregory Gerber (75tl), Andre Bonn 75(tc), Creative Family 75(tr),Tyler Olson 77cl, Dream79 78(t), Kobby Dagan 79(t), Andrey_Popov 80(t), alejandro dans neergaard 81(t), Tyler Olson 81(e), Monkey Business Images 81(b), BlueOrange Studio 82(a), Monkey Business Images 82(b), hxdbzxy 82-83c, Catwalker 84(t), Corepics VOF 87r, Anatoliy Lukich 87cl, otomobil 89(t), Atiketta Sangasaeng 94-95, blvdone 98(tl), Irina Schmidt 98tr, f11photo 99(tc), Filipe Frazao 99(tr), Prath 100(t), Rtimages100(d), bikeriderlondon 101(t), Anastasiia 103(t), I AM NIKON 108(t), Alex Brylov 109(t), Florin Stana 109b, Rawpixel.com 110(t), wanphen chawarung 111(t), Syda Productions 112(tr), wavebreakmedia 113(t), Sergey Nivens 115(t), Pudi Studio 117cr, hugolacasse 118(t), Sarunyu_foto 119(t), Rawpixel.com 121(t), Goran Djukanovic 122(a), Robert Kneschke 123(t), Monkey Business Images 123bl, Siwabud Veerapaisarn 124(t), David Acosta Allely 125(t), XiXinXing 152(a), Monkey Business Images 152(b), Oleg Zabielin 152(c), kurhan 152(d), gamble19 152(e), antb 152(f), VR Photos 152(g), Syda Productions 152(h), Andrey Burmakin 152(i), Robert Kneschke 152(k), Alexander Raths 152(l), Goodluz 152(m), Junial Enterprises 152(o), Lucky Business 153(d), Igor Kolos 153(g), Deklofenak 153(i) Diego Cervo 153(f), Liviu Ionut Pantelimon 154(2), Pelfophoto 154(3), Niderlander 154(4), Mariia Sats 154 (6), Triff 154(8), Monkey Business Images 154(11), Philip Lange 155(a), Alexandra Lande 155(c), Bullet74 155(e), IM_photo 155(f), Andrea Muscatello 155(i), Federico Rostagno 155(j), David Fowler 155(k), Thor Jorgen Udvang 155(l), Vibrant Image Studio 155(m), Brian Prawl 155(n), eurobanks 155 (aspirin bottle), Dan Scandal 155 (alarm clock), f9photos 155 (backpack), James Clarke 155 (binoculars), Masalski Maksim 155 (digital camera), Coprid 155 (hat), Sasimoto 155 (money belt), Fatih Kocyildir 155 (notepad), design56 155 (soap), HomeStudio 155 (street map), Fotonium 155 (suitcase), g215 155 (umbrella), Olena Zaskochenko 155 (waterproof jacket), Jocek Chabraszewski 156 (a), dotshock 156(d), Ljupco Smokovski 156(g), michaeljung 156(h), bikeriderlondon 156 (i), Dima Fadeev 156 (j), EpicStockMedia 156 (k), Maridav 156 (l), Dionisvera 157 (apple), Maks Narodenko 157 (bananas), ifong 157 (barley corn), Mny-Jhee 157 (biscuits), Ninell157 (broccoli), Jessmine 157 (cabbage), Laboko 157 (cream), Swellphotography 157 (coffe), Ruth Black 157 (cupcake), Yevgen Romanenko 157 (cheese), O. Bellini 157 (fizzy drink), Evgeny Karandaev 157 (grapes), nito 157 (jelly), Alex Staroseltsev 157 (kiwi), Viktar Malyshchyts 157 (lemon), Gavran333 157 (lettuce), Edward Westmacott 157 (lobster), Valentyn Volkov 157 (mango), Viktar Malyshchyts 157 (melon), urfin 157 (milk), Zcw 157 (Mussels), Olga Popova 157 (oats), EM Arts 157 (onion), Valentina Razumova 157 (orange), Evgeny Karandaev 157 (orange juice), Alex Staroseltsev157 (pineapple), Denis Dryashkin 157 (potatoes), Nattika 157 (plum), Sergio Martinez 157 (roast chicken), Dionisvera 157 (spinach), Africa Studio 157 (tea), Bochkarev Photography 157 Studio (fish), Valentyn Volkov 157 (watermelon), Repina Valeriya 157 (wheat), Pogonici 157 (yoghurt), Sebastian Kaulitzki 158(b), Brian A Jackson 158 (d), Aleksandar, Todorovic 158 (e), Christopher Boswell 158 (g), Jim Barber 158 (h), Mariusz S. Jurgielewicz 158 (coastline), Pichugin Dmitry 158 (desert), Procy 158 (glacier), Celso Pupo 158 (lake), Gary Yim 158 (mountain range), Perspectives Jeff Smith 158 (ocean), puwanai 158 (rain forest), Veniamin Kraskov 158 (river), Vadim Petrakov 158 (waterfall), davidpstephens 159 (a), FineShine 159t (b), Xavier Marchant 159t (c), Ian Rentoul 159 (d), Mogens Trolle 159t (e), Tiago Jorge da Silva Estima 159t (f), My Good Images 159t (h), Naypong 159 (i), paytai 159 (j), claffra 159t (k), Peter Gudella 159t (l), irin-k 159t (m), Kamira 159t (n), Luis CÃ © sar Tejo 159t (o), Volodymyr Goinyk 159t (p), Ronnie Howard 159t (s), Stephane Bidouze 159t (t), Mike Price 159t (u), Jacinto Yoder 159t (v), Anke van Wyk 159t (w), smereka 159t (x), Aleksandar, Todorovic 159t (y), Raj Krish 159t (z); **SuperStock:** imagebroker. net 29c, LatitudeStock/ Capture Ltd 54-55, Robert Harding Picture Library 74-75 (background), AxiomPhotographic/ Design Pics 99, Westend61 107l, Corbis 107cr, 112, Juice Images 154 (9); **The Kobal Collection:** Recorded Picture Company 47l, River Road Paramount 48tr, Recorded Picture Company 48tl, Miramax/ Dimension Films / Tweedie, Penny 49tl, Riama-Pathe 117t, Mediapro Studios 118bl, Warner Bros 118br, Video Vision Entertainment/ Distant Horizon /Pathe 118tl, Marvel/ Paramount 118tr; **www.imagesource.com:** Photolibrary 20(a), www. imagesource.com 154(l).

All other images © Pearson Education

Every effort has been made to trace the copyright holders and we apologise in advance for any unintentional omissions. We would be pleased to insert the appropriate acknowledgement in any subsequent edition of this publication.